HOUGHTON MIFFLIN

WORLD REGIONAL STUDIES

Unless we know about the traditions and ways of life of people in other nations, we cannot develop an adequate understanding of the present-day world. The goal of the World Regional Studies series is to provide a well-rounded picture of human experience in six major areas of the world:

> The Middle East
> Africa
> China
> India
> Japan
> Russia

Using history as the organizing principle, the books in this series incorporate concepts and skills from the social sciences and from the humanities. Political and economic systems, geography, social organization and human values, the fine arts, and religion are all discussed in depth.

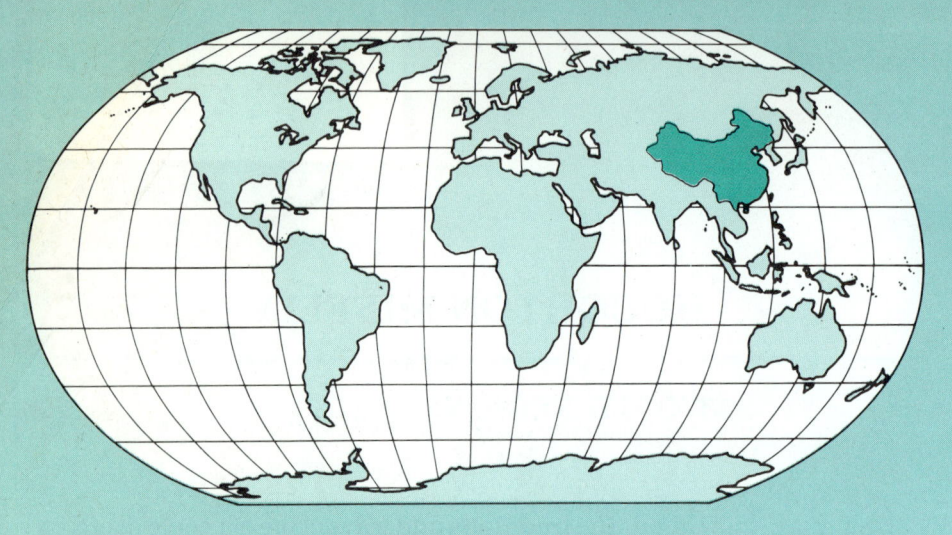

WORLD REGIONAL STUDIES

China

Third Edition

Michael Kublin
Hyman Kublin

HOUGHTON MIFFLIN COMPANY / Boston

Atlanta / Dallas / Geneva, Illinois / Palo Alto / Princeton / Toronto

Michael Kublin

Dr. Kublin received his Ph.D in History from New York University. He also has an MBA from Pace University. He is currently Assistant Professor of International Business at the University of New Haven and taught history previously at Kingsborough Community College in Brooklyn, New York. Dr. Kublin is also general editor for the Houghton Mifflin World Regional Studies series.

Hyman Kublin

A specialist in non-Western history, the elder Dr. Kublin received his Ph.D from Harvard University. Formerly Associate Dean of Graduate Studies of the City University of New York, he taught history at Brooklyn College, the University of California (Berkeley), the University of Delaware, and the University of Hawaii. He was a Fulbright Research Professor at Waseda University in Japan.

Howard R. Anderson

Dr. Anderson, consulting editor, taught social studies in Michigan, Iowa, and New York. He also taught at the University of Iowa and at Cornell University, and served as President of the National Council for the Social Studies.

For invaluable suggestions the author is indebted to Melissa Walt Thompson and Caryn White of the Council on East Asian Studies, Yale University. Alison Lipniki and Chris Walnycky, Reference Librarians at the University of New Haven Library provided unflagging cooperation and assistance. My wife, Janet Blaustein Kublin, provided research, editorial, and typing support as well as unending encouragement.

Cover photo: The Great Wall of China

The chapter opener art on the first page of every chapter depicts a traditional ornamental Chinese key design.

Please see page 281 for acknowledgments of permissions to reprint copyrighted material.

Copyright © 1991 by Houghton Mifflin Company. All rights reserved.

No part of this work may be reproduced or transmitted in any form or by any means, electronic or mechanical, including photocopying and recording, or by an information storage or retrieval system without the prior written permission of Houghton Mifflin Company unless such copying is expressly permitted by federal copyright law. Address inquiries to School Permissions, Houghton Mifflin Company, One Beacon Street, MA 02108.

Printed in the U.S.A.

ISBN: 0-395-47078-1

ABCDEFGHIJ-M-99876543210

CONTENTS

Introduction *ix*

1 China and the Chinese *1*

1. China—A Land of Variety *2*
2. China's Major Rivers *12*
   SIDELIGHT TO HISTORY: China's Floating Population *13*
3. Food Production in China *15*
4. A Common Way of Life *18*
5. A Land of Complex Languages *24*
   SIDELIGHT TO HISTORY: Chinese into English *25*
6. China's System of Writing *28*

2 The Ancient World of China *33*

1. The Development of Chinese Civilization *34*
   SIDELIGHT TO HISTORY: China's City Walls *36*
2. The Zhou Period *40*
3. China's Classical Age *43*
4. Other Teachings in the Zhou Period *47*

3 The Early Imperial Age *54*

1. The Qin, Han, and Tang Dynasties *55*
   SIDELIGHT TO HISTORY: The Silk Road *59*
2. Domination of Confucianism in Chinese Life *62*
3. The Framework of Chinese Society *65*
4. The Spread of Buddhism in China *69*
   SIDELIGHT TO HISTORY: The Only Female Emperor *71*

4 The Late Imperial Age—From Song to Ming *76*

1. Dynastic Struggles for Power *77*
2. China As a Seafaring Power *81*
3. Chinese Contributions to World Civilization *83*
   SIDELIGHT TO HISTORY: Invented in China *88*
4. Philosophy, Art, and Literature *89*

5. Challenges to Ming China's Security 93
   SIDELIGHT TO HISTORY: Which Way Is East? 95

5 The Late Imperial Age—The Qing 99

1. The Manchu Conquest of China 100
   SIDELIGHT TO HISTORY: Notable Qing Emperors 104
2. Problems of Peaceful Times 106
3. The Qing Domain 109
4. European Pressures on Qing China 112

6 The End of the Chinese Empire 119

1. Revolts in the mid–1800's 120
   SIDELIGHT TO HISTORY: The Taiping Rebel Army 122
2. Foreign Pressures on China 124
3. The Empress Dowager and Movements Toward Reform 128
4. Japanese Inroads Against the Qing 134
5. Attempts at Reform in China 138

7 The Struggling Republic 145

1. The Republic's Shaky Foundation 146
2. Increased Friction Between China and Foreign Nations 152
3. Changes in Chinese Life Following World War I 156
4. Sun Yat-sen—Founder of the Chinese Nationalist Revolution 159
5. Chiang Kai-shek's Leadership of the Kuomintang 164

8 China—From Nationalist to Communist 172

1. The Conflict Between Chinese Nationalism and Japanese Imperialism 173
2. Revival of the Chinese Communist Movement 177
3. The Kuomintang Attempts at Reform 181
4. War with Japan 184
   SIDELIGHT TO HISTORY: Support for Free China 187
5. Communist Control of China 193

9 China Under Mao Zedong   201

1. China As a Totalitarian State   202
2. The Economic Transformation of China   207
3. Social Changes in Communist China   214
   SIDELIGHT TO HISTORY: Village Doctors   218
4. The Great Proletarian Cultural Revolution   220
5. China's International Relations Under Mao   226
   SIDELIGHT TO HISTORY: The Republic of China on Taiwan   234

10 China Under Deng Xiaoping   240

1. The Rise of Deng Xiaoping   241
2. Economic Progress Under Deng   250
3. China's Foreign Policy Under Deng   258
   SIDELIGHT TO HISTORY: Hong Kong and China   263

Bibliography   271

Glossary   274

Acknowledgments   281

Index   283

MAPS

Agricultural China   4
The People's Republic of China   8–9
River Valley Populations   18
Ancient China   41
The Early Imperial Age   58
The Mongol Empire   78
The Qing Empire   102
Imperialism in China   125
China, 1926–1934   166
China, 1934–1945   183
China, 1945–1949   194
Industrial Resources of China   212
Transportation in China   212

CHARTS, GRAPHS, AND TABLES

Comparing Population and Land Areas   20
Timetable: Ancient China   35
Timetable: The Early Imperial Age   56
Timetable: Dynasties of the Late Imperial Age   77
Timetable: The Opening Years of Qing Rule   101
Timetable: The Closing Years of Manchu Rule   121
Timetable: The Early Republic   148
Timetable: China Under the Kuomintang   174
Timetable: China Under Mao Zedong   203
Timetable: China Under Deng Xiaoping   242

PHOTO ESSAYS

Growing Rice   16
Minorities in China   19
Wedding Patterns   22
Chinese Characters   29
First Asians   34
Shang and Zhou Art   39
Tang Art   66
Religious Images   70
Mongol Rulers   79
Ming Sea Power   82
Song Porcelain   87
Chinese Painting   90
The Nationalist Army   161
Japan's Early Moves in China   175
War-torn China   186
Allied Support   189
Communist Power   191
The People's Republic   196
Communist Leaders   205
Indoctrination   206
Industrialization   210
Education   216
Health Care   217
Red Guards   222
The Republic of China   232
Nixon's China Visit   235
China's Changing Leadership   243
The Pro–Democracy Movement   249
Changes in China's Economy   253
China in the 1980's   257

INTRODUCTION

Sir Edmund Hillary, a famous mountain climber, was once asked why he had risked his life to scale the world's highest peak. "Because," he answered, "it's there." The same reply might be given to those who wonder why they should study China. Anyone who even glanced at the newspapers or television newscasts in May and June of 1989 knows that China is "there." Furthermore, this gigantic country has been "there" for 40 centuries.

China's Huge Population

China has more people than any other country in the world. In fact, the population of one of China's coastal or river provinces is greater than that of any single country in the world. China's population today is about 1.1 billion, and it may well reach 1.2 billion by the year 2000. The very size of China's landmass and the size of its population severely complicates the task of running the country for China's leaders.

China's Heritage

With its heritage of civilized life extending over a period of several thousand years, China has contributed much to world civilization. A study of human life is incomplete unless China is part of that study. During the past thousands of years, the Chinese people have had more than their share of great people. In the field of government China's rulers and officials often were outstanding administrators. Its foremost philosophers, including Confucius, left an enduring body of thought that has influenced countless people. China's scholars and teachers, painters and poets, and inventors and engineers have made a great many contributions to the world's body of knowledge and its list of achievements.

China's Enduring Civilization

The Chinese way of life is not the oldest in the history of the world. The civilizations that flourished in ancient Babylonia and Egypt and in the Indus River Valley in India were already old before the ancestors of the Chinese began to shake off the conditions of prehistoric life. But these first civilizations have disappeared. The Chinese civilization, on the other hand, has continued to the present.

In recent decades China has undergone great changes. Since 1949 mainland China has had a Communist government. The Communists have tried to root out many traditions of the past. No government, no matter how strictly it exercises control, is able to sweep away long-cherished ideas and customs overnight. Consequently, many traditional elements of Chinese society continue to influence China's social and economic patterns.

Communist China As a World Power

Until the mid-twentieth century, modern China was interested mainly in its own part of the world. Chinese power and influence had rarely extended beyond East and Southeast Asia. What happened in the rest of the world was of little concern to the Chinese or to their leaders.

After the Communist takeover of China, the country's Communist leaders have insisted on playing a major role in world affairs. They have been determined to recapture the position of leadership in Asia long held by their ancestors. The Chinese leaders have also proclaimed their views on such crucial world issues as disarmament, third-world debt, and the refashioning of Communist economic practices.

To reenforce its claims to the status of a major power, Communist China has engaged in a major drive to build up its industry. While China has made impressive gains in this drive, its per capita income still ranks it among the poorer nations of the world. Some experts believe, however, that the time may not be too far off when China becomes an important industrial power.

China's Importance

In the 1700's and 1800's, the Chinese Empire was half a world away from the United States. When the clipper ship *Empress of China* set sail from New York in 1784, it took several months to reach China. After the ship was loaded with tea and other items from China, it returned home, taking more than a year to complete the round trip. For more than a century afterward, any similar trip meant at least several months of travel.

Today the impact of science and technology has reduced travel time between distant parts of the world to hours and days rather than weeks and months. Communications are almost instantaneous. Because time and distance have taken new meanings, so have the age-old geographical distinctions between East and West. With increased contact among world cultures, East–West distinctions are no longer clear-cut and have blurred and begun to disappear.

Contacts between the United States and Communist China were renewed in 1972 when President Richard Nixon visited China. Since then, economic ties have developed and grown. Diplomatic ties were renewed after the United States and China exchanged ambassadors in 1978. Many Americans have visited China since the renewal of ties—economic and diplomatic. Thousands of Chinese students now attend American colleges and universities.

Americans have watched with growing interest the economic flowering of free enterprise in China among many peasants and urban dwellers. Americans cheered when pro-democracy advocates began to gather in Tiananmen Square and urge greater freedom for China. Americans also watched in horror as China's leaders cracked down on student dissidents and other outspoken individuals and instituted programs to reeducate China's people in the values of communism. No matter what course China takes in the 1990's, Americans know they must continue to watch and learn about China, understanding that knowledge of China is an important tool in the shaping of world affairs and world peace.

PINYIN

In January 1979 the People's Republic of China adopted a phonetic alphabet to facilitate the spelling of Chinese names and places in English and all other languages using the standard Roman alphabet. This system is called *Pinyin*. Accordingly in this textbook spellings of Chinese names and places, with a few historical exceptions, are in Pinyin. In addition most names, at the instance of first use, are followed by a pronunciation guide. The list below shows the spellings of names and places in both Pinyin and the former Wade–Giles (traditional) spelling for most of the commonly used terms. Names that have not been changed include Confucius, Taiwan, Taipei, Tao, Taoism, Shanghai, Tibet, and Chiang Kai-shek.

Place Names
Pinyin/Traditional

Anhui/Anhhwei
Beijing/Peking
Chang Jiang/Yangzte River
Chongqing/Chungking
Fujian/Fukien
Fuzhou/Foochow
Guangdong/Kwantung
Guangxi/Kwangsi
Guangzhou/Canton
Guizhou/Kweichow
Hangzhou/Hangchow
Hankou/Hankow
Huang He/Hwang Ho (Yellow River)
Hubei/Hopeh
Jiangsu/Kiangsu
Jiangxi/Kiangsi
Jiaozhou Bay/Kiaochow Bay
Jilin/Kirin
Liaodong/Liaotung
Nanjing/Nanking
Shaanxi/Shensi
Shandong/Shantung
Shenyang/Mukden
Sichuan/Szechwan
Tianjin/Tientsin
Xi/Hsi River
Xinjiang/Sinkiang
Xi'an/Sian

People

Deng Xiaoping/Teng Hsiao-p'ing
Jiang Jing/Chiang Ching
Laozi/Lao-tzu
Li Bo/Li Po
Mao Zedong/Mao Tse-tung
Shihuangdi/Shih–Huang Ti
Zhou Enlai/Chou En-lai

Dynasties

Qin/Ch'in
Qing/Ch'ing
Song/Sung
Tang/T'ang
Zhou/Chou

1

China and the Chinese

Chinese civilization originated and flourished in the easternmost part of Asia, a region far removed from other early centers of **civilization.** Towering mountains, vast deserts, and dense forests isolated this area from other parts of Asia. But, despite its isolation, China enjoyed physical conditions favorable for the development of civilization. Broad plains, fertile valleys and upland plateaus, great rivers, and coastal harbors furnished opportunities for living sufficient to maintain a large population. As a result, China has been heavily populated since ancient times, and its civilization reached a high level of social and technical development very early in its history.

The origins of the Chinese are unclear. Probably some of the ancestors of the people we know as Chinese were inhabitants of East Asia for thousands of years. Others very likely were later arrivals from northern and central Asia. Intermarrying over hundreds of years, these various settlers eventually became the Chinese. All arrivals contributed in one way or another to the development of Chinese civilization.

Like any other civilization, that of the Chinese has changed greatly over the centuries. To be sure, some elements of Chinese life have resisted the pressures of change. But other features of this civilization have gone through a continuous development. Since 1949, the tempo of change has been rapid as China has interacted with the West and has attempted to become a world leader.

1. China—A Land of Variety

The Chinese have had many picturesque names for their country. Probably the most common name has been the *Middle Kingdom*, which in Chinese is Zhung–Guo (JUNG-GWAH). The Chinese people gave their country this name because they believed it to be the center of the universe. To most Europeans, the great land in East Asia became known as China. This name was derived from the Qin (CHIN) **dynasty,** which created the Chinese Empire more than 2,000 years ago.

Today China occupies an area of about 3,700,000 square miles and is the fourth largest country in the world. Only the Soviet Union, Canada, and the United States are larger in area. China's northernmost territories lie in the same degrees of latitude as Labrador in northeastern Canada, and its southernmost regions lie in the same latitude as Cuba. If China were set down in the Atlantic Ocean, it would stretch almost the entire distance between the United States and the British Isles. The vastness of China is also suggested by the length of its frontiers, among the longest in the world. To the north, west, south, and east, China has common borders with a dozen different countries. (See the map on pages 8–9.)

The Vastness of China

China was not always so vast as it is today. About 3,500 years ago it consisted of a number of small states in the area of the Huang He (HWANG HUH), which in English means the Yellow River, because of the color of its water. During the course of many centuries, these various states were slowly welded into a strong and unified **empire.** The rulers of this empire gradually pushed its borders outward in all directions. It was not until the early 1700's that China began to approximate its present size. Its outermost boundaries, however, have often remained vague or in dispute. The border between India and China, for example, has been disputed for many years.

China Proper

The heartland of China has always been the east central section, commonly called **China Proper.** (See map, page 4.) Here the Chinese people have lived since **prehistoric** times. Chinese civilization developed and flourished in China Proper. This was the China that became envied and feared by peoples all over Asia.

China Proper reaches from the Great Wall in the north to the borders of Burma, Laos (LAH-ohs), and Vietnam in the subtropical south. It extends from the shores of the Pacific Ocean in the east to Xinjiang (SHIN-jee-YAHNG) and Qinghai (CHING-HY) in the west. About 900 million people live in China Proper. Since large parts of this region, especially in the south and west, are mountainous, much of the land is uninhabited. The majority of the Chinese in China Proper make their homes in four areas: the North China Plain, which is crossed by the mighty Huang He (Yellow River); the valleys and delta plains of the Chang Jiang (CHAHNG JYAHNG), formerly called the Yangtze, in Central China; the valley of the Xi (SHEE) River, formerly the Hsi, in the south; and the broad plateau of the southwest.

The inhabited areas of China Proper are among the most densely populated parts of the world. (See map on page 18.) More people live on the North China Plain than in the entire United States. The Chinese living in the valley of the Chang Jiang alone outnumber the total population of the Soviet Union.

To govern this huge area, the rulers of China have divided it into administrative units. Currently China is divided into 21 **provinces,** five **autonomous regions,** and three government controlled municipalities—Beijing (bay-JING), Shanghai (SHANG-HY), and Tianjin (tee-YAHN-jin). (See map, pages 8–9.)

Fine yellow soil, or loess, is blown down from Mongolia and deposited, sometimes to great depths, over a wide area of North China. The loess is fertile, and with irrigation, crops thrive in this region.

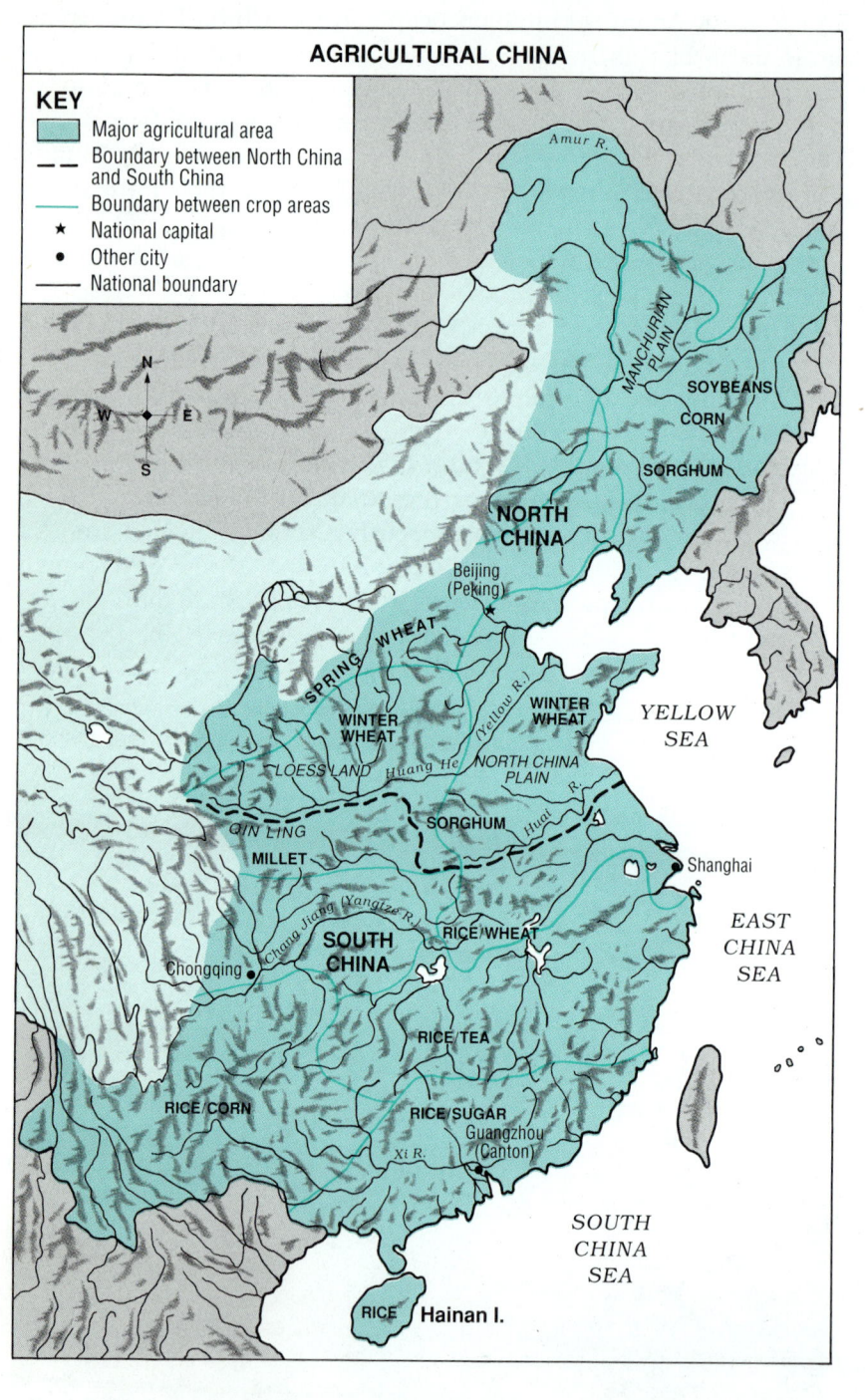

Limestone hills rise almost straight up along both sides of the Xi River as it flows through Guangxi Province. This famous landmark in South China has inspired artists and poets for centuries.

North China

The various regions of China Proper differ greatly in terrain, climate, soil, rainfall, and crops. The main differences are between North and South China, which are divided roughly by the Qinling Shan (Mountains) and the Huai (HWI) River. The mountains act as a barrier between the rainbearing winds from the south and the winds laden with **loess** from the north. The mountains roughly divide the drier wheatlands of North China from the moist ricelands of South China. Rainfall varies from 10 to 25 inches in North China, while South China receives anywhere from 40 to 90 inches a year. Important characteristics also differentiate eastern and western regions.

Summer in North China is warm and at times hot. During the winter, fierce northern winds whip across the area and snowfalls are common. For protection against the cold, people wear heavy quilted clothing. Homes are made of pounded mud

ENVIRONMENT: AGRICULTURAL CHINA. Almost all of agricultural China lies within the area covered by the map on page 4. Although many different types of crops are grown in each region, the map notes only the major crop or crops. The map also shows the major division between North and South China. Which region receives the most rainfall?

or mud brick because forests are scarce in the area and the people have little wood for building.

The farmers in North China have irrigated their lands since ancient times because the area suffers from inadequate rainfall. When the water supply fails, as often happens, drought results. Through the centuries the people of North China have suffered many devastating famines. As a result the very life of North China depends on its water supply.

South China

Geographically South China is a different world from North China. Mountains and forests cover much of South China. The region is warm during most of the year, and most southern parts are hot. Winters are much milder than in North China. In some parts of South China, snow has never fallen. The people of South China build wooden houses that can be easily ventilated because of the high temperatures. During the summer season, from June through September, drenching rains are brought by the **monsoons.** Some areas are so deluged by the monsoon rains that rivers overflow and flood low-lying lands.

The scattered plains of South China were first broken by the plow centuries ago, and farmers have settled in great numbers in the many river valleys. In their constant search for tillable land, they have also farmed strips of land called **terraces** on the sides of hills and mountains. In the southernmost portion of South China the growing season is so long that it lasts the year round. **Double-cropping** is possible. Although famines have not been unknown in South China, they are rarely so critical as those that have ravaged the north.

Autonomous Regions

While the Chinese were spreading their way of life throughout China Proper, they came in contact with non-Chinese people on their borders to the north and west. The way of life of many of these non-Chinese people differed sharply from the more culturally sophisticated way of life of their Chinese neighbors. Nomadic and warlike, the non-Chinese people were both feared and scorned by the Chinese.

From time to time, various non-Chinese groups raided parts of China Proper. Sometimes they even conquered large sections of Chinese territory. For their own safety the Chinese tried to extend their political or military control over the non-Chinese people living along their borders. Usually this was done by setting up **protectorates.** In China's current administrative framework, the sprawling, thinly populated border areas have been designated as autonomous regions. (See map, pages 8–9.) Traditionally these areas have been China's poorest, consisting mainly of minorities, or non-Chinese. They make up about 6 percent (about 60 million) of China's total population. In contrast, the land area of these regions amounts to 60 percent of China's total area. According to China's government, autonomous regions are intended to protect the culture, traditions, and languages of the native peoples who live in them. The government also has set special goals for **modernization,** raising living standards, and increasing productivity in these areas.

Northeast China

Occupying an area of almost 600,000 square miles, Northeast China is considerably larger than Texas, California, and the New England states combined. It is composed of the three provinces of Heilongjiang (HAY-long-jee-YAHNG), Jilin (JEE-lin), and Liaoning (LYOW-NING). Westerners have long called this area Manchuria. Its rich resources have made Northeast China a much sought after territory in modern times. The south and central sections of the region consist of broad fertile plains that are ideal for agriculture. The principal crops harvested in the region are wheat, soybeans, corn, and sorghum—a kind of cereal grain. Because of its abundant deposits of coal and iron, the central part of Northeast China is also a major industrial center.

The well-forested eastern and northern sections of Northeast China provide fine commercial-grade lumber. These sections, however, are still undeveloped and offer few prospects for large-scale settlement. Even less developed is the western section, a land of broad plains and grasslands.

Until recent times the Northeast had a small population. It was the homeland of the Qing (Manchus), a fierce nomadic people who conquered the Chinese Empire in 1644 and founded China's last imperial dynasty. (See page 99.) Numbering scarcely two million at the time, the Qing prohibited their more numerous subjects to the south from settling in their northeastern homeland. The population increased very little, therefore, during the 250 years of Qing rule over China.

In the early twentieth century, however, the Northeast was finally opened for settlement. Today the region has more than 50 million inhabitants, 90 percent of whom are of Chinese descent. Today the region is considered an integral part of China, which relies heavily on the region's industrial resources.

(Continued on page 10)

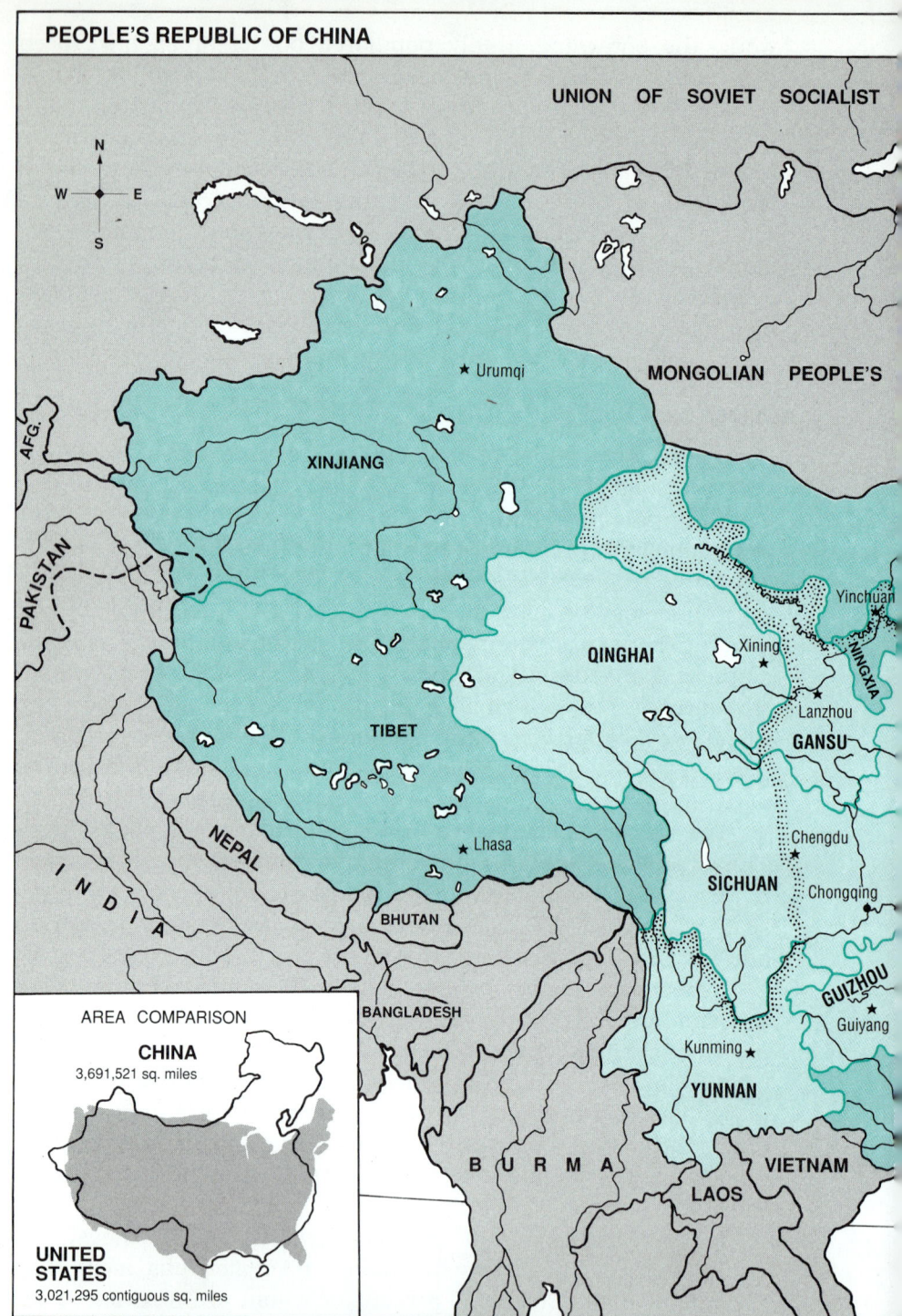

PLACE: THE PEOPLE'S REPUBLIC OF CHINA. Note the outline of traditional China Proper. This is where Chinese civilization developed and flourished over many centuries. The small inset map in the lower left corner compares sizes

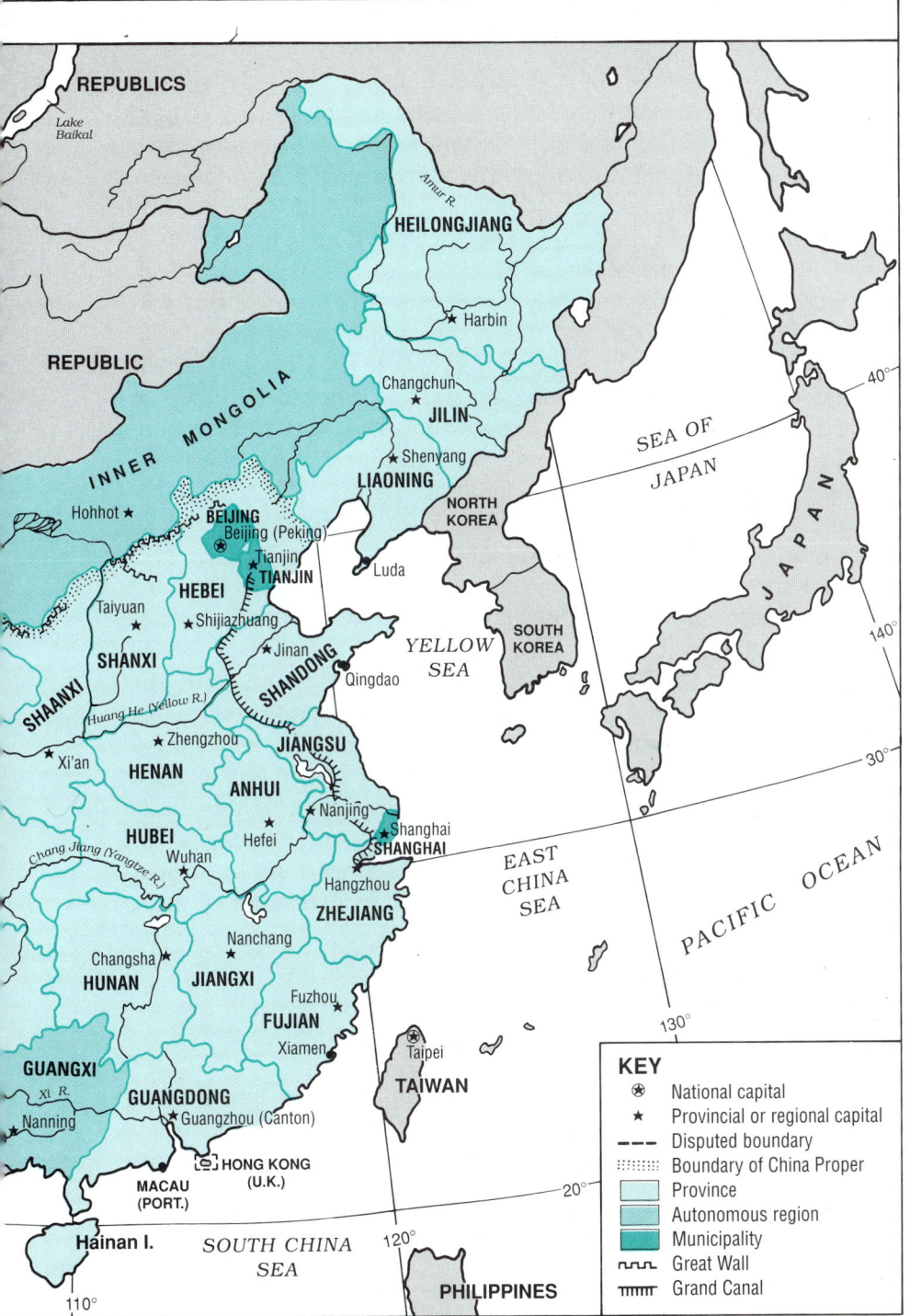

of China and the mainland United States. When Hawaii and Alaska are added to the mainland, the United States is larger than China. Note that Beijing, China's capital, lies at about the same latitude as New York City.

Mongolia

An enormous expanse of territory, Mongolia is thinly settled. Until the twentieth century Mongolian lands covered a territory known simply as Mongolia. It consisted of present-day Inner Mongolia and the country formerly known as Outer Mongolia. Now known as the People's Republic of Mongolia, the country ousted the Chinese and in 1924, declared its independence, which China recognized some 20 years later.

Traditionally most Mongols have dwelt in the northern part where rich grasslands exist. There the people make their livelihood by grazing their herds of sheep, cattle, goats, and camels on the rich grasslands. Within the last few decades, however, a drive for modernization has led to the introduction of mechanized agriculture and some small-scale industry. Thus the traditional way of life has been undergoing a radical change.

The southern part of Mongolia is a wasteland dominated by the Gobi (GOH-bee), which in Mongol means "desert." Many sections of the Gobi have never been explored. The southeastern part is known as Inner Mongolia. Originally inhabited by nomads, Inner Mongolia has in the past few centuries been settled by land-hungry Chinese farmers. Rainfall is uncertain, but the farmers manage to raise crops of wheat and sorghum.

Along the borders of the Gobi, the Chinese have begun a huge tree-planting program in an attempt to stop the forward march of desert sands. But such desert-stopping programs along the Gobi's borders sometimes fall short of their objectives because they are in areas where rainfall is uncertain from year to year. In addition, the programs compete with zealous Chinese immigrants who allow livestock to overgraze or who plow up the land for crops, thereby stripping the land of its plant cover and helping the desert to advance.

Xinjiang

Sitting in the heart of Central Asia, Xinjiang is a barren and forbidding region. In fact the interior of Xinjiang consists of a desert—the Takla Makan (TAHK-lah mah-KAHN). For many centuries merchants made their way along the caravan routes that started in northwest China Proper and then skirted the Takla Makan to north and south. These routes were part of the **Silk Road,** which connected the Chinese Empire with India, Persia (Iran), and the countries bordering the Mediterranean Sea.

The people of Xinjiang, mainly Uighurs (WEE-goors), are distantly related to the Turks and are followers of Islam, the religion founded by Mohammed. The Uighurs live largely in the foothills of the mountain ranges that hem in the desert on all sides except the east.

Tibet

Situated south of Xinjiang and north of India, Tibet has been secluded by geography from the outside world. For most of its history, Tibet has been called the "roof of the world." Few travelers are willing to brave Tibet's towering mountain ranges and barren windswept plateaus. Tibet has an average elevation of over 14,000 feet, but many peaks rise several thousand feet higher. Distantly related to the Chinese, Tibetans number less than two million. Their economy, both in the past and in the present, has combined agriculture, herding, and trade.

In this century, Tibet has experienced many problems. Some stem from competition over its rich resources and its **strategic location.** Others have arisen because of the strong ethnic, cultural, and religious identity of its people. In 1950, the Chinese army (People's Liberation Army) entered the region and established it as a protectorate. In 1959 Tibetans revolted against Chinese domination and reforms. The Chinese fiercely suppressed the uprising. The Dalai Lama, Tibet's religious and secular ruler, fled to India, where he continues to live, and Tibet was made an autonomous region of China. Tibetans continue to resent and resist the Chinese presence as a threat to their unique culture and traditions.

Check Your Understanding

1. Why did the Chinese name their country the "Middle Kingdom"?
2. How does China compare in area with other countries of the world?
3. **a.** What name is given to the heartland of China? **b.** In what four parts of this area do most of the people live? **c.** Contrast the climate and crops of North and South China.
4. **a.** What borderlands are included in China today? **b.** Which of these borderlands are autonomous regions?
5. ***Thinking Critically:*** How does the creation of autonomous regions reflect China's traditional attitude toward non-Chinese people?

2. China's Major Rivers

Rivers are the arteries of China Proper. The three great rivers—the Huang He, the Chang Jiang, and the Xi—have always dominated China Proper and the lives of its millions of people. (See map, pages 8–9.) For 40 centuries water has never been far from the thoughts of the people. Whether living in North or South China, the people have always kept a watchful eye on the skies and the streams that water their land.

The Huang He—North China's Lifeline

Like many great rivers of Asia, the Huang He has its source in Tibet. Flowing about 3,000 miles in an easterly direction, it cuts a jagged course through the lofty mountains of northwest China and then meanders across the North China Plain.

One of the longest rivers in the world, the Huang He takes its name from the yellowish color of its waters, which are constantly muddied by silt eroded from the loess soil of the Northwest. Although the Huang He is largely useless for navigation, its waters are vital for millions of farmers. Held back by massive dikes, the waters are released as needed into the centuries-old irrigation systems of North China.

In recent decades two great bridges spanning the Huang He have been constructed, the first at Wuhan and the second at Nanjing (below). Completed in 1968, the Nanjing bridge helps to link Beijing and Shanghai.

SIDELIGHT TO HISTORY

China's Floating Population

Though the Chinese are not traditionally a maritime people, rivers and coastal waters have been home for countless Chinese. For many centuries, millions of Chinese have lived out their lives aboard junks and sampans, the most typical kinds of Chinese boats. Earning their livelihood from fishing and the transportation of passengers and goods, China's floating population has long been accustomed to swaying decks underfoot.

The "water people" have been especially numerous in the ports from Shanghai south to Guangzhou. Entire families live aboard these vessels. The houseboats in these harbors are at times crowded so close together that for long distances the sight of water is actually blocked out. In these places, it is possible to move from one boat to another, walking for miles before touching land.

Most people in China have been peasants who for generations have made their living from the earth. But for the water people, houseboats have been and continue to be a traditional way of life.

The Huang He has often burst its dikes and flooded the land. On at least 26 occasions over the last 3,000 years, floods have actually changed the course of the river's flow to the sea. These floods have been a mixed blessing. As the waters recede, they leave behind a fertile layer of silt. But because of the terrible damage inflicted by its floodwaters, the Huang He is often called "China's Sorrow."

The Chang Jiang—China's Most Important River

The Chang Jiang in the central part of China is the fourth largest river in the world. Fed by the melting snows of glaciers in Tibet, this giant stream bisects China Proper from east to west. Several great cities lie along the Chang Jiang. Shanghai, China's most well-known seaport, lies near the river's mouth. About 100 miles upstream from the sea is Nanjing (NAHN-JING), once China's capital city. Other major cities located along the Chang Jiang are Wuhan and Chongqing (CHOONG-CHING), China's capital during World War II.

Unlike the Huang He farther north, the Chang Jiang is navigable for almost 1,000 miles inland from its mouth. Oceangoing vessels constantly make their way from one river port to the next. Above Wuhan, where the descending waters rush from the western mountains, special steamers are used to navigate the miles of rapids.

The Chang Jiang and its many tributaries carry an enormous volume of water. Yet at times, the river system's seemingly unlimited capacity is inadequate. On the other hand, during the late spring and summer, if much water runs down from the distant glaciers and rainfall is heavy, the Chang Jiang and its tributaries overflow. The resulting floods cause great destruction. Today a series of dams is under construction, which will help control flooding and provide urgently needed hydroelectric power for China's developing industries.

The Xi—Southern China's Great River

Located in the far south, the Xi flows through rugged terrain for almost 1,700 miles. Guangzhou (GWANG-JOH), formerly called Canton by Westerners, is an old and famous seaport, that lies near the river's mouth. Not far beyond in the open sea is the important island of Hong Kong. (See page 263.) The lower stretch of the Xi is navigable, making the river a major transportation route into the interior.

Other Transportation Links

Because China's key rivers flow from west to east, the Chinese have found it easier to travel and transport goods between the eastern and western parts of China than between the northern and the southern sectons. To ease north-south travel, the Chinese more than 1,300 years ago built the Grand Canal. (See map, pages 8–9.) Connecting the lower Chang Jiang with the Huang He, the Grand Canal is one of the longest constructed waterways in the world. Today the 1,500-mile-long Grand Canal serves mainly local businesses. A plan is under consideration, however, to make the canal a part of a project to divert water to drought-plagued North China by equipping the canal with locks and pumps.

In the twentieth century China has become the world's major railroad constructor, building a total of 33,000 miles of railroad track to link almost all parts of China. These railway lines are mainly in China Proper. Supplemented by coastal shipping and airlines, the railroads have served to bind the regions of China Proper more closely together.

Check Your Understanding

1. What are China's three major rivers?
2. What problems are associated with China's great rivers?
3. **a.** How were North China and South China linked long ago? **b.** What other links have been added in recent times?
4. **Thinking Critically:** Why are the rivers of China vital to its existence? Why is the Chang Jiang more important than the Huang He?

3. Food Production in China

For centuries China Proper has been one of the world's greatest producers of food. Faced with the need to support a population of a billion people, Chinese farmers have always raised many crops. Rice has topped the list, but it is by no means the only important crop raised. Rice is cultivated in areas enjoying a warm climate and abundant water, but in large parts of China Proper these conditions do not exist. In fact, many Chinese have never eaten rice.

Wheatlands of North China

For centuries the principal foodstuff of North China has been wheat. Largely because of North China's production, the annual wheat crop of China Proper is exceeded only by those of the Soviet Union and the United States. In the summertime, the broad fields of the North China Plain are shaped into thousands of acres of waving grains, including barley, millet, and sorghum. From these cereal grains, the Chinese make such foods as noodles, porridge, dumplings, and pancakes.

Ricelands of South China

Rice **paddies** are a part of just about every farming plot in South China. The farmers flood the paddies at periodic intervals during the year and then transplant young rice plants, which have been grown from seed in nursery beds. Because South China has a long growing season, the farmers prepare the paddies for another planting as soon as the first rice crop is harvested. In this way, they can grow two or three crops annually. For this reason, China is the world's leading producer of rice.

GROWING RICE. Chinese rice sowers scatter the precious seed as evenly as possible over the nursery beds (above). After 30 or 40 days, the seedlings are transplanted to paddies. Usually workers must handle each young plant, but the worker at right is using a transplanting machine invented by Chinese engineers.

Still, hunger and even famine are no strangers to South China. Such tragedies have occurred when too much or too little rain has caused floods or drought. At times, too, it has been difficult to transport surplus stocks of grain to areas where shortages existed. On the whole, however, the people of South China have seldom experienced the terrible famines that sometimes occur in the north.

Other Crops

Crops characteristic of both North and South are grown in the central part of China Proper, but the region is best known as the center for two special products—tea and silk. China's finest teas grow here, for the hilly country south of the Chang Jiang is well suited for cultivation of tea bushes. Conditions in the region are also favorable for the growth of the white mulberry, a tree with leaves specially valued as food for silkworms. As a result, China's world-famous silks are produced in this area.

A few crops important to the Chinese diet and economy have been cultivated nearly everywhere in China Proper. China is one of the world's largest producers of cotton, raising enough cotton to satisfy its basic needs. China is also a major producer of soybeans, which were first domesticated in China about 3,000 years ago. Rich in protein, soybeans can be boiled and crushed to produce soy milk. The soy milk is formed into curds, which when pressed produce tofu, one of China's most popular foods. Tofu can be baked, steamed, smoked, marinated, and deep-fried. It can be sliced, shredded, and made into bread, cake, and candy. The Chinese also raise sweet potatoes, peanuts, and oil-bearing seeds. Native varieties of certain fruits, such as apples, oranges, and watermelons, are grown as luxuries for those who can afford to buy them, not as dietary staples.

A Simple Diet

Despite the fame of Chinese cooking, most Chinese through the centuries have subsisted on a monotonous diet. As much as three fourths of an individual's daily food has been cereal grains, while the rest has usually consisted of vegetables. The Chinese diet has lacked milk, butter, and cheese, for few herds of cattle have been raised. Chinese farmers have used the available land to raise crops for humans rather than fodder for animals. Meat, therefore, has also been in short supply.

The small amount of protein in the typical Chinese diet has come principally from fish, pork, or chicken. People living near the seacoast round out their meals with fish. But even though China is one of the world's major fishing nations, the demand has always exceeded the supply. Chinese unable to afford fish may enjoy an occasional piece of pork or chicken. Pigs and fowl are much easier and cheaper to raise than cattle.

Check Your Understanding

1. Name the chief food crops of each of the following areas: **a.** North China, **b.** South China, **c.** Central China.
2. **a.** Describe the typical diet of most Chinese. **b.** Why are meat and dairy products scarce?
3. ***Thinking Critically:*** Explain how China leads the world in the production of rice but sometimes suffers famine.

4. A Common Way of Life

Ways of living vary all over the world, and there is usually good reason for these variations. A Chinese proverb sums up the matter well: "If you see something strange and do not consider it strange, its strangeness disappears." Learning the background of unfamiliar ways of living also helps to take away strangeness.

Many Types of Chinese

The Chinese people include not only the inhabitants of China, but also the millions of citizens of China who are regarded as "non-Chinese." These people are listed in the latest available Chinese census (1982) under more than 50 headings. Anthropologists, however, commonly stress two elements in describing the Chinese people. These elements are culture and language.

PLACE: RIVER VALLEY POPULATION. While China has an average population density of 288 people per square mile, the population density of its major river valleys is much higher. About how many people live on each square mile along the Chang Jiang and in parts of the North China Plain?

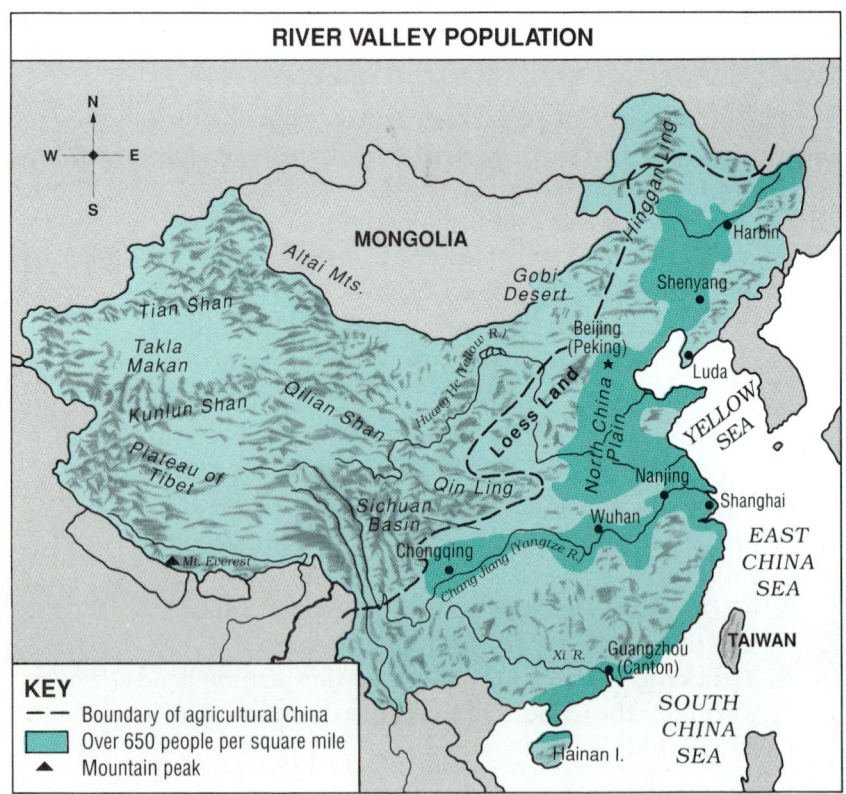

MINORITIES IN CHINA.
Some 45 million citizens of China are racially non-Chinese. A few of these "minority nationalities" are shown here. Left, Kazakh women of Xinjiang. Below (left to right): Tibetan; Li (on Hainan Island); Benlong (in southwest China).

The great majority of Chinese people (94 percent) belong to the Han ethnic group (named after the great Han dynasty). Below, these Han teenagers, in Western-style clothes, stroll down a street in the city of Chengdu.

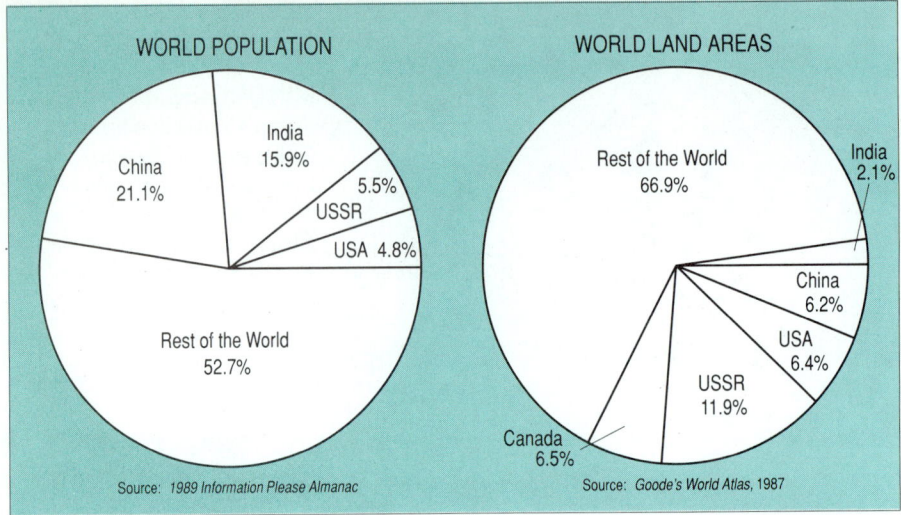

COMPARING PEOPLE AND LAND. A little more than 21 percent of the world's population lives in China. This means that on average one out of every five persons in the world lives in China. What percent of the world's total land area does China have?

A study of the photographs on page 19 reveals that there are many types of Chinese. For one thing, skin coloring varies. In the northern parts of China complexions are often light or cream-colored, while in the south they range over many dark shades. When the Portuguese, themselves swarthy, came to eastern Asia in the sixteenth century, they often referred to the Chinese as a light-skinned people. In some parts of China only a minority of the inhabitants have almond-shaped eyes.

The Chinese Way of Life

The way of life of any group of people may be said to be the sum total of the ideals they have set for themselves in life and the adjustments they have made to the problems of living. It includes their attitude toward nature and the universe and their traditions, customs, and patterns of behavior. Their way of life also embraces the procedures of government, methods of social organization, means of earning a living, and forms of artistic expression.

As a whole this book is concerned with the history and development of the Chinese way of life, but many of the elements just listed will be treated in later chapters. In this section we will deal only with certain common features of the traditional Chinese civilization.

Acceptance of Nature

Until very recent times, the Chinese people had almost no interest in trying to pit their strength against nature. They sought more to live in harmony with nature than to make themselves master of it and develop a scientific way of thinking. The Chinese objective in life was to live in peace with nature and its forces, which they respected and feared. In their view, people were merely a small cog in the great universe of the natural world. The Chinese point of view was superbly demonstrated in their famous landscape paintings, which often displayed tiny human figures overshadowed by towering mountain peaks and other natural features.

Chinese Society

During most of China's long history the family has been the most important unit of society. The traditional Chinese family was patrilineal with descent traced through the father. It often extended five generations in each direction, including a father's ancestors back to his great-great-grandparents and his descendants to his great-great-grandchildren. The center of authority was the oldest direct-line male, such as the grandfather or great-grandfather. Female elders also had authority, especially over their sons and daughters-in-law. In theory, the elders determined what crops were to be raised, when lands were to be mortgaged, which children were to be sent to school, and whether single family members should marry. In practice, most of the adult members of the household would usually have a voice in such decisions.

Old age and childhood were considered the happiest times in the life of the Chinese. Old age was venerated, and elderly parents could expect to receive good care and respect for as long as they lived. Children were welcomed, especially boys, since only they could continue the family line and name. Girls were not as welcome as boys because they would eventually leave home to become members of other families. The birth of too many daughters was regarded as punishment from heaven, and in time of famine baby girls were sometimes abandoned and allowed to die.

Ideally, all living generations lived in the same household. Few Chinese families, however, could actually afford such an arrangement, since most farms were too small to support a large number of people. Usually a family consisted of the parents, their unmarried children, and perhaps the eldest son, his wife, and their children.

Marriage Patterns

Until the mid-twentieth century in China, young people had no say about whom they would marry. Parents and elders sought brides and grooms who could advance the family's interests. The search was conducted by members of the family or, more commonly, by a professional matchmaker. When a suitable bride or groom was found, the two families completed the formalities for the marriage. There was no courtship for the couple; in most cases they first met on their wedding day. Since the wedding

WEDDING PATTERNS.
Differences in the wedding ceremony symbolize old and new China. In the traditional wedding (left), embroidered silk robes veiled the bride, who was carried to her new husband's home in a sedan chair. The couple below did not have an elaborate ceremony, as their wedding attire shows. But most likely bride and groom were able to choose their marriage partner, rather than having to follow their parents' choices.

festivities were elaborate, whenever a family lost a daughter through marriage, it might well acquire a heavy debt in return.

The bride generally faced trying times. She went to live with her husband's family, where she was expected to be a dutiful daughter-in-law. Although divorce was infrequent, a husband could discard his wife if she failed to have children. Moreover, the wife could be sent home in disgrace if she acted disrespectfully to her husband's parents or if she talked too much. To make matters worse, Chinese mothers-in-law were notoriously critical of new wives. The standing of the daughter-in-law improved, however, as she bore children, especially boys.

Village Ties

Most Chinese lived in villages, and seldom did a man leave the village of his birth. In China, a country of farmers, about the only way to get land was to inherit it. Thus, the Chinese did not often leave home in search of a better life. They were reluctant to be separated from family. Only disaster and desperation would drive a Chinese from his home village.

Respect for ancestors also kept the Chinese at home. Departed forebears were so venerated that the head of a household had as a main duty the care of family graves. A Chinese could be sure of similar respect from his descendants. Even if he left his village, he hoped to return before he died so that he might be buried with his ancestors.

The attitudes of the Chinese toward themselves and other peoples were influenced by their isolation from other civilized societies. For centuries the people of neighboring lands were eager to borrow Chinese customs and ideas. The confidence of the Chinese in their cultural superiority was not seriously shaken until recent times.

Valuing the Past

By stressing the value of the past as a source of wisdom, the teachings of the great philosopher Confucius (kun-FYOO-shus) turned the attention of one generation after another to antiquity. The veneration of ancestors also reflected Chinese respect for past generations and their achievements. Thus, the Chinese people attached great importance to historical writing. For 2,000 years scholars compiled a detailed record of the events of one dynasty after another. No other people possess so long and continuous a written record of their past as the Chinese.

After evolving over 4,000 years, Chinese civilization in this century has undergone many political, social, and cultural upheavals. To be sure, the Chinese way of life did not remain unaltered until modern times. Like any civilization, over the course of centuries it was continuously undergoing change. Yet the upheavals in the twentieth century have probably been greater than all the changes of the preceding centuries. As we shall see later in this textbook, changes since 1949 have been especially drastic.

Check Your Understanding

1. **a.** Who are included in the phrase *the Chinese people*? **b.** What two elements does the textbook stress in describing the Chinese people?
2. What is meant by the Chinese way of life?
3. What was the traditional attitude of the Chinese toward nature?
4. **a.** Describe the traditional Chinese household. **b.** Contrast the position of young and old. **c.** What status did women have?
5. What was the traditional Chinese attitude toward ancestors and the past?
6. **Thinking Critically:** What is the relationship between the Chinese proverb quoted at the beginning of this section and non-Chinese views about the Chinese people?

5. A Land of Complex Languages

Knowing something about a people's means of expression is one way to learn something about the people themselves. Therefore studying some of the characteristics of the Chinese language will add to an understanding of Chinese civilization.

The Chinese Language Family

Chinese belongs to the Sinitic, or Sino–Tibetan, language family. Other languages in this family are Tibetan, Burmese, and Thai. The Sinitic tongues have a number of common characteristics, and probably all of them derive from a single ancestor language of the distant past. The average person cannot detect the similarities among the various members of a language family. But language experts can identify these relationships through study of grammar and vocabulary.

SIDELIGHT TO HISTORY

Chinese into English

Though the Chinese have had contacts with English-speaking peoples for several centuries, few Chinese words have entered the English language. Those that have, however, are quite colorful. Following are some examples:

chop suey: "Odds and ends" in Chinese.

chow mein: "Fried noodles" in Chinese.

kowtow: To show slavish respect; in Chinese means "to knock the head" on the ground in a deep bow.

lychee nuts: Nut-shaped fruit eaten fresh or dried.

pekoe: A popular tea.

pongee: A silk cloth.

sampan: A small flat-bottomed boat, usually with a single sail and a cabin made of mats.

shantung: A silk cloth.

tong: An association or club.

typhoon: "Big wind" in Chinese.

By far the most important of the Sinitic tongues is Mandarin Chinese, the everyday speech of about three fourths of the Chinese people. During the language reforms of the 1920's, this **dialect** was given the name *guoyu*, (GWOH-YOO) meaning "national language." The current name for the dialect, however, is *putonghua* (poo-TONG-gwah), meaning "common spoken language." It is based upon the northern dialect and the pronunciation of Beijing.

This language and its dialects are spoken in the northern and western parts of China. Throughout the southeastern part of the country, many other languages are in common use. They too are often called dialects, even though they are actually different enough from *putonghua* to be considered separate languages altogether.

These so-called dialects are all Sinitic languages. But they are as different from each other as French is different from the other Romance languages—Spanish, Italian, and Portuguese. Chinese people who speak any of these southeastern dialects ordinarily cannot be understood by those speaking any of the others or by people using *putonghua*, the national language. Educated people in southeastern China, therefore, usually have learned the common spoken language in addition to their native language.

Spoken Chinese

The great majority of words in *putonghua*, as well as in all the Chinese dialects, are composed of single syllables. For this reason, the language has often been called monosyllabic.

This feature may be illustrated with the names of places and persons. *Shanghai,* for example, is a combination of two single-syllable words, *shang* meaning "above" and *hai* meaning "sea." The name of the Communist leader Mao Zedong (MOW dzuh-DOONG), like that of most Chinese, is composed of three elements. The family name, which comes first, is *Mao;* it means "hair" or "fur." *Zedong,* the personal name, consists of two parts, equivalent to the first and middle names in Western custom. Since there are only a few hundred Chinese family names, millions of people in China have the same surnames. The Chinese have traditionally believed that people with the same surname belong to the same **clan** and are related, however distantly, to each other.

Language Homonyms

Spoken Chinese seems to the untrained ear like an unbroken repetition of the same sounds. This is because the number of syllables in Chinese is relatively small. As a result of this lack of variety in syllables, the Chinese language is full of homonyms—that is, words that are pronounced alike but that have different meanings. Examples in English of homonyms are *to, too, two.* Obviously communication between speakers would be impossible without a way of making clear the differences in meaning of words that are pronounced the same way. Context—the position of the word in a sentence and its use—is one way of making different meanings clear. But still another method of distinguishing meaning is the use of *tone,* which was developed in the Chinese language.

The Importance of Tone

The meaning of a monosyllabic homonym in Chinese depends on two things. First, there is the sound of the word. Second, there is the tone or pitch in which the word is spoken. The latter is all-important. The Mandarin Chinese language generally uses four different tones, a high tone, a rising tone, a tone that combines a falling and rising inflection, and a falling tone. But some of the Chinese dialects have many more variations in tone. In learning a new word in Mandarin or in one of the other Chinese dialects, it is necessary to know both the word's sound and its tone. A word that is pronounced with a rising tone may mean something entirely different from a word with the same sound but uttered in a falling tone. These tones give spoken Chinese its lilting quality.

A Changing Language

The Chinese languages may seem complicated to the Westerner, but for the Chinese people these languages have been an effective means of expression. Until the twentieth century foreign languages were rarely studied in China. The local languages provided all the existing vocabulary needed for the study of philosophy, history, and literature. Furthermore, the existing vocabulary could always be enlarged and adapted to cover new needs. Two or more words were usually put together to express a new idea or to describe a new object. In recent years, however, the problem has become serious as the Chinese have had to cope with many new and unfamiliar terms that apply to science, technology, and ideology.

The Chinese have responded to the challenge in several ways. Sometimes foreign words simply have been borrowed and pronounced as much like the originals as possible. Sometimes new words have been coined. Thus, in Chinese the word for airplane is literally "fly-machine." Train is "fire-wagon," and atom bomb is "origin-element-explosive." A third approach has been to increase emphasis on the study of foreign languages in the schools and universities of China.

Check Your Understanding

1. **a.** To what language family does Chinese belong?
   b. What other languages belong to this family?
   c. What language is most widely spoken in China?
2. Many Chinese words sound alike. How are Chinese able to distinguish between similar sounding words when speaking?
3. How have the Chinese tried to develop a vocabulary adequate for studying modern technology?
4. **Thinking Critically:** How has language been a barrier to unity among the Chinese?

6. China's System of Writing

Originating more than 3,500 years ago, the Chinese system of writing was fully developed before the beginning of the Christian era. This marvelous but intricate method of writing has had a far-reaching influence on the development of Chinese civilization. Furthermore, the Chinese script spread beyond the frontiers of China itself through a process called **cultural diffusion.** The only system of writing in East Asia for many centuries, the Chinese system was borrowed by the Koreans, Japanese, and Vietnamese, who adapted the written system to their own languages in another significant and important process known as **acculturation.**

Development from Pictographs

Like the early writing of Egypt and the Middle East, Chinese writing began with the drawing of rough but recognizable pictures of objects. Even today it is possible to guess the meaning of some of the ancient Chinese **pictographs.** In time the ancestors of the Chinese developed a means of expressing *ideas* in writing. The symbol for an idea was generally formed by combining pictographs that suggested the idea. For instance, the combination of the characters for "woman" and "child" means "good." The symbols for "sun" and "moon" together denote "light" or "bright." Such symbols, when used in combinations, are called **ideographs** (see page 29).

Other characters in Chinese writing are composed of a "meaning" symbol and a "sound" symbol. The "meaning" symbol, obviously, gives a clue to meaning, while the "sound" symbol suggests the pronunciation. Most of the characters in present-day Chinese writing are of this kind.

Chinese writing includes more than 50,000 characters. The great majority of these characters are rarely used and are unknown even to many well educated people. But a knowledge of 1,000 to 1,500 characters is necessary for even elementary reading and writing.

Unifying Effect of the Writing System

Few features of the Chinese civilization had as much of a unifying effect as did this system of writing. Since the meanings of the written characters depended on form and not on sound, they could be used anywhere that a Chinese language was spoken. Peoples speaking different dialects did not develop separate methods of writing. The same written characters were used

A Chinese calligrapher holds his brush pen upright in writing characters (above). The samples below show how Chinese characters combine to form other characters with more abstract meanings. Note the pronunciations under the characters that indicate how these words are spoken in *putonghua*, the most widely used Chinese language. The tone used in pronouncing similarly spelled words differentiates them. The markings tell the Chinese which of four tones to use.

日		月		明
YUĒ		YUÈ		MÍNG
(sun)	+	(moon)	=	(bright)

女		子		好
NǓ		CIMU		HAO
(woman)	+	(child)	=	(good)

throughout China even though they were pronounced according to local speech. As long as the meanings of the characters were understood, Chinese writing could be read without regard to pronunciation.

It should be pointed out, however, that for centuries the great majority of people in China never learned to read or write. The need to memorize so many written characters hinders efforts toward **literacy** and serves to perpetuate illiteracy. During the last hundred years efforts have been made to reform the Chinese writing system, but most proposals have solved old problems only to create new ones.

The basic language problem is that so many dialects are spoken throughout China. If the many thousands of characters are replaced with a **phonetic alphabet,** the new written language will be intelligible only to those who knew the particular spoken language on which the alphabet was based. A speaker of the dialect spoken in the city of Guangzhou, for example, will not be able to read the new writing if it is based on *putonghua*, the common spoken language. One way this difficulty could be eliminated, however, is to teach all of the people the common spoken language. Many Chinese, however, are reluctant to give up their local speech.

Promoting Literacy

Since coming into power the leaders of the Chinese government have been encouraging education for the young and old alike. They know that **industrialization**—one of the major goals in China today—cannot be promoted or advanced without a literate population.

Various methods of teaching people to read have been adopted in modern China. The number of written characters in common use has been reduced to about 1,000. Standard abbreviations have been invented for the more complicated characters. Moreover, people who speak local languages have been required to study Mandarin. Finally, the Western alphabet has been adopted as the basis of a phonetic script known as **Pinyin.** To reduce the confusion caused by the many homonyms, a phonetic mark indicates the tone of pronunciation to be used with each homonym.

Check Your Understanding

1. **a.** How did the Chinese system of writing evolve?
   b. How does Chinese writing differ from ours?
   c. What other Asian countries based their systems of writing on the Chinese system?
2. How has the Chinese system of writing helped to unify the Chinese people?
3. How has the Chinese system of writing contributed to illiteracy among the Chinese people?
4. *Thinking Critically:* Why has it been difficult to increase literacy in China?

CHAPTER REVIEW

■ Chapter Summary

Section 1. To understand the history of the Chinese people, one must keep in mind the huge size of their country. China Proper alone is larger than most Western nations. With its borderlands of Manchuria, Inner Mongolia, Xinjiang, and Tibet, China is the fourth largest country in the world. As a result, China enjoys a range of geographical regions that is typical of continents. The population of China is far greater than that of any other country.

Section 2. For centuries the lives of the Chinese people have been influenced by rivers—especially the Huang He, the Chang Jiang, and the Xi, together with their tributaries. To the Chinese, these river systems have been both a blessing and a curse. They furnish life-giving water to areas often threatened by drought. But frequent floods have brought great hardship and suffering to the people.

Section 3. Most people in China have been farmers. Adapting themselves to widely different conditions of soil, temperature, and rainfall, the Chinese have raised wheat, rice, other grains, tea, silkworms, and a variety of vegetables. Despite the tremendous amount of foodstuffs raised in China, however, demand has often exceeded supply.

Section 4. The millions of Chinese differ widely in height, skin color, and other physical features. It is impossible to describe a "typical" Chinese. The Chinese "way of life" is not easily defined either, for many different elements entered into the development of the Chinese civilization. Some of the more notable features of this civilization were a life close to nature, a strong loyalty to family, veneration of ancestors, and a deep awareness of and respect for the past.

Section 5. Many languages are spoken in China, most of which belong to the Sino–Tibetan language family. Three fourths of the people speak *putonghua,* or Mandarin, while the rest speak dialects of Mandarin or other languages related to it. The majority of Chinese words are monosyllabic. To differentiate between homonyms, the Chinese use four tones.

Section 6. Despite the lack of unity in spoken language, a single system of writing has been used throughout China. Chinese writing developed more than 3,500 years ago and influenced other civilizations beyond China's frontiers. Although Chinese writing combines more than 50,000 characters, a knowledge of only about 1,500 is necessary for literacy. Because of its intricacy and great number of characters, however, few Chinese have learned to read and write. In recent years, serious efforts have been made to spread literacy in China.

■ Vocabulary Review

Define: civilization, dynasty, empire, China Proper, prehistoric, province, autonomous region, loess, monsoon, terrace, double-cropping, protectorate, modernization, Silk Road, strategic location, paddy, dialect, clan, cultural diffusion, acculturation, pictograph, ideograph, literacy, phonetic alphabet, industrialization, Pinyin

■ Places to Locate

Locate: Middle Kingdom, Huang He, Great Wall, Chang Jiang, Xi River, North China, South China, Manchuria, Tibet, Inner Mongolia, Grand Canal

■ People to Know

Identify: Qin, Manchus, Uighurs

■ Thinking Critically

1. Compare North China with South China in terms of its people, its topography, and its productivity.
2. In what ways have China's three major rivers shaped China's history and life?
3. Why have parts of China periodically suffered from famine even though the country leads in the production of wheat, rice, and other food grains?
4. How have culture and language helped shape a common way of life for the Chinese people?

■ Extending and Applying Your Knowledge

1. Find out more about the geographic role of the Huang He, Chang Jiang, and Xi River. Choose one of these rivers to explore further, investigating how the river itself and its use by the people of China has changed through time.
2. Discover how a person in China uses a Chinese dictionary. Also find out how it is possible to print Chinese newspapers and books. A book on the history of printing may be useful.

2
The Ancient World of China

For many years the only available knowledge of ancient Chinese civilization was derived from myths, traditions, and official histories. In the twentieth century these legends and histories were enriched by finds from archaeological excavations. Together the traditional material and the modern discoveries tell the story of China's development. They also trace the succession of China's dynasties from the first and perhaps mythical rule of the Xia (SHEE-uh) to the powerful state of the Qin rulers (221–206 B.C.).

During the more than 1,500 years covered by these early dynasties, there emerged many of the customs and ideas that have characterized Chinese civilization to the present. For instance, our earliest knowledge shows Chinese living together in close-knit family groups or clans. Love of family and loyalty to relatives are ideals that have endured throughout Chinese history. We also know that quite early the Chinese invented a system of writing and developed a tradition of accomplished artisans, a talent especially demonstrated in beautiful objects cast in bronze. Furthermore, China's first intellectual flowering occurred in the latter part of China's ancient period. Confucius and his disciples shaped Chinese ideas about the proper relationships among people. The Taoists also deeply influenced Chinese thought, as their teachings became the basis for many works of literature and art. Thus, these early centuries were among the most formative and productive of China's history.

33

1. The Development of Chinese Civilization

Some 70 years ago Western and Chinese archaeologists began their search for information about the China of prehistoric times. They and other scholars found many important remains of ancient Chinese life in East Asia, the area that includes China, Japan, and Korea. As a result both the prehistoric age in East Asia and the earliest periods of Chinese civilization have become much better known.

One of the World's Oldest Inhabited Areas

Skeletal remains estimated by scientists to be about 200,000 to 500,000 years old were discovered in North China in 1927. Known as Peking Man, this specimen is representative of a whole group of people and provides China's link to the Old Stone Age, or Paleolithic Era, when stone tools were first used. Peking Man and others like him were probably more like *Homo sapiens*, as modern humans are called by scientists. Archaeologists believe that Peking Man lived in caves, hunted for food, used rough stone tools, and knew the use of fire. The search for remains of other early people continues. In 1964 archaeolo-

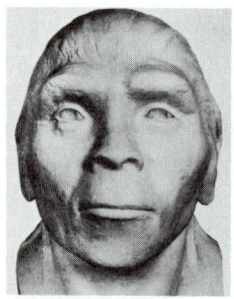

FIRST ASIANS. A reconstruction based on ancient skull fragments shows what Peking Man probably looked like (left). These short, heavy-browed people may have been the first human beings in Asia. Archaeologists found their skeletal remains in the vicinity of the cave shown below, about 30 miles southwest of Beijing. Chinese archaeologists have carried out further excavation of caves in the area.

TIMETABLE

Ancient China

B.C.
1994–1523	Xia dynasty
1523–1028	Shang dynasty
1028–256	Zhou dynasty
551–479	Lifetime of Confucius
403–221	Period of Warring States
221–206	Qin dynasty

gists discovered remains that were 100,000 years older than Peking Man. Older still are fossil teeth discovered in 1965 and estimated to be 1.7 million years old.

Remains of later prehistoric people have also been found in East Asia. It is impossible to say whether these remains represent descendants of Peking Man or ancestors of the Chinese people. They might have been both. But the archaeological record does prove that people have been living continuously in East Asia since long before the dawn of recorded history.

The early inhabitants of China were probably joined from time to time by peoples who emigrated from other parts of Asia. About 5,000 or 6,000 years ago some of these prehistoric peoples, particularly those settled in the northern part of the land, were making many changes in their ways of living. They had learned how to make more efficient weapons and tools of stone than earlier people and thus were able to live in greater security and comfort. These New Stone Age, or Neolithic, people differed from their Paleolithic predecessors. The New Stone Age people lived in small villages and practiced a more settled life of hunting, herding, and farming. From these communities a number of small states gradually emerged in the valleys of northwest China and on the broad North China Plain.

Sources of Information

For many centuries traditions, legends, and myths have been handed down from one generation of Chinese to the next, forming China's rich **oral tradition.** Historians have found oral tradition an important but not always accurate source of information about early China. Until some of this material was set in writing, China's early history was known exclusively from these oral

SIDELIGHT TO HISTORY

China's City Walls

High, massive walls surrounding many cities and towns in China have been a common sight since ancient times. These walls have been repaired, strengthened, and extended so many times that it is usually impossible to say when any of them were originally built. To the early Chinese a wall was so necessary for a settlement that they used the same word—*cheng*—to mean either "city" or "wall."

An early Shang city is said to have had a wall more than 2,000 feet long, 60 feet wide, and 30 feet high. Such a wall might have taken as long as 18 years to complete with 10,000 laborers working as many as 330 days a year.

Chinese city walls are a reminder of the insecurity of life and property so common in the Middle Kingdom for long periods of time. The frequent appearance of marauding armies and rampaging invaders compelled people living in cities and towns to look after their own defenses. The inhabitants of the many tiny villages were less fortunate. They could find safety only in flight.

The huge gates of some of these city walls are among China's most precious architectural treasures. Many city walls and gates have been torn down to make way for modern needs, but fortunately others have been preserved.

---

sources. A more accurate source of information was a series of Chinese histories, the earliest of which were written about 2,000 years ago. Even these must be evaluated carefully, however, because the authors relied a great deal on oral tradition for their sources.

According to some of these ancient histories, about 4,000 years ago many of the Chinese communities came under the control of a strong state. The rulers of this state, who were called the Xia, are generally considered China's first dynasty. But some modern scholars have been reluctant to believe that the Xia state ever existed. Archaeologists have never discovered its location, nor have they found any object that can be proved to have been made by its people.

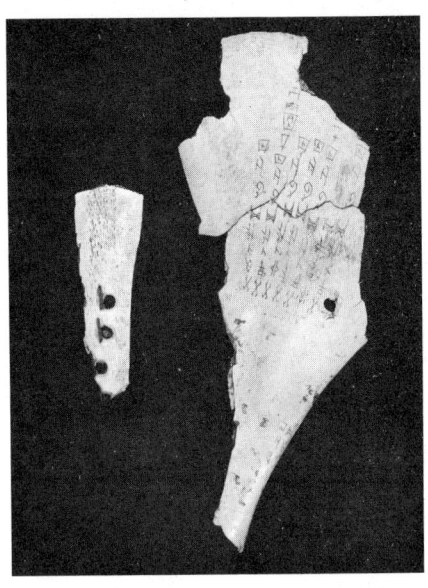

Dragon bones show the inscription of Shang priests who tried to foretell the future.

A few years ago, however, these scholars were given cause to wonder. For the same reasons that they doubted the existence of the Xia, they also doubted the existence of the Shang (SHAHNG) dynasty. According to tradition, the Shang had been China's second dynasty, reigning from about 1523 B.C. to about 1028 B.C. In the late 1920's archaeologists discovered the buried remains of one of the capital cities of the Shang, thus proving that this dynasty did indeed exist. Given the continuing interest in China's ancient history by archaeologists, it seems probable that the Xia dynasty's existence will some day be proven.

Historical Evidence of the Shang

For centuries objects known as "dragon bones" or "oracle bones," were highly prized by people in China. Ground into powder, these ancient tortoise shells and shoulder bones of oxen and deer were used to make remedies for nervous disorders and other ailments. In the early 1900's Chinese scholars became interested in the strange scratches on many preserved dragon bones. Careful study revealed these marks to be early forms of Chinese writing. The bones were traced to Anyang (AHN-YAHNG), a town in North China. From them, scholars deciphered most of what is known about the history, culture, and religion of the Shang. Exploratory excavations at Anyang soon uncovered the ruins of the ancient capital of the Shang dynasty. This discovery not only confirmed the existence of the second Chinese dynasty but also revealed a high level of culture.

Ancient Anyang contained many imposing buildings. It was evident that artisans practiced their crafts in the capital city, and some trade was carried on. Most of the people who lived outside Anyang's walls were farmers. The members of the Shang **aristocracy**, who were warriors and priests, lived in Anyang and other cities and towns. The Shang state was ruled by a succession of 35 monarchs who passed on their position and power to other members of their families.

Highly Skilled Artisans

Many of the Shang objects unearthed at Anyang have impressed scholars with their artistic and technical mastery. These artifacts have also raised some tantalizing questions. The Shang people were skilled at writing, the casting of bronze, and the use of the potter's wheel to produce utensils from clay. Were these skills developed by the people of Shang, or had they gradually learned them from centers of civilization in other parts of Asia? Centuries before the Shang existed, many of the techniques eventually used by their artisans had been known to the peoples of Egypt, the Middle East, and the Indus River valley in India. How and when this knowledge spread to China—and *if* it spread—are questions that are still unanswered.

Writing and Religion

Most of the deciphered written records of Shang times have a close connection with religion. The Shang rulers believed in supernatural spirits and sought their help on important problems. To consult the spirits, they practiced **divination.** Questions for which they wanted answers—such as whether rain would fall, whether crops would be bountiful, or if war could be expected—were inscribed on flat pieces of bone. A hot poker was then thrust into holes drilled in the bones. This made cracks appear, and the priests then divined, or interpreted, the answer by examining the pattern of cracks. Inscribed with the original questions (and frequently the answers), the bones were then stored away. In the centuries following the Shang dynasty, the bones were dispersed over a wide area. Farmers frequently uncovered them while plowing their fields. These were the "dragon bones," or "oracle bones," that several thousand years later led scholars to the site of ancient Anyang.

Bronze Work

Although the people of Shang China were masters in the working of bronze, they fashioned most of their tools from stone and

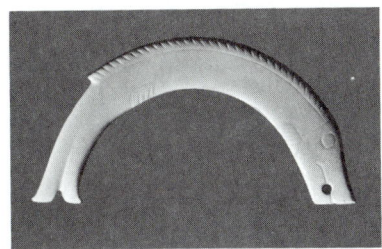

SHANG AND ZHOU ART.

A Shang artisan gave a tiger face to the bronze ceremonial vessel at upper left. A squared spiral design called the thunder pattern can be seen in the clay vase above, which was excavated at Anyang, the Shang capital. Chinese artisans have long excelled in carving jade ornaments. Left, a white jade fish pendant from the Zhou period. Zhou artisans also fashioned beautiful objects of bronze. Below, a Zhou bronze tapir has a playful look. A stylized dragon design, typical of many Chinese art objects, appears on the bronze back of the Zhou mirror at lower left.

wood. Bronze, an alloy of copper and tin, was so scarce and valuable that its use was restricted. In the Shang era, and indeed for some centuries afterward, bronze was used primarily for vessels needed in religious ceremonies and for weapons. Bronze articles filled with wine and food were buried in large tombs. These bronzes are now extremely rare, for many centuries ago the tombs were rifled by grave-robbers. Bronze objects of the Shang era are today highly valued, but not only because they are old and rare. Collectors also prize them for their superb technical mastery and great beauty. Some admirers of these bronzes claim that in the techniques of casting and artistic decoration the Shang artisans have never been surpassed.

Check Your Understanding

1. What information have archaeological excavations revealed about Old Stone Age and New Stone Age people in China?
2. How do scholars know about the existence of the Xia dynasty?
3. What did scholars discover about the culture of the Shang?
4. **Thinking Critically:** Why are archaeological findings more accurate as sources of information than sources based on oral tradition?

2. The Zhou Period

During the 1100's B.C. the Shang dynasty was overthrown by peoples from western China. These conquerors of the Shang founded the Zhou (JOH) dynasty. This was the first—or second—of many changes in the ruling houses of China over the next 3,000 years. Counting the still unconfirmed first ruling house (the Xia), there have been 25 official dynasties in China's long history.

A Long But Weak Reign

No other family in all Chinese history had so long a reign as the Zhou. One might think from their long **sovereignty** that the rulers of this dynasty enjoyed great power. But such a conclusion would be wrong. Although the Zhou rulers held the title of emperor and maintained their claim to imperial position for

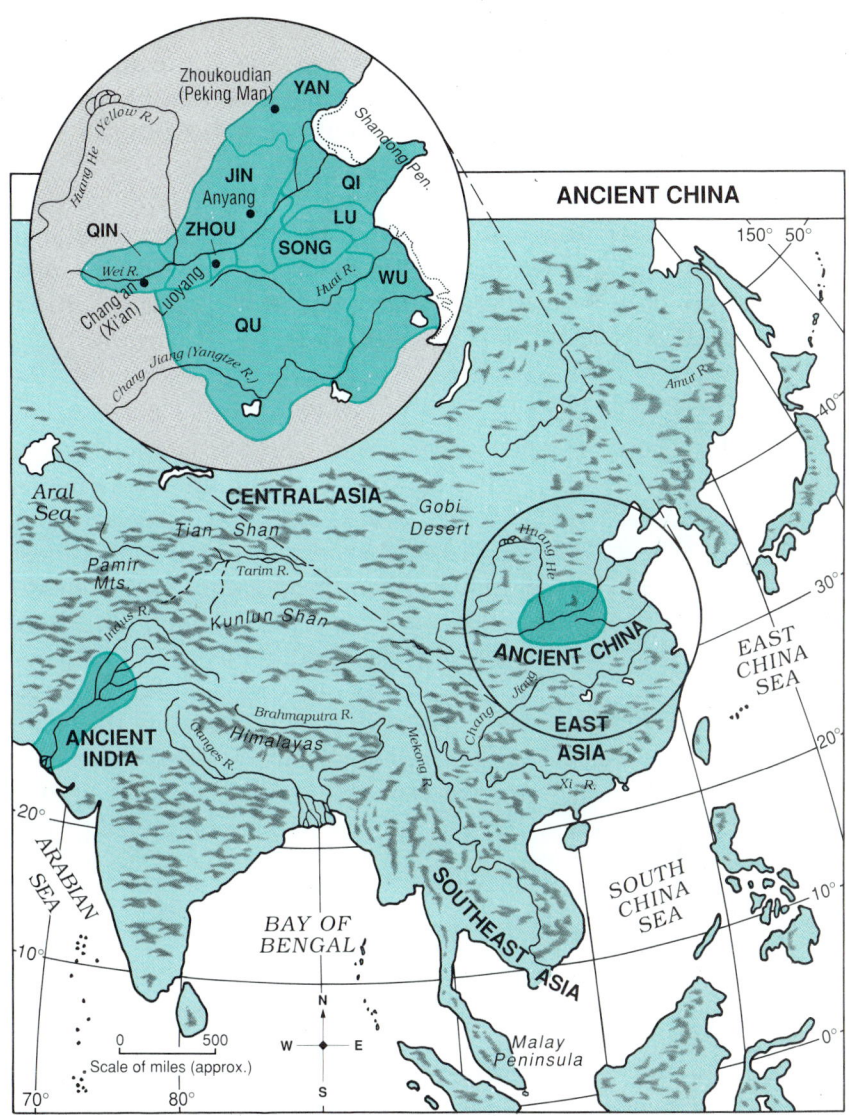

PLACE: ANCIENT CHINA. The main map shows two ancient cradles of civilization—the Huang He in China and the Indus River in India. Vast distances, mountains, and deserts separated these two centers. The inset map highlights the North China Plain during the Zhou period. Note the names of other Chinese feudal states that existed during the Warring States period. In the third century B.C., the Qin vanquished the Zhou and united China in a single empire. The dotted line offshore on the inset map indicates the deposits of soil that have built up the coastline since ancient times.

over 700 years, most of them were political figureheads. Within a few centuries after the conquest of the Shang, invaders from beyond the frontier shattered the strength of the Zhou monarchs. Thereafter, during the long Zhou period, China was an empire only in name.

The Zhou rulers contributed little to the history of their times. But during the nearly 800 years they held the title of emperor, Chinese life was constantly changing. The Chinese people were building a new and richer way of life on the foundations laid down during the Shang era.

The Iron Age

During the Zhou dynasty artisans continued to fashion bronze objects as they had in earlier centuries. For a while production of bronze vessels and weapons rivaled that of Shang artisans.

About 600 B.C. the use of iron began in China. The Chinese probably learned the technique of iron production from nomadic peoples of Central Asia. (See map, page 41.) Though the new metal never replaced bronze in the fashioning of art objects, ironworking had a far-reaching effect on Chinese life. Because iron is harder than bronze, ironworking made possible the manufacture of superior weapons and tools. Iron-tipped plows, for example, were much more efficient than wooden plows. By the end of the Zhou period the use of iron had become fairly widespread in China.

The Chinese Feudal System

Another development of the Zhou period was the appearance of political organization similar to European **feudalism.** In Western Europe, feudalism was a system in which nobles, or lords, were granted the use of lands that legally belonged to the king. In return, the nobles owed loyalty and military service to the king and protection to the peasant farmers (serfs) who lived on and worked their estates (fiefs).

In Western Europe feudalism was associated with a period of several centuries beginning about A.D. 900. At this time the collapse of the great empire of Charlemagne forced people to accept the rule of strong lords in return for protection. Distinct differences existed, however, between the feudal-like system of political organization that developed in China and medieval European feudalism. One difference is that feudalism came earlier to China, probably during the Zhou period. More important, unlike the rulers of Western Europe who had few family ties to unite them, the Zhou ruling class was principally united by family ties. The Zhou ruling class was all part of a vast, widely dispersed family, with the monarch as head. Kinship ties gradually weakened, however, and by the sixth and fifth centuries B.C., the Zhou Empire was made up of a number of independent and fairly strong feudal states. (See map, page 41.) The rulers of these states ignored the authority claimed by the Zhou emperors and continually warred among themselves. This strife became especially turbulent during the years 403–221 B.C., a time known as the Warring States period.

The crumbling of Zhou authority during the Warring States period and the chaotic struggles among the states caused great concern among thoughtful people in China. Many believed that their civilization was headed for ruin. But the troubles of the period were actually the growing pains of a changing society. The economy expanded during these years, trade flourished, and the population grew. Great advances were made in agriculture and technology. Many irrigation projects were built and iron was used to make weapons and tools. The Zhou state finally disappeared in 256 B.C. It was soon to be followed by a new empire founded by a new dynasty.

Check Your Understanding

1. **a.** What dynasty followed the Shang? **b.** Why were the rulers of the new dynasty emperors in name only?
2. **a.** How did the Chinese come to use iron? **b.** What advantage did iron have over bronze?
3. **Thinking Critically:** Compare European feudalism with the type of feudalism that existed in China at this time.

3. China's Classical Age

Despite the political chaos that prevailed, a flowering of Chinese thought took place during the last few centuries of the Zhou period. These centuries have been called China's Classical Age in honor of the period's long-lasting influence over Chinese thought and culture. In reality the period is China's first Zhou **classical age** because in later times brilliant writers and thinkers ushered in still other ages of long-standing importance. But the Chinese have held the earliest of their great thinkers in the highest esteem.

The Importance of Confucianism

Confucius (kun-FYOO-shus) usually ranks first among China's outstanding **philosophers.** Born in northeast China, probably about 551 B.C., Confucius lived less than a century before Socrates, the great philosopher of ancient Greece, and about the same time as the Buddha (BOO-da), India's great philosopher-teacher. (See page 69.) During his boyhood Confucius studied extensively. He took particular interest in history, court ceremonies, and music. As a young man he became a government employee but also spent much time teaching.

After reflecting on the confused state of Zhou society, Confucius reached some conclusions about what he thought to be the causes of the disorder. Although he had solutions to propose, his efforts to persuade feudal princes to adopt his ideas were unsuccessful. Confucius spent the rest of his life teaching a small but loyal group of followers. He died in 479 B.C., but his teachings formed the basis of Chinese education for 2,000 years.

Confucianism, the philosophy based on the teachings of this man, has probably influenced the lives of more people than any other body of thought in all history. It is an **ethical system** rather than a religion. As such, it focuses on the right and wrong of human conduct. Confucius was primarily concerned with the behavior of human beings in this world. He paid little attention to such matters as sin, salvation, and the nature and fate of the soul. He believed that not until people learned to behave properly in this life could they turn their minds to problems of the afterlife. Confucianism may thus be considered a guide to proper behavior based on ethical principles. Confucius' aim was to help people improve themselves so that both the individual and society would benefit.

The Five Relationships

Confucius hoped that if people knew what was expected of them in their relations with other people, they would behave correctly. He therefore singled out five principal relationships in which people might be involved. Confucius believed that if everyone acted in the recommended way in each of these social relationships, peace and harmony would result. Individuals, families, communities, and country would benefit.

The first relationship was between the ruler and his ministers. Confucius placed a heavy burden of responsibility on the ruler of a country. The ruler was expected to be an outstanding example of proper social behavior for all Chinese subjects. If the ruler's conduct was good-hearted, just, and dignified, officials and ministers would be inspired to behave similarly. If, on the other hand, the ruler was wicked, brutal, ruthless, and dishonest, no one could expect the ministers or the people themselves to behave properly.

The second relationship was that of father and son. In the same way, Confucius called on fathers and sons to understand their obligations to each other. One of the foremost duties of a father was to be a worthy model for his children. It was his responsibility to guide their behavior and to develop their character along the right lines. Thus, a father could justly claim credit for the accomplishments of his children, but he could also be called to account if his sons and daughters strayed from the path of acceptable behavior. As for the son, his duties were to honor his parents while they lived and to respect their memory after death. This was known as **filial piety,** the highest virtue in the Confucian ideal of good behavior.

Two of the remaining social relationships also concerned the family. The third relationship concerned husbands and wives. The husband was head of the family. His responsibility was to see that the memory of ancestors was respected and that the good reputation of the family was preserved. It was also the husband's duty to ensure that the family name was passed on to the next generation. This meant that the first duty of the wife was to bear sons. Daughters were loved but not so highly prized as boys because they would eventually marry and leave the family.

In the fourth relationship Confucius emphasized harmony between older and younger brothers. The older son, who would someday become head of the family, had to learn to be a model of behavior for his younger brothers. In turn, the brothers were expected to accept without complaint the special position of the oldest son in the family.

The final relationship was between members of the community. Confucius had a "Golden Rule" to cover the various types of behavior in this relationship. "Do not do to others," he said, "what you would not want them to do to you." This instruction was a plea for honorable behavior by the individual towards all other members of the community.

Teachings of Confucius

Confucius was a shrewd teacher. That he recognized the strengths and weaknesses of human character is evident from his many sayings that have been handed down over more than

2,000 years. Many of his richest pieces of wisdom are short and witty statements like the following:

> Knowing what he knows and knowing what he doesn't know is characteristic of the person who knows.
>
> Making a mistake and not correcting it is making another mistake.
>
> The superior man blames himself; the inferior man blames others.
>
> He who learns but does not think is lost; he who thinks but does not learn is in danger.
>
> To go too far is as wrong as to fall short.

Confucianism was not widely accepted until after the death of its originator. The rulers of the many states of Zhou China were tough-minded politicians and had little regard for Confucius' philosophy. But students of Confucius kept his teachings alive. To the books which Confucius had prepared (largely by collecting the writings of earlier times), his disciples added others. They tried not only to preserve the wisdom of the "Great Master" but also to advance ideas of their own. These books, known as the *Confucian Classics,* are a treasury of social and ethical philosophy. They are part of the cultural heritage of China and of all humankind.

Mencius (MEN-shee-us), who was born about a century after the death of Confucius, was the greatest disciple of the famous sage. Like Confucius, Mencius had faith in the basic goodness of people and hoped to rescue them from the evil ways of society. Especially interested in the welfare of the people and in just government, Mencius held that people were not obliged to be loyal to wicked rulers. In fact, he maintained that oppressive and incapable rulers had no right to rule. Chinese beliefs held that no person could become a ruler without spiritual approval—the **Mandate of Heaven.** Mencius, who was concerned with the welfare of the people, expanded the concept. In his view a ruler earned the Mandate of Heaven by providing for the well-being of the people, thus winning their support. Mencius even taught that people had the right to revolt against monarchs who abused their power and neglected their responsibilities. In later centuries when rebellions against emperors broke out, Mencius' doctrine that "the voice of the people is the voice of Heaven" was often quoted.

Check Your Understanding

1. **a.** What is Confucianism? **b.** What was its guiding principle?
2. **a.** Name the five principal relationships taught by Confucius. **b.** How was each relationship properly expressed?
3. **a.** Who was the greatest disciple of Confucius? **b.** How did the views of this disciple expand upon the teachings of Confucius?
4. *Thinking Critically:* Why was Confucianism not widely accepted during the lifetime of Confucius? Why has this philosophy been so widely accepted since his death?

4. Other Teachings in the Zhou Period

Confucianism had many rivals. Some thinkers of the late Zhou period differed from Confucius and his followers in their views concerning human nature. Nor did these thinkers agree with the Confucianists on what was wrong with society or what might be done to remedy individual and social problems. Some of these thinkers formulated views that attracted many followers, either immediately or in later times. Other thinkers attracted few followers and because of that had little influence in shaping political and social policies. Two of the more successful philosophies were **Taoism** (DOW-iz-um) and **Legalism.**

Taoism

According to tradition, the first great teacher of the philosophy of Taoism was Laozi (LOW-dzuh). It is claimed that he was a little older than Confucius. There is, however, some doubt that such an individual as Laozi ever lived. Nevertheless, the ideas attributed to him won many disciples during the last centuries of the Zhou dynasty. These ideas were eventually summed up in a small book called the *Tao Te Ching* (DOW-deh-jing), or *The Classic of the Way and Its Power*. The *Tao Te Ching* is the basic text of Taoism.

Taoism is not easily understood because its teachings cannot be conveyed by words alone. Taoism cannot be explained. It must be experienced or felt. Thus, it is often called a mystical philosophy. The difficulty of making clear the meaning of Taoism once inspired a poet to write the following verse about Laozi and the *Tao Te Ching*:

> "Those who speak know nothing;
> Those who know are silent."
> These words, I am told,
> Were spoken by Laozi.
> If we are to believe that Laozi,
>   Was himself *one who knew*,
> How is it that he wrote a book,
>   Of five thousand words?

A Universal View

The Taoists believe that people, in their effort to understand the universe, divide it into many parts. People give everything a name of its own. In doing so, they neglect the universal view, forgetting that the natural world is an integrated whole. Because the phenomena of the universe are so numerous and different, the oneness of the universe is overlooked. Humans, the Taoist points out, are merely one element, no more and no less important than all the other elements of the natural world. Since people generally are confused or ignorant about their own place in the universal view, they do not know how to think and behave properly. They have no peace of mind, therefore, and society is in a troubled state.

If people are ignorant of their best interests in life, the Taoists claim that society itself is largely responsible. They claim that society does not permit human beings to act in a completely natural way. Instead, they say that society distorts the human personality by compelling people to conform to unnatural standards of behavior. Rather than following their natural instincts, the Taoists claim that people strive vainly and unhappily to live according to laws, customs, and traditions that are contrary to the ways of nature.

To escape from this trap set (with the best intentions) by society, people must find the Tao, or "Way," of the universe. The Taoists claim that people should reject formal knowledge and learning and rely more on their senses and instincts. The Taoists argue that people should try to discover the nature and rhythm of the universe so they can seek to rediscover their natural selves. Like the bamboo that sways in the breeze and the cloud that drifts with the wind, people should flow with the "Way." People will have peace of mind, say the Taoists, only when they ignore the legal and moral codes created by government and society and behave naturally and spontaneously.

Government Opposition

Power-seeking princes did not look kindly on the Taoists. From the point of view of China's rulers, the Taoist teaching that government and laws should be ignored seemed dangerous. The lords of the Chinese feudal states thought their subjects should be obedient. They did not want any philosophers to encourage people to behave as each personally thought best. Because of the disapproval of the feudal states, the Taoists found it difficult to practice their beliefs within organized society. The followers of Laozi therefore withdrew to the mountains and forests. Becoming hermits, they sought to live in nature as harmonious parts of their surroundings. In this way they tried to uphold the following teaching of Laozi:

> Man follows the ways of the Earth,
> The Earth follows the ways of Heaven,
> Heaven follows the ways of Tao,
> Tao follows its own ways.

Taoism, with its emphasis on individuality, had a lasting influence on Chinese life and culture. Its contrast with the Confucian demands of political conformity and the rigors of strict Confucian morality made Laozi's views appealing. It mattered little that most people did not formally adopt the teachings of Laozi. In the thinking and behavior of generation after generation of the Chinese people, the influence of Taoism has been strong. Moreover, some of the finest Chinese literature and painting reflects the influence of Laozi and his disciples.

The Legalists

Confucius, Mencius, and other philosophers believed in the basic goodness of human nature and the universe. But contrary beliefs were held by the **Legalists,** whose teachings were developed in the third century B.C. The Legalists took for granted the idea that human nature was inherently bad. They believed that the interests of the state were more important than the welfare of the individual. Only through the enforcement of strict laws could rulers bring security and order to society.

The Legalists believed that severe laws backed by force were necessary to achieve the ruler's goal. Minor crimes and any failure to carry out government decrees were to be ruthlessly punished. The Legalists argued that harsh punishments for small crimes would deter people from committing major violations of the law. As with people, so it was with customs and traditions. To increase the wealth and power of the state, the Legalists thought no ruler should hesitate to trample on the time-honored ways of the people. They taught that any people, ideas, and institutions that stood in the ruler's way shoud be weeded out.

Legalism in Qin

One Chinese feudal state whose rulers followed Legalist thought was that of the Qin (CHIN). In the fifth century B.C. the feudal domain of Qin had established itself in the mountainous country of northwest China. It was not especially strong in comparison with various states to the east on the North China Plain. But, in keeping with Legalist teachings, the rulers of Qin let nothing stand in their way of increasing the power and wealth of the state. Gradually they introduced new policies that solidified their hold on their mountain domain. The hereditary nobles in the Qin state were ruthlessly eliminated. Peasants were given plots of land to hold in private ownership, but in return they had to pay taxes to the central government and to serve when needed in the army. In the course of two centuries the rulers of Qin established a politically stable and militarily powerful state.

Qin rulers frequently waged war against their weaker neighbors and thus continued to acquire new territories and bring them under their control. For a long time the rulers of neighboring states did not recognize the common danger they faced and were slow to unite against the powerful Qin state. When they finally recognized the importance of a united effort, it was too late. The Qin armies overpowered all their rivals. The weak Zhou dynasty came to an inglorious end in 256 B.C. Shortly afterward, the Qin ruler stamped out final efforts at resistance and proclaimed a new imperial line.

A New Era

The establishment of the Qin dynasty in 221 B.C. signaled the beginning of a new era in Chinese history. The formation of the Chinese state mirrored the stages of civilization that other great civilizations had passed through. From village communities, small states had formed, which in turn evolved into great domains during the late Shang and Zhou periods. Under the powerless Zhou dynasty a confederation of states developed. Then, this loose assembly of states was united under the rule of the monarchs of Qin. The conquest of the Zhou dynasty by the Qin was the beginning of the Chinese Empire, which was to endure under a series of dynasties for more than 2,000 years.

Check Your Understanding

1. **a.** Who were the Taoists? **b.** What did they teach? **c.** Why did the rulers of the Chinese states oppose the Taoists?
2. **a.** How did the Qin rulers rise to power? **b.** What philosophy did they follow?
3. **Thinking Critically:** Compare the ideas of the Legalists with the views of the thinkers who came before them. What kind of government today might find the ideas of the Legalists attractive?

CHAPTER REVIEW

■ **Chapter Summary**

Section 1. The China region shares with several other areas of Asia and Africa the distinction of being one of the oldest inhabited places on earth. Although archaeologists began excavations in China only in the twentieth century, their discoveries have yielded important information about the earliest Chinese civilizations. According to legend the Xia was China's first dynasty. But the first dynasty for which archaeologists have found actual physical evidence is that of the Shang. The people of Shang times no longer relied solely on hunting and herding. Their economy was based on agriculture and trade. They practiced religious divination and had developed a system of writing. The Shang were especially noted for their skill in bronze working.

Section 2. The Shang dynasty was replaced by the Zhou. In Chinese history, the 850-year-long Zhou period is known as an age of great ferment that has often been compared to the feudal period of Western Europe. One extremely important development that took place was the introduction of the use of iron. But the Zhou period is memorable above all as the age of great philosophers.

Section 3. Confucius was one of the outstanding thinkers of the Zhou period. His ideals were the establishment of social harmony and the perfection of individual behavior. He sought to instruct his fellow Chinese to behave properly in their family and social relationships and always to conduct themselves in accordance with high ethical standards. Although Confucius had little influence during his lifetime, his teachings ultimately became the standard for Chinese society.

Section 4. The social philosophy of Confucianism had many competitors. Taoism with its stress on harmony and nature had a powerful appeal to many Chinese. Its ideas and outlook continued to influence the Chinese people for centuries. Tough-minded rulers, notably the princes of the state of Qin, were attracted by the ideas of the Legalists. Following Legalist teachings, the Qin sovereigns introduced practices that greatly strengthened their realm. As a result, they were able not only to overwhelm rulers of neighboring states, but also to overthrow and replace the Zhou dynasty. With the rise of the Qin to supreme power, the Chinese Empire began.

■ **Vocabulary Review**

Define: oral tradition, aristocracy, divination, sovereignty, feudalism, classical age, philosopher, Confucianism, ethical system, filial piety, Mandate of Heaven, Taoism, Legalism, Legalist

■ **Places to Locate**

Locate: Anyang, Indus River, East Asia, Central Asia

■ **People to Know**

Identify: Peking Man, Xia, Shang, Zhou, Qin, Confucius, Laozi, Mencius

■ **Thinking Critically**

1. How did the use of iron change Chinese life?
2. Why did people living in urban areas in China build walls around their cities?
3. How did the teachings of Confucius, Mencius, and Laozi each affect the power of rulers?
4. How was the Chinese type of feudalism different from the type of feudalism practiced in Western Europe?

■ **Extending and Applying Your Knowledge**

1. Do research in encyclopaedias and other reference works to find out more about *Homo erectus*, the species with which Peking Man is classified. Share your report with the class.

2. Interesting information about the work of archaeologists and anthropologists is included in several articles found in the October 1988 issue of *National Geographic*, (Vol. 174, No. 4, pages 434–503). Read these articles to compile a report on how modern archaeologists and anthropologists reconstruct the spread of humankind throughout the world from its centers of origin.

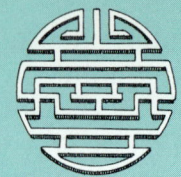

3

The Early Imperial Age

The Early Imperial Age began in 221 B.C. and lasted until A.D. 960. The establishment of the Qin dynasty (221–206 B.C.) signified the end of the Zhou period and the beginning of the Chinese Empire. Although the ruling house of Qin lasted a mere 15 years, its impact on the later history of the Chinese people is immeasurable. The Qin emperors destroyed the many independent states into which China had been split for centuries. The Qin emperors also changed the very foundation of Chinese government and life.

Although peace was an ideal cherished by the Chinese people, the Qin and later dynastic rulers often plunged the country into war to establish and maintain their control over China. One ruler after another used military force to compel respect throughout the empire for the **central government**. Chinese rulers also used armed might to defend their domain against foreign enemies and to encroach on the territories of their neighbors. Despite occasional setbacks, some of them devastating defeats, the empire continued to expand. The height of its power was reached under the Tang dynasty.

Yet the history of imperial China is much more than the overthrow and establishment of a series of ruling houses. It is also the story of the continual development of Chinese civilization. Over the centuries Chinese life has undergone many changes. These changes range over the total spectrum of Chinese life and involve social organization, economic activities, and cultural achievements of lasting value.

1. The Qin, Han, and Tang Dynasties

The establishment of the Chinese Empire was accomplished by the Qin dynasty. Its pattern of a strong centralized government was followed by the Han (HAHN) and Later Han dynasties. After a period of disunity, the height of Chinese power was attained under the Tang (TAHNG) dynasty. The Chinese Empire at this time was rivaled in size and strength only by the new domain of the Arabs in the Middle East.

The Qin Dynasty

Shihuangdi (shir-hwahng-dee), the Qin ruler who founded the Chinese Empire, came to the throne in 246 B.C. Shihuangdi hoped to create the greatest empire ever known. During his reign, armies were on the march constantly. By using his armies effectively, Shihuangdi crushed resistance within the state and overwhelmed non-Chinese inhabitants along the borders. After 25 years, the Qin ruler felt that he had succeeded in creating his eternal empire. In 221 B.C. he formally established the Chinese Empire, adopting the title of Shihuangdi, which means "First Emperor." By the time of his death in 210 B.C., the realm of the First Emperor included most of China Proper.

This section of the Great Wall of China dates to Ming times. In the background appear several of the fortified towers from which Chinese soldiers for centuries guarded against raids from nomads and other invaders.

TIMETABLE

The Early Imperial Age

221 B.C.–206 B.C.	Qin dynasty
206 B.C.–A.D. 8	Han dynasty
25–220	Later Han dynasty
220–589	Age of Disunity
589–618	Sui dynasty
618–907	Tang dynasty

Shihuangdi wanted to protect his conquests against the raids of nomadic warriors from Manchuria and Mongolia. With this purpose in mind, he launched one of the most ambitious construction projects that has ever been undertaken anywhere. This was the building of the Great Wall along the northern frontier of China Proper.

Many smaller barriers had been erected earlier by various Chinese states during the Zhou period. Shihuangdi united, strengthened, and extended these walls, making them into a single massive fortification. Building the Great Wall was a monumental construction project that took thousands of conscripted laborers years to complete by hand. The wall stretched from the coast of northeast China for almost 1,400 miles—the approximate distance between Boston, Massachusetts, and Minneapolis, Minnesota.

Work on the Great Wall continued beyond Qin times. Actually Shihuangdi's "Great Wall" preceded the present Great Wall, which dates from the fourteenth and fifteenth centuries A.D. For some 1,500 years, repair work or new construction has been done on the rambling structure. Visitors to China today are shown a section that was restored and opened to visitors in 1949.

Fall of the Qin Dynasty

Shihuangdi had aroused much resentment by forcing thousands of peasants to carry out his military goals and to toil on the Great Wall and on other public projects. Moreover, many educated Chinese objected to his Legalistic rule. They favored a return to rule based on other philosophical systems. A struggle for the throne followed Shihuangdi's death. Having lost the support of the Chinese people, the Qin dynasty fell. By 206 B.C., only a few years after the First Emperor's death, the dynasty came to an end. During its short rule, the Qin had shown that China could be united under a centralized government. Thus the Qin dynasty proved to be one of the most important periods of Chinese history.

Rise of the Han Dynasty

The winner of the struggle for imperial power established the Han dynasty (206 B.C.–A.D. 8). Under this regime and that of its successor, the Later Han (A.D. 25–220), Chinese military power was felt by many people. The very name of these two dynasties has continued to evoke images of military grandeur among the Chinese. In tribute to the feats of these empire-builders, the Chinese to this day call themselves "the Han people" or "the Sons of Han."

The Han rulers made their greatest advances in Central Asia. Chinese troops pressed into the mountain and desert regions of Xinjiang, occupying important towns and establishing military bases. By controlling these strategic points, they dominated the caravan routes that connected northwestern China Proper with the trading centers of India, Persia, and the Mediterranean world. These avenues of commerce, one of which was the famed Silk Road, enabled the Chinese to trade with peoples as far distant as the Romans. (See map, page 58; Sidelight to History, page 59.) Even after the Later Han dynasty fell from power, the flow of goods between China and the West did not completely come to an end.

The Han dynasty developed a **tributary system** to deal with the non-Chinese border states. As long as the local rulers of these states paid **tribute** in the form of money and goods, the Han permitted them to remain in power and rule as they wished. The rulers of the border states sent their sons to the Han capital at Chang'an where the sons received a Chinese education and married Chinese princesses. The tributary system allowed the Han dynasty to promote its political and social objectives and to develop some familial ties in areas beyond its borders. The tributary system remained in use throughout China's imperial history.

The Age of Disunity

The 400-year period after the disappearance of the Later Han dynasty became known as the Age of Disunity. During this period, China broke up into several independent states. At first the Chinese Empire was divided into three monarchies—the Wu, the

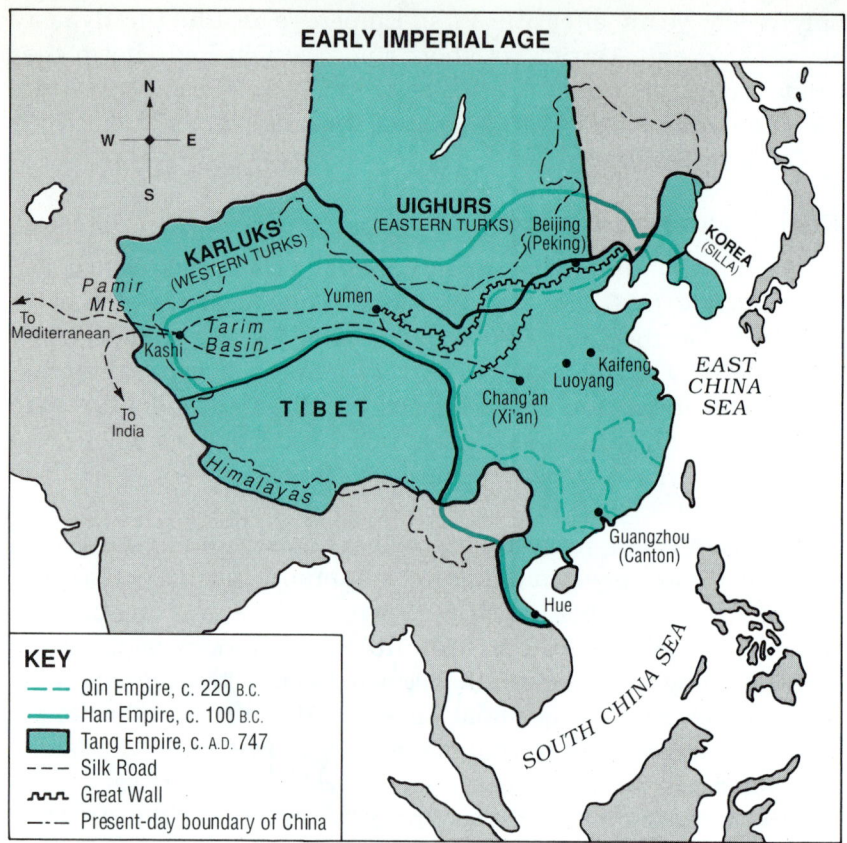

MOVEMENT: THE EARLY IMPERIAL AGE. This map shows the varying extent of the Chinese Empire under the three great dynasties of the period. Some parts of the Tang Empire—for example, Tibet and Silla (Korea)—were vassal states of the Chinese emperor. Note the route of the Silk Road, which extended west from Chang'an around the Takla Makan desert in the Tarim Basin.

Wei, and the Shu Han. The rulers of these three monarchies battled and intrigued among themselves for supremacy. The exploits of these times stirred the imagination of the Chinese people in later centuries. They transformed the great commanders and warriors into legendary heroes, telling tales of their daring deeds over and over again in their homes and teahouses. After many centuries these traditional tales were collected and written down in *The Romance of the Three Kingdoms,* one of China's greatest novels.

The period of the three monarchies seemed especially glorious to the Chinese people because of the unhappy period that followed for the next few centuries. While the contenders for the throne wasted their strength fighting one another, invaders managed to burst through the frontier defenses and overrun much

SIDELIGHT TO HISTORY

The Silk Road

A westward journey along the Silk Road began at the Han capital of Chang'an, now Xi'an. The caravan route extended in a northwesterly direction toward Gansu and then headed across Central Asia. Merchants avoided the perilous desert of the Takla Makan by skirting north and south of it to follow strings of oases. At Kashi the Silk Road again split. One branch led westward toward the Mediterranean and one southward to India.

The Mediterranean branch ended at Antioch in Syria. Over the Silk Road flowed goods and cultural influences between two great empires—Han China and the Roman Empire, then at its height. Merchant caravans on the Silk Road brought precious Chinese silks to the outposts of the Roman Empire's Asian provinces. From these outposts, traders then carried the silks to many other parts of the Roman Empire. The silks were so famous that the Romans called China the "silk country," or Serica. On their part, the Chinese gave the name *Ta Ch'in,* meaning "Great Ch'in," to that part of the Roman Empire they knew about. In return for the silks, the Chinese received woolen and linen cloth, glass, horses, precious stones, and ivory. Along with the goods, however, ideas and influences also traveled back and forth between East Asia and the West. The Chinese introduced people of the West to rhubarb, peaches, apricots, and other fruits. News about gunpowder and papermaking, inventions that began in China, probably traveled along the Silk Road as well.

Contacts between China and India to the southwest led to the introduction of Buddhism, probably by merchants traveling the southwestern branch of the Silk Road. Once the Chinese learned about Buddhism, the religion spread rapidly. (See pages 69–73.)

---

of North China. For a time China became the prize of foreign invaders, but it was eventually reunited under the Sui (SWIH) dynasty. There were just two emperors of this dynasty, and their reign lasted only from 589 to 618. The Sui dynasty laid the foundation for the long period of peace and prosperity that followed. A strong centralized government was established. In addition, the Great Wall was reconstructed and expanded to facilitate the movement of goods and communication between the north and the south.

Unfortunately the able first Sui ruler, Emperor Wen, was succeeded on the throne by his less-talented son, Emperor Yang. Yang's overambitious building projects and attempts to expand the empire drained the country's resources and greatly weakened Yang's control. He fled to South China where he was assassinated in 618.

The Tang Dynasty

During the early years of the seventh century a dynasty was founded that was just as powerful as the Han. This was the Tang, a family that ruled from A.D. 618 to 907. The greatness of the Tang age rests partly on the size of its far-flung empire, which spread over East and Central Asia. (See map, page 58.) More important, however, during this period Chinese civilization came into full bloom. Trade and commerce flourished as never before. Brilliant literature, painting, sculpture, architecture, music, and dance brought a new richness to the life of the country. The people of nearby Korea and Japan eagerly borrowed and imitated the Tang culture. Moreover, travelers, merchants, and missionaries came from all over Asia to admire the wonders of Chinese civilization.

A Golden Age of Prose and Poetry

The vigor of Tang literature is revealed in the writings of Han Yu (HAHN YOO). A master of literary form and celebrated for his polished style, he was widely imitated not only by Tang writers but also by scholars of later periods in China's history. His most famous essay, "Memorial on the Bone of Buddha," protested the display in the imperial palace of a supposed bone of Buddha. The strong anti-Buddhist and anti-foreign tone of the essay nearly cost Han Yu his life, but later Confucian philosophers heralded his work.

Poets of the Tang era rank among the world's masters. Li Bo (LEE BOH) can perhaps be considered the greatest of these poets. About 1,800 of the 20,000 poems he is reported to have written have survived. Li Bo had the reputation of a carefree fellow, who was fond of travel, but in some of his poems he shows a poignant sadness. Whatever caught Li Bo's mood of the moment was quickly captured in verses of rich imagery and delicate beauty. The flavor of his work is suggested by this translation of one of his poems. Entitled "Quiet Thoughts at Night," this 20–character poem, in perfect tonal and grammatical symmetry, traditionally has been memorized by every Chinese school child:

> So bright a gleam on the foot of my bed—
> Could there have been a frost already?
> Lifting myself up to look, I found that it was moonlight.
> Sinking back again, I thought suddenly of home.
> [Witter Bynner, trans. *The Jade Mountain: A Chinese Anthology.*]

Another famous poet who lived at the same time as Li Bo was Du Fu (DOO FOO). Du Fu's verses are less lilting and lyrical than Li Bo's, probably because Du Fu had experienced much personal tragedy. The reader can sense in his poetry a deep compassion for human suffering. Bo Zhuyi (BOH JOO-EE), the third of the great triumvirate of Tang poets, lived at a time when the dynasty had entered its fateful decline. His compositions were simple in language and often taught a moral lesson. Po Zhuyi's poems are still favorites of the Chinese people.

Literary achievements of the Tang golden age, however, could not stop rebellions at home nor the pressure of invasions along the borders during the last half of the dynastic period. Political decline set in. The death blow came in 907 when rebels ousted the last of the Tang emperors from the imperial throne, thus ending the Early Imperial Age.

Check Your Understanding

1. **a.** What were Shihuangdi's two major ambitions? **b.** How successful was he in attaining them? **c.** What led to the fall of the Qin dynasty? **d.** Why was the Qin one of the most important periods in China's history?
2. **a.** Why were the areas conquered by the Han particularly important to China? **b.** How did the Han keep these areas under control?
3. **a.** What happened when the Later Han dynasty lost power? **b.** What images do Chinese have of this period? **c.** What dynasty reunited China?
4. Why is the period of the Tang dynasty referred to as a golden age of literature and poetry?
5. *Thinking Critically:* Why was the Silk Road an important part of the development of Chinese civilization and power?

2. Domination of Confucianism in Chinese Life

"An empire can be conquered on horseback, but it cannot be ruled from horseback." So a scholar warned the first Han emperor. Not all successors to the Han appreciated this wisdom. But those who did built up enduring empires. They realized it was easier to defeat an enemy on the battlefield than to achieve victory and maintain control in the political arena. Every dynasty, from the Qin on, was confronted with governing a huge territory inhabited by a large population. As the empire grew in size, the problems of administration naturally increased.

Confucianism Under the Qin

The question of how to rule a huge empire was one of great importance to every dynasty. The Qin rulers, determined to create a centralized government, followed the rigorous doctrines of Legalism. (See page 49.) The Qin rulers recognized that to establish their own authority, they had to destroy both the Zhou system of tributary states that was kept under loose central control and the hereditary nobility. Local leaders who refused to accept the policies of the Qin were ruthlessly crushed. The Confucian scholars protested against the imperial government's brutal methods and disregard for **tradition.** But the Qin rulers retaliated. Copies of the Confucian Classics were destroyed, and many of the scholars fell victim to the emperors' fury. According to legend, the Qin rulers had a number of scholars buried alive. These extreme measures badly hurt the Qin cause. Since Confucianists were about the only Chinese trained for public service, the dynasty was hard put to find experienced officials to serve the government.

Confucianism Under the Han

As we have seen, the Han emperors enlarged the empire and therefore added to the challenges of administration. Wiser than the Qin rulers who had single-mindedly practiced Legalism, the Han emperors carefully assessed the value of the Confucian scholars and teachings. The Han concluded that Confucianism, which emphasized respect for tradition, customs, and age, could be used to promote peace and stability. Therefore, the Han rulers adopted the teachings of Confucius as the official philosophy of the state. At the same time, Confucian scholars were appointed to administrative positions in the government. For the next 2,000 years Confucianism and government were inseparable in China.

These four terracotta figures from the Tang dynasty show women of the court playing polo. During this dynasty, women enjoyed greater freedom than in later times. Beginning with the Song dynasty, the activities of women were mainly restricted to the home.

Civil Service Examinations

To make certain that the state would have the service of properly trained and educated administrators, a system of regular examinations was introduced during Han times. Candidates for high government positions were required to take a series of rigorous tests. The test questions were based on Confucian philosophy and the Confucian interpretation of history, which emphasized morality in human affairs. Attention was also paid to literary style and skill in **calligraphy.** The examinations placed little value on technical knowledge and skills. It was assumed that the scholar-officials who had mastered Confucian thought were capable of governing wisely. Those who passed these difficult examinations became eligible for official appointments.

During most of the Early Imperial Age, only male members of aristocratic families were recommended for civil service examinations. The upper classes had no intention of sharing political power with the common people. For many centuries the aristocrats were strong enough to block any efforts by the state to open the examinations to all candidates regardless of **social class.** In the late Tang period, however, rebellions and wars greatly weakened the aristocratic families. The government then succeeded in breaking the **monopoly** of the old and wealthy families on government offices. From then on, until the Confucian examination system was abolished in 1905, all male subjects of the emperor were eligible to compete for appointment to high political positions.

Importance of Education

"A small man with education is of use to the state; of what use is a tall man who knows nothing?" Many proverbs like this one point to the traditional Chinese respect for learning. In imperial China, education came to mean Confucianism and its related arts and skills. By mastering the teachings of Confucius and the explanations of his philosophy by outstanding scholars, students could pass the government examinations and achieve high positions. The inseparable combination of imperial government and Confucianism thus rested on maintaining the educational system.

Schooling in China had as its main aim the preparation of students for the civil service examinations. No sacrifice was considered too great by families anxious to see their sons get ahead in the world. From the moment the sons were able to toddle around, the parents directed their attention to Confucian learning. But only wealthy families could afford to allow their sons to spend years in study instead of work. Because few schools existed, most students were educated by tutors.

The Demands of Confucian Education

There were few short cuts in the Confucian educational system. Students started their education with three primers called the *Trimetrical Classic,* the *Classic of Filial Piety,* and the *Thousand-Character Classic.* They then went on to wrestle with the Confucian Classics themselves. All the while they had to learn the many complex characters of Chinese writing, to develop appropriate literary style, and to acquire the arts of calligraphy and composition of poetry. After 15 years or more of concentrated study, the hopeful scholars, who by this time were 30 years old or older, took the first of many series of tests. If they survived the first examination, which was given in their own community, they became eligible to compete on higher levels. The final examinations were held in the imperial capital, where successful candidates were interviewed by the emperor himself.

Passing these difficult tests made a scholar eligible for office. It did not, however, guarantee appointment. The scholar assigned to government service was fortunate. Generally these **scholar-officials** could look forward to lives of usefulness, comfort, and wealth. Not to be overlooked was the credit reflected on their families and communities. Scholars who failed to pass the examinations did not easily give up. Many of them took the tests again and again, regardless of repeated failure. To support themselves while preparing for the next round of examinations, scholars often became teachers. Scholars who realized they lacked the ability to be able to pass the higher level examinations often did the next best thing and became clerks, scribes, and recordkeepers at lower levels of the bureaucracy.

Check Your Understanding

1. What means were used by Chinese emperors to find qualified men for government posts?
2. What skills or knowledge did a man need to become a government official?
3. *Thinking Critically:* Compare the way Qin rulers regarded Confucianism with the way Han rulers regarded it. Why do you think the Han rulers differed from the Qin in this regard?

3. The Framework of Chinese Society

In the Confucian view, Chinese society was divided into certain classes. These four traditional classes were scholars, peasants, artisans, and merchants. Supposedly each person could be classified as a member of one of these groups. Yet, despite the Confucian teachings, China's **social order** was not rigidly fixed. Occasionally people moved from one social class to another. Moreover, there were some groups of people who did not fit into any slot in the Confucian class system.

Scholars

In no other country were scholars so highly esteemed as in China. Those unusually gifted intellectuals who became officeholders were especially respected. From the point of view of the Confucianist state, these scholar-officials contributed most to the administration of the government by keeping the affairs of state in order. Furthermore, the scholar-officials were responsible for enriching the country's arts and learning because they were also expected to be historians, philosophers, poets, painters, and musicians.

In actual practice the scholar-officials varied considerably in ability and performance of duties. Many scholar-officials were honest and just, and some even had monuments erected in their memory. But other scholar-officials abused their power. Part of this problem stemmed from their low pay. On their low salaries

TANG ART. Tang artists, many of them scholar-officials, excelled in painting and sculpture. A Tang scholar-official of high rank painted the figures at right as part of a scroll depicting 13 emperors of earlier dynasties. Although worn with age, the scroll still ranks among the finest of Chinese figure paintings.

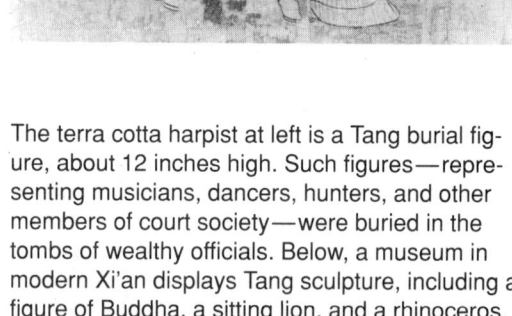

The terra cotta harpist at left is a Tang burial figure, about 12 inches high. Such figures—representing musicians, dancers, hunters, and other members of court society—were buried in the tombs of wealthy officials. Below, a museum in modern Xi'an displays Tang sculpture, including a figure of Buddha, a sitting lion, and a rhinoceros.

they had to support families and staffs and had to repay their parents and friends for the expenses of their education. To meet their expenses, some scholar-officials resorted to bribery and other corrupt practices. Such dishonest officials cost the state dearly.

Peasants

As the providers of food for all, peasants were highly respected in theory. In reality, however, the high social classification of the peasantry was meaningless. Since more than 80 percent of the population derived their livelihood from the land, the peasantry made up the mass of the people. Actually, peasants varied in their economic well-being. Some were wealthy, and others made a comfortable living. But most were hopelessly poor. A farmer who owned two and a half acres of land, the minimum amount necessary for the support of a family of five or six, was considered lucky. Many peasants, however, owned no land at all and had little hope of ever owning any.

Some of the peasant's difficulties stemmed from Chinese customs and practices. For example, when peasants who were the heads of a household died, their property was divided among their male descendants. Thus, after a few generations, farming plots were split into many small strips. With insufficient land to earn a living, many peasants had to work for low wages or lease additional plots at high rentals. The peasants also had to pay heavy taxes. And when peasants needed loans to tide them over during lean months, moneylenders charged high interest rates. Once indebted to moneylenders, the peasants were rarely able to pay off their debts. Usually they lost the little land they may have had.

When farming offered no hope for even a meager living, peasants in their desperation sometimes became bandits. They then roamed and terrorized the countryside, robbing travelers and merchants and preying on defenseless villagers. Occasionally bold and daring leaders organized peasants engaged in banditry into large bands or even armies strong enough to challenge the imperial troops. Even the most powerful dynasties never completely succeeded in stamping out these peasant rebels.

Artisans

Artisans constituted the third class in Confucian society. Like the cultivators of the land, artisans were considered to be productive members of society and in theory were well regarded. Artisans made articles that were needed by both rich and poor.

Living in the cities and towns, artisans often carried on their work in the same buildings where they had their homes. Their **factories** also served as retail shops, where the artisans displayed their wares and where people bought the handmade articles they produced. The businesses and skills of the artisans were passed on within the family from generation to generation. Tools and techniques changed very slowly, and many families carefully guarded the secrets of production that distinguished their goods from the work of other artisans.

Merchants

Merchants composed the last of the four social classes in Confucian society. From the Confucian point of view, the merchants contributed little or nothing to the welfare of society because they were regarded as parasites who accumulated their wealth by trading and selling goods that were created by the labor of others. At best, the merchants were considered a necessary evil. This view reflected the limited economic knowledge and experience of the scholar-officials as well as the **prejudice** of the people who venerated the land and its products. The contempt of the Confucianists for the merchants was partly a result of fear. The scholar-officials realized that the merchants' riches could be used to change or even destroy the traditional social order. To prevent any overturning of the social order, Confucian scholar-officials favored the enactment of laws to restrict the operations of businesspeople.

Even though merchants were held in low esteem by the scholar-officials and peasants, many townspeople admired the person who lived well and was skillful in accumulating wealth. People were eager to offer their children as brides and grooms for the children of prosperous businesspeople. Successful businesspeople were envied by many less fortunate townspeople.

Outsiders

One group of people who had no place within the Confucian social system consisted of military men. Soldiers were stationed throughout imperial China and in garrisons along the frontiers. Not only the scholar-officials but also many common people despised the men of the army. "Good iron is not used for nails, and good men are not used for soldiers," stated a well-known saying. Few Chinese joined the army voluntarily. During times of confusion and rebellion, the government frequently lost control of the army. Then bands of soldiers became as feared as peasant bandits and robbers. But during time of law and order, soldiers were praised.

There were others besides soldiers who had no place in the Confucian social order. The imperial nobility, for instance, formed its own social group. So too did the priests of the various religions and cults. Also, a small number of people were domestic slaves, but they accounted for only a tiny percentage of the population.

Check Your Understanding

1. **a.** Describe the four classes of people that made up the framework of Chinese society. **b.** What groups were considered outside the framework of Chinese society?
2. Why did scholar-officials look down on the merchant class?
3. What group was mainly responsible for China's cultural achievements in the Early Imperial Age?
4. *Thinking Critically:* Which group consisted of the highest proportion of Chinese society? Why, do you think, were most of the people in this group helplessly poor?

4. The Spread of Buddhism in China

Before and during the Early Imperial Age, teachers of many faiths tried with varying success to convert the Chinese people to their beliefs. Some of these religions arose within China; others were introduced by missionaries from foreign lands. The Chinese were tolerant in matters of faith and would listen politely to these various spiritual messages. "Every truth has its sect," they said, "and every sect has its truth." No religion, however, ever seized the imagination of the Chinese more strongly than Buddhism. Confucianism appealed to the rational side of human nature. In contrast, Buddhism won favor with the spiritual side of the Chinese people.

Buddha's Search for Enlightenment

Gautama (GAW-tuh-muh), the founder of Buddhism, was born about 567 B.C. in a small kingdom in northern India that today is part of Nepal. A prince by birth, Gautama according to tradi-

RELIGIOUS IMAGES. One of the most popular Buddhist saints or deities (top left) has been the Goddess of Mercy or Guanyin. Eleven angry-looking faces adorn the headdress of this eighth-century sculpture. A 50-foot-high statue of Buddha (below), flanked by other Buddhist deities, sits in a cave temple at the foot of a cliff in Henan province. A stone rubbing of Confucius (top right) was done centuries after his death. No real likeness of Confucius exists.

SIDELIGHT TO HISTORY

The Only Female Emperor

Buddhism thrived in China under the early Tang rulers. One of its most ardent supporters was the only woman ever to become emperor of China. When one of the Tang emperors died in 683, his widow—the Empress Wu—seized power. For a time she was the "power behind the throne" while two successive **puppet emperors** held the imperial title.

Then in 690, she assumed the title of emperor herself and ruled until 705. Through the ages other shrewd women at times held power in the Chinese court, but the Empress Wu was the only woman ever to bear the actual title of "emperor."

---

tion led a sheltered life during his youth. When he first saw sickness, poverty, and death, he was deeply shocked. Gautama began to brood about the nature and purpose of life. Unable to find satisfactory answers, he decided to leave his home and family and search for the truth. After many years of wandering, studying, and thinking, the answer that Gautama had been seeking came to him through intuition. With this knowledge he became the Buddha, the Enlightened One.

The Buddha's Enlightenment began with acceptance of the Four Noble Truths. The first truth is that sorrow and suffering are a part of life. The second truth states that desire and yearning for the goods of this world make people unhappy. According to the third truth, people must end their attachments to things on earth and their yearnings for things they do not have in order to find peace. The fourth truth explains how believers can escape the pain and suffering to which they are doomed in this world. According to this truth, believers must lead a life of moderation and follow the Noble Eightfold Path—right views, right intentions, right speech, right action, right occupation, right effort, right concentration, and right meditation.

Buddha also taught that at death a person's soul is reborn into another body, and in fact, that people will go through many rebirths before attaining the final reward of **nirvana.** When they have attained nirvana, people are freed from the cycle of rebirth.

Buddha devoted his life to spreading the truth he had found, winning many faithful disciples.

Buddhism's Hold in China

Buddhism spread throughout India and then into Central Asia, where many converts were won. During the Age of Disunity, merchants and missionaries brought Buddhism over the caravan routes into China. Some Chinese converts, eager to learn more about their new faith, made pilgrimages to India during the sixth and seventh centuries. After studying at Buddhist centers for many years, the converts returned to China. They translated the Buddhist scriptures into Chinese and founded monasteries to preserve and carry on the Buddha's gospel.

Countless Chinese accepted the Buddhist faith. Buddhism's teachings of moral behavior and mercy toward fellow human beings had a powerful appeal. So did its promise of eventual peace, for life to most of the Chinese people meant a daily struggle for survival. Buddhism also enriched Chinese culture. Buddhist monasteries and pagodas were built throughout the empire. Many of them were adorned with exquisite statues of the Buddha in wood, stone, and bronze. Painters portrayed the Buddha and his saints and illustrated inspiring events of their lives. Buddhist themes also appeared in literature and poetry.

Opposition to Buddhism

Confucianists in the Chinese government eventually became fearful over the popularity of Buddhism. They did not oppose its teachings, but its growing political and economic influence alarmed them. Because lands turned over to Buddhist monasteries as gifts were exempt from taxes, the government lost a great deal of revenue. It also was deprived of able-bodied soldiers when men became Buddhist monks, since monks did not have to serve in the army. Moreover, Buddhist monks and nuns were bound by religious vows not to marry. Thus, by not having children, they limited the growth of China. Then, too, many philosophers shifted their attention from Confucianism to Buddhism. Since it seemed for a while that Buddhism might sweep away all other loyalties, the Confucian scholars accused the Buddhists of forming a state within the state.

During the ninth century, the Tang state launched a series of persecutions that severely weakened Buddhist influence in China. Although Buddhism was not outlawed, thousands of monasteries, temples, and shrines were destroyed. The property was confiscated, and many Buddhist monks and nuns were compelled to give up their religious life. Thereafter Buddhism declined as an organized religion, and it never fully recovered from the blows delivered by the jealous Tang dynasty.

Other Religions in China

A number of other great philosophies and religions of the world were to be found in Tang China. The two great Chinese philosophies, Confucianism and Taoism, were already more than 1,000 years old. Until the government-led persecutions, centers of Buddhist faith and learning flourished. Tradition places the arrival of Jews in China during the first centuries of the Imperial Age, and their appearance in the cities of North China during Tang times is definitely known. Moreover, Christianity was brought to China during the Tang era.

Islam, the religion of the Arabs, filtered into China a little more than a century after the death of its great prophet, Mohammed. In their great expansion eastward, Arab soldiers and their converts had driven far into Central Asia. There they not only gained many new followers but also clashed with the troops of the Tang Empire. From bases in Central Asia, Islam was brought into China by merchants and travelers. It is still deeply rooted in Xinjiang and the northwestern provinces.

During the Early Imperial Age, Buddhism and Islam were the only foreign religions to gain many converts in China. The Christian sects disappeared soon after the Tang dynasty broke up, and the Jews did not seek converts to their religion. Neither Buddhism nor Islam succeeded in displacing Confucianism as the dominant philosophy in Chinese life. Confucianism, however, incorporated many of the spiritual ideas of both faiths into the body of its philosophical teachings.

Check Your Understanding

1. How did Buddha come to found his religion?
2. What were the central ideas of Buddhism?
3. How did Buddhism spread to China?
4. What contributions did Buddhism make to Chinese culture?
5. ***Thinking Critically:*** How did Confucianism manage to maintain its dominance in Chinese life in spite of the spread of Buddhism and other religions to China?

CHAPTER REVIEW

■ **Chapter Summary**

Section 1. After the foundation of the Qin dynasty, the Chinese Empire emerged as a powerful state. Established by Shihuangdi, the Qin dynasty ruled for only a short time before it gave way to the Han dynasty. China's tributary system, which was developed by the Han dynasty, remained in use throughout China's imperial history. The disruption of the Age of Disunity was followed by the short-lived Sui dynasty. The most powerful dynasty of the Early Imperial Age—the Tang—then came to power. During the period of Tang rule, literature and arts flourished, giving China a golden age of brilliant cultural achievements. The works of such poets as Li Bo rank high among the masterpieces of world literature.

Section 2. During the Han dynastic period of the Early Imperial Age, Confucianism began its domination of Chinese life. In imperial China, education came to mean Confucianism and its related arts and skills. Confucian scholars were appointed to government posts after passing a series of grueling tests on Confucian philosophy and Chinese history.

Section 3. The framework of Chinese society revolved around four traditional classes of the social order: scholars, peasants, artisans, and merchants. While scholars were held in the highest esteem because of the Chinese respect for learning, merchants were held in lowest esteem because they made profits from the labors of others. Soldiers, aristocrats, and others, however, did not fit neatly into the Confucians' social order and remained outside the social framework of Confucian society.

Section 4. Buddhism came into China from India during the first centuries of the Early Imperial Age, and won many followers. During the later years of the Tang dynasty, however, Confucians became alarmed by Buddhism's growth and initiated a series of persecutions that effectively stopped its spread. Monasteries, temples, and shrines were destroyed, and property was seized, forcing many Buddhist monks and nuns to leave religious life. Nevertheless, Buddhist ideals permanently influenced many aspects of Chinese life. Other foreign religions—Islam, Christianity, and Judaism, were also introduced during the Tang dynastic period.

■ **Vocabulary Review**

Define: central government, tributary system, tribute, tradition, calligraphy, social class, monopoly, scholar-official, social order, factory, prejudice, puppet emperor, nirvana

■ **Place to Locate**

Locate: Silk Road, Kashi, Xi'an, Chang'an, Tarim Basin

■ **People to Know**

Identify: Shihuangdi, Emperor Wen, Emperor Yang, Han Yu, Li Bo, Du Fu, Bo Zhuyi, Gautama, Confucianist, Buddhist

■ **Thinking Critically**

1. Explain the meaning of the proverb, *An empire can be conquered on horseback, but it cannot be ruled from horseback.* What experiences of the Chinese probably led to creation of this proverb?
2. What weaknesses does the dynastic history of China reveal during the Early Imperial Age? What relationship does this weakness have to the length of a dynasty's rule?
3. Even though dynasties rose and fell during China's imperial history, the system of scholar-officials remained to administer the empire. What were the strengths and weaknesses of this administrative system? Assess the importance of this system to the length of China's imperial history.
4. Why did Buddhism attract many Chinese believers?

■ **Extending and Applying Your Knowledge**

1. Research and write a report on the Great Wall of China and how it protected China.
2. Compare illustrations of Chinese art before and after the introduction of Buddhism into China. Look for new themes or ideas attributable to Buddhism's influence.

4

The Late Imperial Age—From Song to Ming

It has been said of the Chinese that they always absorb their conquerors. Conquerors are usually in a position to impose their traditions, customs, and languages on the conquered peoples. Although the Chinese people often had to submit to the occupation of their country by foreign armies, the conquerors usually adopted the ways of their Chinese subjects, rather than the Chinese adapting to the ways of their conquerors.

During their long history the Chinese people were often overpowered by invaders from the northern and western borderlands. In an effort to keep these warlike nomads outside the frontier, the rulers of China constructed fortifications and stationed troops at key points. Sometimes Chinese armies invaded the lands beyond their borders and destroyed bases there. At other times, the Chinese tried diplomacy to keep foreigners at bay or used the tactics of divide and rule. Yet no matter what measures they tried, the Chinese were periodically overwhelmed by foreign peoples.

Conquerors ruled large parts of China during the Late Imperial Age—from the end of the Tang dynasty in 907 to the end of the empire in 1912. The history of these 1,000 years reveals that some conquerors succumbed quickly to the Chinese way of life. A few showed resistance to Chinese ways. In spite of foreign conquests, however, Chinese civilization endured.

1. Dynastic Struggles for Power

The downfall of a Chinese dynasty was always followed by a bitter struggle for power. The collapse of the Tang dynasty was no exception. Following the Tang collapse, years of conflict set in with the empire split into several warring states. The Chinese Empire remained divided for 300 years. It was finally reunited, but not by a Chinese dynasty. Conquerors from beyond its borders rather than a line of Chinese rulers eventually made the Middle Kingdom part of the largest empire in human history.

The Song Struggle

Soon after the downfall of the Tang, another Chinese ruling family succeeded in founding a new imperial dynasty. From 960 to 1279 the Song (SOONG) reigned over an area consisting mainly of China Proper. During the Song era, a people from Mongolia called the Khitan (KEE TAHN) broke through the Great Wall and gained control over large parts of Chinese territory. (*Kitai*, the Russian word for China, and *Cathay*, the old English word for China, come from the name of this empire.) In the western borderlands a people related to the Tibetans created a strong state in what is now Xinjiang.

The Song state fought desperate battles with the surrounding monarchies, but the Chinese could neither conquer nor absorb their enemies. In the early 1100's the power of the Khitan was at last shattered, but they were conquered by people from Manchuria, not the Song. The people from Manchuria continued their drive into China. In 1127, they forced the Song dynasty to abandon all its northern territory. Thereafter the Chinese ruling house, with its capital in the delta area of the Chang Jiang, was known as the Southern Song. Its domain embraced only a part of central and southern China Proper. The Southern Song dynasty lasted for 150 years.

TIMETABLE

Dynasties of the Late Imperial Age

960–1127	Song
1127–1279	Southern Song
1279–1368	Yuan (Mongol)
1368–1644	Ming
1644–1912	Qing (Manchu)

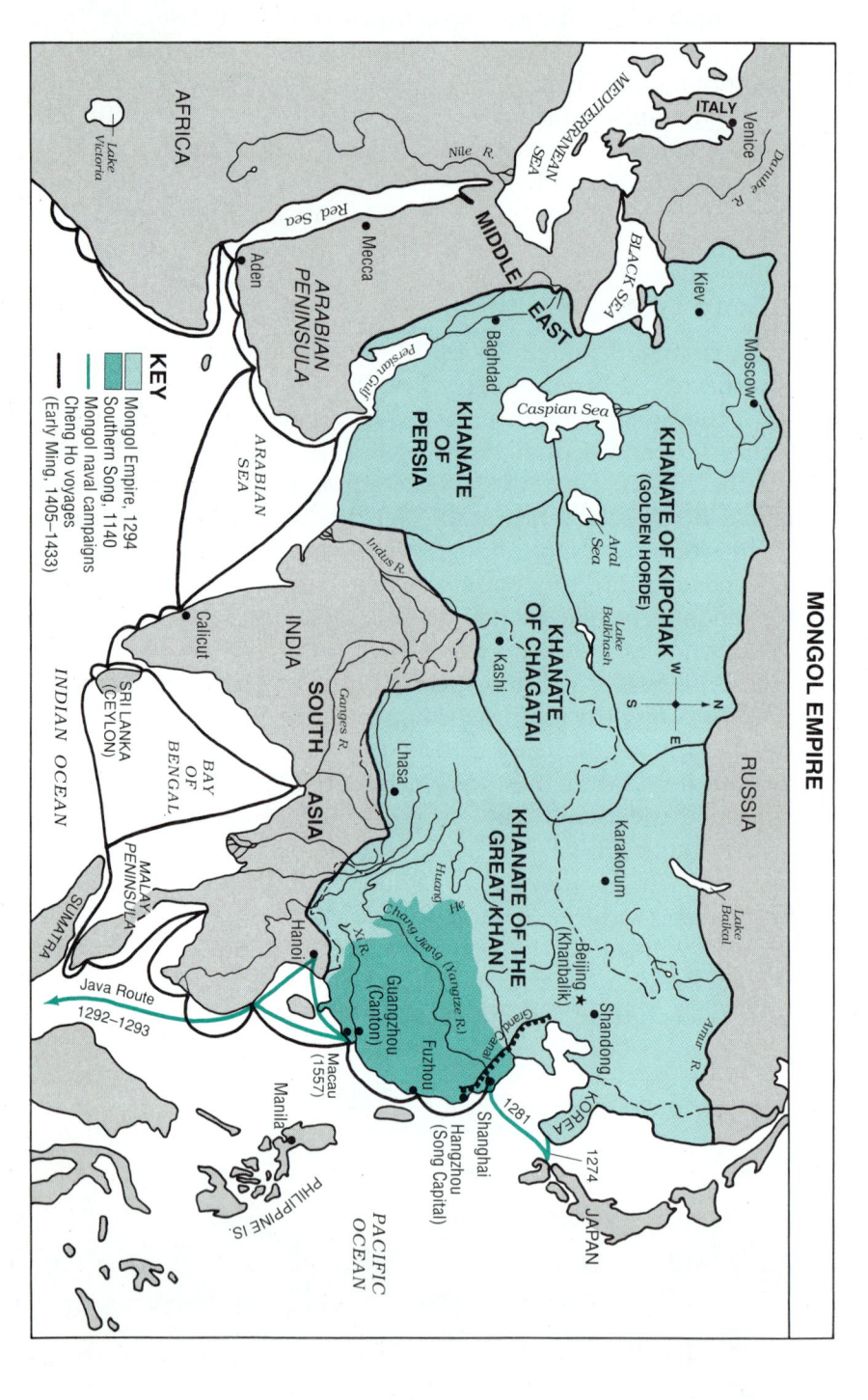

MONGOL RULERS. An old Chinese drawing (left) represents Genghis Khan, who united the Mongol tribes and conquered much of Asia. The illustration below appeared in an early French edition of Marco Polo's account of his travels and is supposed to show Kublai Khan receiving Marco Polo and his father and uncle. Who was Marco Polo?

The Mongol Horde and Genghis Khan

In the 1200's, the Mongol cavalry, the most fearless and brutal horsemen ever to ride into battle, swept as a whirlwind across Asia and eastern Europe. One by one, many states from Korea in the east to Russia in the west fell to the Mongol armies led by Genghis Khan (JENG-gis KAHN) and his descendants. From Tibet eastward to the Pacific, only Japan and monarchies in South and Southeast Asia escaped Mongol rule.

Temujin (TEM-oo-jihn), the given name of Genghis Khan, was born about 1165. Although he was the son and heir of a Mongol chieftain, Temujin's tribe rejected his claim to leadership when his father died. Thereafter, he was hunted and hounded by numerous enemies. But Temujin gathered an army of devoted warriors and fought his way to undisputed leadership of the **khans,** or princes, of Mongolia. In 1206 he capped his victories by adopting the title of Genghis Khan, which means "Ruler of the Universe." The galloping Mongol horsemen rode roughshod over

REGION: THE MONGOL EMPIRE. Mongol warriors spread over Asia and even into Europe, creating the superstate shown on the map to the left. The khanates were divisions of the Mongol Empire. Kublai Khan was known as the Great Khan because he was overlord of the entire Mongol Empire, although his sovereignty was disputed in some areas. The dashed lines show China's modern boundaries. Of which khanate did China make up the major portion?

the monarchs of Asia. Long before Genghis Khan died in 1227, his name was said with fear and awe throughout the civilized world. It was Genghis Khan's grandson, Kublai (KOO-bly) Khan (1215–1294) who in 1279 defeated the last of the Southern Song rulers and brought all of China into the great Mongol Empire.

The Mongol Empire reached its greatest extent under Kublai Khan. In 1271, eight years before the actual overthrow of the Southern Song dynasty in 1279, Kublai Khan established a new imperial dynasty called the Yuan (yoo-AHN). The Mongol Empire was simply too vast to be efficiently administered and had already begun to decline. Economic, military, and administrative problems combined with a series of earthquakes, floods, and famines to deal the Yuan dynasty a death blow in 1368.

The Ming Dynasty

Long before the Mongols were ousted from power, revolts had broken out in many parts of China. Bands of rebels roamed through the valley of the Chang Jiang and the south, throwing the country into turmoil. A Buddhist monk finally united the various rebel forces and led them to victory over the Mongols. The monk then established a new dynasty—the Ming (MIHNG), which lasted from 1368 to 1644.

The new emperor and his successors dispatched Chinese troops into border regions far to the north and west. For a brief time Chinese power was once more supreme. After centuries of rule by non-Chinese, the Chinese were once again masters of their own land. Government administration was set in order, and the destruction caused by years of war and rebellion was repaired. Trade and commerce were encouraged. Traditional arts and crafts showed a new vigor, and Chinese scholars and writers equaled or surpassed the accomplishments of their ancestors.

Check Your Understanding

1. **a.** What happened to the Chinese Empire after the fall of the Song dynasty? **b.** Why were the Song unable to hold the empire together?
2. **a.** How was China conquered by the Mongols? **b.** Describe the extent of the Mongol Empire.
3. ***Thinking Critically:*** Compare the decline and fall of the Mongol Empire with the decline and fall of earlier dynasties in China. Is the pattern of disruption similar or different? Explain.

2. China As a Seafaring Power

China is not usually thought of as a seafaring nation. Indeed, until the end of the Tang dynasty, the Chinese had rarely been tempted to sail the seas off their coasts. The expansion and defense of the empire had focused Chinese attention on the border regions to the north and west. Maritime trade with China had been carried on largely by Arab and Indian merchants who traveled between the Middle East and East Asia. But China's lack of attention to the potentially rich sea trade changed drastically during the 500 years following the fall of the Tang.

Maritime Activities Under the Song

As large parts of the north came under the rule of nomadic peoples from the borderlands, many Chinese fled to the coastal regions of Central and South China. They settled in these areas and brought under cultivation large tracts of land. From Shanghai south to Guangzhou, little towns became busy ports. The sea, foreign trade, and naval power were now appreciated as a means of livelihood. Maritime activities also provided a valuable source of income for the imperial government. And the Song rulers maintained strongly armed fleets for the defense of their shrunken empire.

Most of the Chinese overseas trade was conducted with Southeast Asia. Here Chinese merchants exchanged goods with Arab and Indian traders, and new seaports soon developed in the region. During the Song era emigrants from China settled in Southeast Asia, laying the foundations for the large Chinese communities that still exist there. As Chinese seafarers acquired skill in navigation, they ventured westward from the Malay Peninsula to trade directly with the monarchies of India. Chinese merchants prospered from this trade. Moreover, the geographical horizons of the Chinese people were tremendously expanded. In other parts of Asia the Chinese came in contact with many lands and peoples previously unknown to them. Thus the Chinese enlarged their knowledge of the world.

Mongol and Ming Sea Power

Under the Mongols, merchants enjoyed greater security and freedom of movement than ever before, for Mongol rule extended from the Pacific Ocean to eastern Europe. Although the flow of people and goods along the caravan routes increased sharply, overseas trade did not suffer. The Mongols quickly acquired an understanding of the sea, and trade between China and South

MING SEA POWER. Drawings from a Chinese book published in 1522 suggest what the vessels used by the seafaring Ming looked like. Official mail and passengers were carried on the government ship shown at left. The other, equipped with outriggers to provide balance, was a troop ship.

and Southeast Asia continued to flourish. The Mongols also used the seas to extend their empire, even launching large-scale naval campaigns against Japan and Java.

The exploits of Chinese sea power under the Ming dynasty were especially impressive. In the early 1400's, at about the same time that Prince Henry of Portugal was sending ships to explore the west coast of Africa, the government of China dispatched great fleets to survey the seas and lands of South and Southeast Asia. Under the command of a great captain called Zheng He (JUNG HUH), seven huge expeditions between 1405 and 1433 made their way to the northern shores of the Indian Ocean. These expeditions of Chinese armadas were incredible feats of sailing. The first expedition had as many as 62 vessels and 28,000 troops and sailors. The armadas crossed the Indian Ocean nearly 100 years before the Portuguese rounded Africa. As a result of these expeditions, the Chinese established a network of trading relations, reaching places as distant as northeast Africa.

By the middle of the 1400's, however, the Ming emperors began to cut back their maritime interests. New troubles along the northern and western frontiers diverted their resources and energies from the sea. As we shall see in the next chapter, the Manchu conquerors of China were more interested in expanding their empire in Central Asia than in pursuing ocean trade with faraway lands.

Check Your Understanding

1. **a.** What caused China to become a maritime nation? **b.** With whom did China trade?
2. Why did the Mongols build up China's trade and sea power?
3. **a.** When did China's overseas trade reach its greatest extent? **b.** Why did China's trade begin to decline?
4. *Thinking Critically:* Why should it not be surprising that China became a sea power when it did in the 1400's?

3. Chinese Contributions to World Civilization

During the early centuries of the Late Imperial Age, the desire to sail the seas safely and to protect China's territory from enemy attacks stimulated Chinese inventiveness. As a result of this inventiveness, the Chinese of the Late Imperial Age made many lasting contributions to the world.

Navigation and Shipbuilding

For hundreds of years the Chinese had known about the compass. But it was not until 1119 in the Song period that they discovered its usefulness as an instrument of navigation at sea. The Chinese also built many new kinds of ships for commerce and warfare. Equipped with great sails and huge oars, Chinese vessels were the ocean liners and battleships of their age. A Chinese writer of the Song period described them in the following way:

> The ships which sail the Southern Sea and south of it are like houses. When their sails are spread, they are like great clouds in the sky. Their rudders are several tens of feet long. A single ship carries several hundred men. It has stored on board a year's supply of grain. They feed pigs and ferment liquors. There is no . . . going back to the mainland when once they have entered the dark blue sea. . . . To the people on board all is hidden, mountains, landmarks, the countries of the foreigners, all are lost in space. [*Chau Ju-kua: His Work on the Chinese and Arab Trade in the Twelfth and Thirteenth Centuries,* trans. by Friedrich Hirth and W. W. Rockhill.]

Chinese armies in the 1230's used rockets as a secret weapon against the fierce assaults of the Mongol cavalry. The Chinese called these weapons "arrows of flying fire" or "long snake crush enemy." The rocket-propelled arrows were dangerous, but not always accurate.

Firearms

The Chinese first learned how to manufacture gunpowder about A.D. 600. For several hundred years they used gunpowder to make firecrackers, unaware of gunpowder's military potential. Then when the Song armies found it difficult to withstand the wild charges of the Mongol cavalry, the Chinese used gunpowder to make explosive weapons. They first devised crude bombs that were flung through the air by **catapults.** Later they learned how to propel explosive missiles from metal tubes. In this way, the Chinese developed cannon and other firearms.

Paper, Printing, and Paper Money

The Chinese first produced paper about A.D. 100. The method of its manufacture took more than 1,000 years to spread across western Asia into Europe. During the Tang period, the Chinese also developed the technique of **block printing.** As a result, many Confucian, Buddhist, and Taoist classics were published as books. The Chinese continued to produce books during the Late Imperial Age, turning out works ranging from serious philosophical studies to popular mystery stories. It has been estimated that by the mid–1700's, more books had been printed in China than in all the rest of the world.

The invention of paper and block printing led to the introduction of paper money. For centuries metal coins had been used in many parts of the world as a medium of exchange. But paper currency was first introduced in Song China. Under the Mongols this type of money came into widespread use. Marco Polo, the Venetian who spent several years living in China during the late 1200's, described paper money to amazed Europeans after his return from East Asia:

> In this city of Khanbalik [the Mongol capital, now Beijing] is the mint of the grand khan. He may truly be said to possess the secret of the alchemists, as he has the art of producing money by the following process. He causes the bark to be stripped from ... mulberry-trees, the leaves of which are used for feeding silk-worms, and takes from it that thin inner rind which lies between the coarser bark and the wood of the tree. This being steeped, and afterwards pounded in a mortar, until reduced to a pulp, is made into paper.... When ready for use, he has it cut into pieces of money of different sizes, nearly square, but somewhat longer than they are wide.... The coinage of this paper money is authenticated with as much form and ceremony as if it were actually of pure gold or silver. To each note a number of officers, specially appointed, not only subscribe their names, but affix their seals also.... When thus coined in large quantities, this paper currency is circulated in every part of the grand khan's dominions; no person, at the peril of his life, dares refuse to accept it in payment. All his subjects receive it without hesitation, because, wherever their business may call them, they can dispose of it again in the purchase of merchandise ... such as pearls, jewels, gold, or silver. With it, in short, every article may be procured. [Marco Polo, *The Travels of Marco Polo the Venetian.*]

Chinese Silk and Porcelain

Since the first centuries of the Early Imperial Age, two Chinese commodities were especially prized in the markets of Asia and Europe. Chinese silk never failed to arouse the appreciation and wonder of customers. The silk was elegant, versatile, and durable. Its qualities were never matched before the modern age of synthetic textiles. Even the gods and goddesses, it was widely believed, clothed themselves in garments of Chinese silk. Since transportation costs along the Silk Road of Central Asia were extremely high, lack of bulk and light weight made silk the favorite merchandise of caravan merchants. With the expansion of seaborne commerce in the Late Imperial Age, even larger quantities of silk, both unfinished and processed, were exported.

The second Chinese product praised for its beauty and great durability was porcelain. The tradition of ceramic arts in China began in the New Stone Age when storage jars were produced for holding food and liquid. But the greatest advance was made when potters perfected porcelain—hard, translucent pottery fired at high temperatures. China's mastery of porcelain production preceded its successful manufacture in the West by 1,000 years. The West still acknowledges China's great technological feat by referring to porcelain as "china." Porcelain remained a Chinese monopoly until the 1700's when German potters succeeded in duplicating it.

Brilliantly white or colored, finished with a fine glaze, and translucent as a jewel, this unique pottery was an object of marvel and mystery to the Westerners who first viewed it. The Chinese learned how to produce fine porcelain during the Han period. By mixing potter's clay with certain minerals and baking the fashioned vessels at extremely high temperatures, artisans produced chinaware fit for an emperor's palace.

The Yuan and Ming dynasties were also periods of great artistic and technical innovation in ceramics. During the Yuan period, some ceramic artisans began to adorn the simple white porcelain with bold pictorial decoration in a technique that is known as underglaze painting. This technique revolutionized Chinese ceramics. Blue pigment, which was derived from cobalt

A Song painting on a silk scroll shows ladies of the imperial court preparing silk. The handscroll is read right to left, beginning on page 87. The four women at the far right are pounding silk strands to soften them for spinning. The first seated figure is spinning silk strands into thread, while the second seated figure is sewing the silk. The third seated figure is fanning a charcoal brazier. Hot coals will fill the iron used to remove wrinkles from the silk. The four standing figures are ironing a length of raw silk, while a child plays beneath the silk.

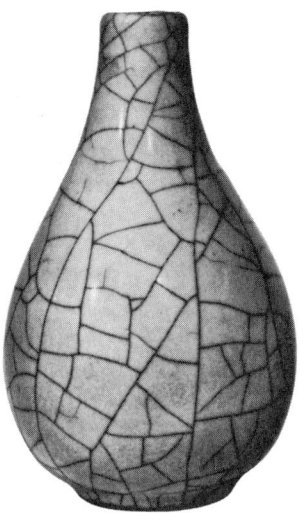

SONG PORCELAIN. The Song porcelain vase at left shows "crackle." Although accidental in some early porcelain, crackle became a desired effect as Chinese potters learned to control its use. A dragon design appears on the Song bowl below. Why was porcelain sought by people in Europe?

ore, was painted directly onto the unfired porcelain body. It was covered with a colorless glaze and then fired in a kiln at a temperature of more than 1,280 degrees Centigrade. At that very high temperature the pottery, pigment, and glaze fuse into a glassy finish. During the Ming period, other colors were added to the blue of the Yuan period, increasing the beauty and variety of the finished pieces.

At first china was produced for patrons in the Middle East. But during the Ming dynasty the domestic market developed. Ming porcelain was avidly sought in other overseas markets,

SIDELIGHT TO HISTORY

Invented in China

Acupuncture: First developed in China, acupuncture is a medical treatment that inserts needles of varying lengths into the body at appropriate points to relieve pain and other forms of physical distress. The Chinese often combined acupuncture with herbal remedies.

Celestial clock: In the A.D. 100's Zhang Heng built a celestial globe that duplicated the movement of the natural celestial sphere. In the 700's, Yi Xing and Liang Lingzan added a mechanical clock. Then in 1088 Su Song improved on the invention with a water-driven device that showed the movement of heavenly bodies.

Ephedrine: The active component of a desert herb used medically in China for thousands of years, ephedrine today is most commonly used to prevent mild attacks of bronchial asthma and to relieve nasal congestion and symptoms of hay fever and other allergies.

Kites: The Chinese have made kites for centuries, stretching silk and then paper over lightweight frames. The Chinese are thought to be the first to explore with kites the effects of the aerodynamic action of wind. The Chinese also used kites for signalling purposes during a battle in the sixth century A.D. Kites were also used to distribute propaganda leaflets urging the defection of soldiers during the Qing dynasty.

Movable type: Movable wooden type began to be used in China in the 1300's. Wang Zhen invented a rotating frame to hold trays of uniformly-sized type. The rotating frames allowed the typesetter to stay in one place while selecting a desired character. The device also simplified the return of each character to its proper tray.

Playing cards: Playing cards were well known in China in the A.D. 900's, but they did not appear in Europe until the mid-1300's. It is likely that playing cards were one of the products carried by the caravans that travelled the Silk Road.

Umbrella: The umbrella is said to have first been used in ancient China as a protection against the sun. It also became a symbol of aristocratic or noble rank. In the Western world, umbrellas did not really become popular until the 1800's.

especially Japan and Europe. Today Chinese achievements in ceramic arts of the Yuan and Ming periods are admired throughout the world and are prized possessions of their owners.

Check Your Understanding

1. What contributions to seafaring were made by the Chinese?
2. What were some of the ways in which the Chinese made use of gunpowder?
3. Why were silk and porcelain important commodities in China's trade with the West?
4. *Thinking Critically:* Why are printing and paper-making regarded as Chinese inventions? How did the Chinese come to use paper money? What other contributions to world civilization are considered Chinese inventions?

4. Philosophy, Art, and Literature

The Late Imperial Age was for a while a period of cultural brilliance. Great works in philosophy, literature, and painting added new treasures to the heritage of Chinese civilization. As in the past, the people of surrounding lands greatly admired Chinese accomplishments. In Japan and Korea especially, Chinese cultural achievements inspired other intellectual and artistic works of great importance.

Neo-Confucianism

One of the reasons for the attacks on Buddhism during the late Tang period had been a renewed interest in the thought of Confucius. (See page 62.) The ideal of a politically organized society was strengthened through such institutions as the examination system. Buddhist emphasis on the afterlife and Taoist escape to nature were rejected as anti-social and anti-political. Buddhist and Taoist ideas did not disappear, but their influence was limited to artistic and cultural spheres and to the realm of popular religion.

Although there were many schools of Confucian thought, one of the great philosophers of the Late Imperial Age was Zhuxi (joo-SHEE), who lived from 1130 to 1200. He sought to combine the teachings of Confucianism, Buddhism, and Taoism into a

CHINESE PAINTING. "Streams and Mountains Without End" is the title of the Song landscape from which this scene is taken (left). Craggy mountains rise in the background, but the overall effect is one of serenity. Landscapes were a highly regarded subject for paintings and often showed humans as an element in the scene. In a Ming emperor's painting of afghan dogs (below), realistic detail is suggested by a few skillful brush strokes. For centuries Chinese artists suppressed their personal tastes and individual styles to follow traditional styles.

unified system. The result was **Neo-Confucianism,** or "new" Confucianism. Zhuxi taught that human nature is good but that it must be polished by education and self-cultivation. The idea that human nature needed improvement through education was also applied to government, for even a perfect ruler needed the advice of well-educated counselors. Thus, the ideal of the Chinese scholar-official regained importance. Until its decline in the twentieth century, Neo-Confucianism dominated Chinese thought. Its attitudes also strongly influenced intellectual development in Vietnam, Korea, and Japan. Zhuxi's influence on the development of Neo-Confucianism was so extensive that the philosophy is sometimes referred to as Zhuxi-ism.

Landscape Painting

During the Song period artists did not give as much attention to Buddhist and other religious subjects as earlier artists had. They turned to nature for themes and inspiration. For example, Guo Xi (GWOH SHIH), who lived from 1020 to 1090, painted haunting winter landscapes and scenes of massive, rugged landscapes. Artists saw an ideal world in nature and tried to express that world through their paintings. Often they did this by painting one small part of nature, perhaps a branch or flower blossom. To them the branch or blossom represented a world in miniature. Unusually imaginative, these artists sought to capture the spirit rather than the form of their subject. Their paintings represented what the artist saw with the mind's eye. Many of these Song paintings, especially those by landscape artists, used various shades of one color. Such paintings were called monochromes.

Landscape painting was also the dominant art form of the Ming period. Painting was often taken up by scholar-officials and became part of the Confucian ideal of the well-developed person. Besides painting pictures themselves, many wealthy Chinese collected paintings and calligraphy by other artists and surrounded themselves with beautiful objects made of jade, porcelain, and bronze.

Poetry, Literature, and Drama

The Song period saw a renewal of interest in China's past. Imperial historians revised and corrected older works and wrote new ones to update Chinese history. The true genius of Song literature, however, was expressed in its poems. Poets wrote simple but beautiful lyric verses to be sung with old Chinese tunes. This poetic form was called the Zi (TZUH).

Although historical study and poetry declined during the Ming period, literature flourished in the form of short stories and novels. This age is most notable for the rise of popular literature. Many of the stories were taken from folk tales that had been told for centuries. They were full of realistic detail, but they often romantically described the exploits of knights and bandits. Three of the most famous novels of Chinese literature were written during the Ming period. *Romance of the Three Kingdoms,* first published in 1522, is a fictionalized retelling of the political events that took place during the Later Han period (A.D. 184–220). *Water Margin,* or *All Men Are Brothers,* which dates from about 1540, is a tale of 108 outlaws who oppose the corrupt social system. The story is set in the Southern Song period about the twelfth century. *Journey to the West,* also known as *Monkey,* was first published in 1592. It is an entertaining tale of a Buddhist monk and his two companions—a cowardly pig and a magical monkey.

Although Chinese art, poetry, and prose all achieved great heights during the Late Imperial Age, drama added a new element to Chinese culture. Chinese drama developed much as Greek drama had. It began as groups of singers telling a story and answering one another as they narrated it. Women took some of the roles. Later, during the Qing period, female actors were banned from the stage. At some point in the development of the drama, one actor sang the principal story, while the other members of the cast recited as a chorus. By the Mongol period the form of Chinese drama had been established. Plays were written in four acts, most of the themes dealt with filial piety and loyalty, and the movements and costumes of actors had become stylized.

Check Your Understanding

1. Who was Zhuxi?
2. What influence did Zhuxi have on Chinese thought and attitudes?
3. What were the main characteristics of Chinese painting during the Song and Ming periods?
4. **Thinking Critically:** Cite evidence from this chapter that will prove or disprove the following statement: *The Late Imperial Age was a period of cultural brilliance.*

5. Challenges to Ming China's Security

After the mid-1400's, the frontiers of Ming China were subjected to constantly mounting pressures. The appearance of new invaders in China's coastal waters made it difficult for the Ming to concentrate their strength on controlling the restless peoples beyond the Great Wall. The Chinese Empire found itself caught between two relentless pressures.

Japanese Pirates

For several centuries Japanese pirates had been prowling in China's offshore waters in search of booty. These pirates were in the service of Japanese feudal lords and sailed in fleets of hundreds of ships and thousands of men. By the late Ming period they had become the terror of the East Asian seas. Not content with attacking trading vessels, the pirates landed raiding parties and sacked Chinese cities and towns. No measures taken by the harassed Chinese succeeded in eliminating this menace. The marauders were finally suppressed in the 1600's, when a new Japanese government took action to cope with this kind of lawlessness.

An even more dangerous threat than the pirate raids was Hideyoshi (HEE-duh-YOH-shee), an ambitious Japanese warrior. During the late 1500's, Hideyoshi succeeded in uniting the Japanese islands, which had been politically divided. Looking for new worlds to conquer, Hideyoshi decided to attack the Chinese Empire. In 1592 he sent Japanese armies to Korea as the first step in an overland invasion of China.

Responding to Korean pleas for help, the Ming government rushed reinforcements to its neighbor. After much bloody fighting, combined Chinese and Korean armies checked Hideyoshi's troops, and an armistice was concluded. In 1597, however, the struggle was resumed. Following Hideyoshi's death in 1598, Japanese troops returned home. But the struggle had devastated Korea and greatly weakened Ming China.

Portuguese Visitors

The rulers of Ming China also had to deal with approaches from Western peoples. Merchants and missionaries from the West had visited China in earlier times, especially during the days of the Mongol empire. The most famous of these was Marco Polo. Travelers from Europe made the long journey overland, following the Silk Road and other well-established caravan routes across Central Asia.

Later European visitors, however, approached China from the sea. The first of these were the Portuguese who, in the fifteenth century, had launched an ambitious program of maritime exploration. Begun by Prince Henry the Navigator, these efforts bore fruit in 1498 when Vasco da Gama discovered a new sea route from Europe to the East. After rounding Africa's Cape of Good Hope, da Gama sailed on to India. Less than 15 years later, Portuguese seafarers sailing from India dropped anchor in the Chinese port of Guangzhou.

The Portuguese at first made a poor impression on the Chinese. Ignorant of Chinese customs of behavior, the Portuguese greatly offended the Chinese who concluded that Europeans were no different from Japanese pirates. But, despite its initial distaste for the Portuguese, the Chinese government in 1557 allowed them to establish a trading post at Macau (muh-KOW), a small peninsula and two islands near Guangzhou. Portugal eventually annexed Macau, holding it for well over 400 years. According to a Sino–Portuguese agreement signed in 1987, Macau will revert to China's possession in 1997.

The Jesuit priests were respected by the Chinese as men of wisdom and knowledge. Father Adam Schall, a German Jesuit, became chief astronomer at the imperial court. He is pictured here in the dress of a Chinese scholar-official. Note the astronomical instruments and the map of the world in the background. Why did many Jesuits adopt the Chinese style of dress?

SIDELIGHT TO HISTORY

Which Way Is East?

To the Portuguese and some other Europeans in the 1500's and 1600's, routes to East Asia by land or by sea extended far to the east. Therefore, they called this area the Far East, a name that made sense from the European point of view. But other Westerners reached China and Japan by routes heading in the opposite direction. Spaniards sailed their ships westward across the Pacific, for example, from Spanish bases in Latin America. At a later time vessels from the United States also sailed across the Pacific to reach Asian ports.

The Spanish and Americans might reasonably have called East Asia the *Far West*. But adopting the European term, they called the region comprised of China and neighboring countries the *Far East*. In the years since World War II, however, Westerners have become aware that in the modern world of shrunken distances, the Far East is not so far after all. In addition, the use of the word *far* suggested that West was the center of the universe. For these reasons the term *East Asia* has now replaced the earlier expression.

Other European Rivals

Because of its head start in the Asian trade, Portugal became wealthy during the 1500's. Portuguese traders carried spices, textiles, porcelain, and silk around the Cape of Good Hope and sold them at handsome profits in the markets of Europe. But other Europeans soon became rivals of the Portuguese. First were the Spanish, who won a foothold in the Philippines in 1565. For many years afterwards, Spanish galleons sailing from Manila carried Chinese goods to the Americas and from there to Europe. In 1598 the Dutch, anxious to share in the profitable commerce with the East, dispatched their own ships to India, Southeast Asia, and China. Then, in the early 1600's, the Dutch, the French, and the English organized great companies to carry on what was called the East India trade.

Still other Europeans, most notably the Russians, reached the frontiers of the Chinese Empire by traveling overland. A few years after the downfall of the Ming dynasty, Russian traders and explorers crossed the vast stretches of Siberia and came in touch with peoples in the Chinese borderlands.

Catholic Missionaries

Portuguese merchants in East Asia were soon followed by Roman Catholic missionaries who hoped to convert the Chinese to Christianity. Francis Xavier, a member of the Society of Jesus, a religious order popularly called the Jesuits, worked for some years as a missionary in India, the East Indies, and Japan. Encouraged by his success in Japan, Xavier sought permission from the imperial government to enter China. His efforts failed, and in 1552 he died without seeing China. Xavier had pointed the way, however, and other Jesuits pursued his goal of bringing Christianity to China. In the closing years of the Ming era, a few missionaries finally succeeded in entering China.

Matteo Ricci (REET-chih), an Italian missionary, was the first Jesuit to gain access to China. He and other Jesuits were impressed by Chinese civilization. Ricci founded a mission at Beijing in 1601 and soon became a friend of the emperor. The Italian's admiration for Chinese culture won him the confidence of many Chinese people. Ricci himself had a high respect for learning and was well-versed in law, mathematics, science, and mapmaking. He was also adept at practical mechanics. When Ricci noticed the respect accorded men of learning by the Chinese, he began to dress like a Confucian scholar. Ricci also urged other Jesuits to learn the Chinese language, as he had done, and to study Chinese history, philosophy, and culture. Many missionaries followed Ricci's advice. As a result, they were able to associate with leaders in Chinese life and also to secure access to the imperial court.

The religious message of the Jesuits had little appeal for the Chinese, however, and the missionaries won few converts. But the Chinese greatly respected the Jesuits' scientific and technical knowledge. The missionaries' skill in astronomy, for example, enabled them to correct the Chinese calendar. The Chinese also appreciated the Jesuits' knowledge of mathematics, surveying, and mapmaking. A map of the Chinese Empire that the Jesuits prepared for the imperial government was one of the best ever made. The versatile missionaries even cast bronze cannon, some of the finest ever seen in East Asia. Despite these services, the Jesuits failed to achieve their great dream—the conversion of China to Christianity. In the early 1700's a ruling against the Jesuits concerning the authority of the Pope and the Chinese emperor led to the expulsion of the Jesuits from China.

Check Your Understanding

1. **a.** How were the pirate raids along China's coast stopped? **b.** Why did Hideyoshi threaten the security of China during the Ming dynasty?
2. **a.** Who were the first Europeans to reach China by sea? **b.** What were their interests in China?
3. ***Thinking Critically:*** How did Jesuit missionaries become interested in China? Why were they not successful in converting China to Christianity?

CHAPTER REVIEW

■ Chapter Summary

Section 1. Invasions were a persistent problem for the Chinese throughout the Late Imperial Age. Years of conflict followed the downfall of the Tang Empire. A new dynasty, the Song, was founded. It eventually fell, however, to the overwhelming force of invading Mongol armies. Under Kublai Khan, China became the center of the huge Mongol Empire. But the Chinese regained control of their own land when the founders of the Ming dynasty ousted the Mongols.

Section 2. During centuries of changing control, invasions in the north forced many Chinese to migrate to areas south of the Chang Jiang. New cities and towns flourished in the coastal regions as China became a seafaring nation and developed an overseas trade that made it the leading sea power in East Asia.

Section 3. The Chinese of the Late Imperial Age made many notable scientific and technological discoveries and inventions. Among their achievements were the use of the compass in navigation, the development of new oceangoing vessels, the use of gunpowder as a military weapon, the invention of printing, and the production of paper. Silk and porcelain were Chinese products that were especially prized by other peoples in both Asia and Europe.

Section 4. Chinese civilization during the Late Imperial Age was also marked by achievements in philosophy, literature, and art. The development of Neo–Confucianism had a profound influence on Chinese government and society.

In the realm of literature and painting, the work of Song and Ming writers and artists has rarely been excelled.

Section 5. During the 1500's and 1600's the Ming rulers had to face new pressures from outside China. Japanese pirates attacked Chinese ships and raided coastal settlements. Hideyoshi, the Japanese warrior-ruler, attempted to invade China. When Hideyoshi died, the Japanese troops were called home. European seafarers opened trade with China, and the Jesuits, a Catholic missionary order, attempted unsuccessfully to convert China to Christianity.

■ **Vocabulary Review**

Define: khan, catapult, block printing, Neo–Confucianism

■ **Places to Locate**

Locate: Guanghzhou, Malay Peninsula, Macau, India

■ **People to Know**

Identify: Song, Mongols, Genghis Khan, Kublai Khan, Yuan, Ming, Hideyoshi, Francis Xavier, Matteo Ricci

■ **Thinking Critically**

1. Why was the Ming period an outstanding one in Chinese history?
2. Why did the Chinese become a seafaring people after the fall of the Tang? How important were the Chinese contributions to navigation and shipbuilding?
3. What threats to China's security came from the Japanese? How successfully were these threats handled?
4. Why did the Jesuits enter China? How did China benefit from the presence of the Christian missionaries? Did the missionaries receive any benefits from China? Explain.

■ **Extending and Applying Your Knowledge**

1. Look up the history of one or more of the Chinese inventions and discoveries mentioned in this chapter or choose one not mentioned. Write a brief paper on how the invention or discovery eventually made its way to the West.
2. Communities of Chinese have settled in various parts of the world, notably India, Africa, and the United States. Find out how one or more of these communities were treated and explore some of the problems they have encountered. Share your findings with your classmates.

5

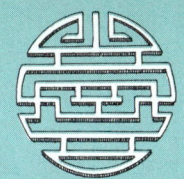

The Late Imperial Age—The Qing

"China," a French philosopher wrote in 1769, "offers an enchanting picture of what the whole world might become if the laws of that empire were to become the laws of all nations. Go to Peking [Beijing]! Gaze upon the mightiest of mortals [the emperor of China]. He is the true and perfect image of Heaven."

The emperor of China at this time was one of the Qing rulers, the dynasty founded by the Manchu conquerors of China. By the late 1700's the Qing dynasty was at the height of its might and magnificence. For years Europeans had known about the splendors of Chinese civilization, chiefly from the accounts of Jesuit visitors to Asia. The missionaries' descriptions of China may not always have been accurate, but their enthusiasm for Chinese civilization was well-founded. China unquestionably ranked as one of the world's great states in the 1600's and 1700's.

In the early 1800's, signs of danger for the Qing dynasty appeared. These came in the form of peasant uprisings. On many occasions during China's long history, such outbreaks had warned the imperial government of trouble. In the 1800's, the Qing rulers were able to put down these uprisings, but they made little effort to eliminate the causes of the unrest that had led the peasants to rebel. At a time when China's rulers could least afford new problems, Europeans began to press against the frontiers of the empire. European demands for freer trade with China signaled more trouble for the Qing dynasty.

1. The Manchu Conquest of China

Of all the outsiders who besieged Ming China, the Manchus were the most successful. In the early 1600's the people of the plains and forests of Manchuria were gradually united by able leaders. Their military might greatly increased when they entered into alliances with Mongol tribes to the west. Although this confederation of outsiders soon ousted the Chinese from the northern borderlands, their advance was brought to a halt by the garrisons along the Great Wall.

A long stalemate between the Ming and the Manchus followed, but it was finally broken by events within China. In many parts of the country peasant rebels challenged the authority of the imperial government. The government rapidly weakened, as it had to divide its forces to deal with foes within the empire as well as aggressors along the frontier. In 1644 Chinese rebel armies entered Beijing, and the last of the Ming emperors fled southward for safety. With the Manchus in front and with rebels to the rear, the Chinese commander of the Great Wall defenses decided to unite his forces with the Manchus to destroy the rebels. Once the Manchus had entered China Proper, they refused to leave.

The Manchus conquered and ruled China with remarkably few men. These northerners numbered no more than two million people—barely one-fiftieth the total Chinese population at that time. In part the Manchu success in snatching control from the rebels who overthrew the last Ming emperor was due to the help of allies. Mounted troops from Mongolia, for example, fought alongside Manchu cavalry. Another source of aid was the support of those Chinese generals who allied themselves with the Manchus in hopes of gaining political favors after the conquest. Nevertheless, the Manchu conquest was impressive—and even more impressive was the success of the Manchus in holding on to their conquered empire for as long as they did.

Manchu Military Might

The most significant factor in the success of the Manchus was their military might. This was provided by the fighting groups set up by Nurhachi (NOOR-hah-chee), the founder of the Manchu state. Nurhachi (1559–1626) grouped the highly skilled Manchu warriors into four divisions, or **banners.** Banners were a significant development in Manchu history because their development marked a movement away from tribal organization toward state-administered units. Each division was identified by its flag;

TIMETABLE

The Opening Years of Qing Rule

1644	Manchu seizure of Beijing
1661–1722	Reign of Kangxi
1736–1796	Reign of Qian Long
1795–1804	White Lotus Rebellion
1839–1842	Opium War ended by Treaty of Nanjing

hence the name *banner*. The four banners grew to eight and eventually, with the addition of eight Chinese and eight Mongol banners, to 24. After their conquest of China was complete, the Manchus used the banners to police the empire. By stationing banners in the larger cities and at strategic points, the Manchus made effective use of a relatively small army.

Nurhachi built up a strong Manchu state, but he died before conquering China. His descendants, however, expanded Manchu power into North China and eventually into the south. In 1644 the Manchus seized Beijing and over the next 40 years consolidated their rule over China. The new emperors adopted the name of Qing for the dynasty they established.

Continued Use of Scholar–Officials

Lacking the experience necessary for governing their huge domain, the Manchu conquerors depended heavily on the Chinese for help. They were especially eager to win the cooperation of the Chinese scholar-officials. The Manchus continued, therefore, the traditional civil service examinations. Also, the Manchus filled many of the highest posts, both in the central government at Beijing and in the provinces, with Chinese civil servants.

The Qing emperors did not, however, give their Chinese aides a free hand. They made certain that their own people held a majority of seats on all important councils and committees. Special examinations were held for Manchus, and those who passed were assigned to positions where they could check on the activities of the Chinese officials. The Manchus allowed no Chinese officials to serve in their native provinces where they might count on political backing from relatives and friends. Also, the Manchus constantly rotated Chinese administrators of high rank. Seldom did any Chinese official hold the same position for more than three years.

Government Under the Qing

Like earlier dynasties, the Qing discovered that its empire was too huge and complex to be administered directly. Most of the provinces were far from the capital and transportation was slow. Therefore, the imperial scholar-officials were assigned to posts only in important cities and towns. As a result, local administrators had a good deal of freedom in many affairs of government.

The Qing divided China into 18 provinces, each with a governor. With some exceptions, a governor-general oversaw every two provinces. Typically the provincial governor was Chinese and the governor-general was Manchu. This system of dual control by

REGION: THE QING EMPIRE. China under the early Manchu rulers of the Qing dynasty was the mightiest empire in the world. The Qing emperors not only reigned over China Proper, their homeland of Manchuria, and the borderlands of Mongolia, Xinjiang, and Tibet but also were acknowledged as overlords by many tributary states. Note that Japan remained outside the tributary system.

Manchu and Chinese was typical of the Qing dynasty. There were also many other checks on the power of Chinese officials.

The principal checks on provincial civil servants were laws and local traditions. Another check was the **censor system,** a practice that the Qing emperors borrowed from earlier Chinese dynasties. **Censors** were traveling investigators who acted as the "eyes and ears" of the emperor. These censors were responsible for searching out abuses of power and corruption in government. They were also supposed to advise against unwise policies, even if the policies were favored by the emperor himself.

China had (and still has) tens of thousands of small rural communities. The number of people in these rural centers might range from several hundred to a few thousand. The Qing government did not send officials to every village. The villagers looked after their own political affairs, solved their own problems, and decided how imperial orders were to be carried out. Many of the villages were governed by an administrator and a council of elders. Though these administrators were chosen in different ways, they were often from the most important families in the community. They looked after the public records, supervised the care of public works, and maintained law and order. They also settled most local disputes, using tradition as their principal guide. If a dispute was especially serious, however, it might be taken for settlement to a government official.

Effect on Villagers

Generally villagers could expect to hear from the government on only two matters—taxes and military service. At harvest time, the peasants knew that the tax collector was nearby. If taxes were not paid on time, the peasants could expect a visit from an official of the provincial governor. Officials also visited the villages to recruit men for the army of the Green Standard, a police force separate from the banners. The Army of the Green Standard was mainly used to suppress local bandits.

To ordinary Chinese peasants the change from Ming rule to Qing rule meant little. They continued to live as their ancestors had for centuries, and they were hardly aware that the government had changed. They had neighbors and rulers, but their first loyalty was to their families. If they advanced in life, part of their satisfaction came from the knowledge that their achievements reflected credit on their families. If misfortune came, they knew that they could depend on their families for help and comfort. None of this was changed by the Manchu conquest of China.

SIDELIGHT TO HISTORY

Notable Qing Emperors

Only four Qing emperors sat upon the throne of China from 1644 to 1796. All were capable leaders. The government was extremely stable during the critical years when the Chinese Empire was being united and extended by the Manchu rulers. Kangxi and Qian Long, the second and fourth of the Qing emperors respectively, rank among the greatest in Chinese history.

Kangxi (KAHNG-SHEE), who ruled from 1661 to 1722, subjugated South China for the Manchus and annexed Taiwan. He personally led his troops against a confederation of Western Mongols in 1696–1697, achieving a great victory against them. During his reign, Chinese border problems with Russia were solved and a strict balance was maintained between Manchus and Chinese in the government.

But Kangxi was also interested in learning, especially Western learning. He permitted Jesuit missionaries to live at his court, and he employed them to map the empire and to teach mathematics and astronomy. Kangxi earned a reputation as a wise and benevolent ruler mainly with the people, by his repeated tax reductions. During his reign, he supported the publication of an official Ming history and two large dictionaries.

Qian Long (CHEE-en LOONGH) assumed the imperial throne in 1736 when he was 25 years old and reigned for 60 years. Under Qian Long, the Chinese Empire attained its maximum territorial expansion. To win the respect of Chinese scholars, Qian Long organized an army of scholars to compile a great imperial library of the best Chinese writings of the previous centuries. But Qian Long ordered the burning of most of the books that contained insulting references to the Manchus or other non-Chinese peoples. Scholars who objected to the book-burning were arrested, their property seized, and their own works destroyed. When finished, the library was called *The Complete Library of the Four Treasuries* and contained over 36,000 volumes.

During the later years of his reign, the empire suffered from corruption, military inefficiency, and other problems. Qian Long abdicated three years before his death at the age of 88.

Emperor Kangxi, the grandfather of Emperor Qian Long, encouraged literature and learning and was himself a student of the Chinese classics. He also studied Western science, mathematics, and music with the Jesuits who lived at his court.

Preserving Manchu Traditions

Like the Chinese, the Manchus were proud of their own way of life and did not want it changed. They did everything possible to preserve it. They kept their own names, spoke their own language as much as possible, and made an effort to retain their own customs. Periodically the Manchu emperors and banners returned to their homeland to live in the manner of their ancestors. The Qing rulers prohibited intermarriage between the Manchu people and the Chinese and forbade the Manchu people to dress like the Chinese. In addition, Manchuria was closed to Chinese settlement. But the Qing rulers compelled the Chinese to wear their hair in a **queue,** as a sign of subjugation for the Chinese. Chinese who violated the order were liable to severe punishment. For more than 250 years, only Chinese rebels against the dynasty let their hair hang loose, as had been the custom in Ming times and before. When the Qing was finally overthrown in the 1900's, enthusiastic rebels clipped off the queues of those still wearing them. Today queues are seldom seen in China. These various practices and regulations kept the conquered and the conquerors apart.

While preserving their own way of life, the Manchus recognized the superiority of the Chinese in arts and learning. In fact, the Qing rulers encouraged and supported Chinese culture. The

Qing emperors and their chief advisers learned the Chinese language, practiced calligraphy, and studied Chinese history, philosophy, and literature. Throughout the empire scholarship and learning were thus greatly stimulated, especially under Kangxi and Qian Long.

Check Your Understanding

1. **a.** How were the Manchus able to conquer China? **b.** What enabled them to maintain their rule?
2. **a.** How did the Manchus win the support of the scholar-officials? **b.** How were they able to control them?
3. What effect did Manchu rule have on Chinese villagers?
4. *Thinking Critically:* Why do you think the Manchu rulers were generally successful in maintaining their own way of life? Do you think they could have been successful without also showing respect for Chinese culture?

2. Problems of Peaceful Times

Once the Manchu conquerors of the Middle Kingdom had consolidated their power, the Chinese people settled down to a long period of quiet and peace. Partly as a result of peaceful conditions from the late 1600's on, there was a steady rise in the population. It has been estimated that the number of people in China in 1700 stood at nearly 142 million, and over the next 110 years it is estimated that the population may have tripled to as much as 432 million.

China had good government under the early Manchu rulers. Voltaire, the renowned French philosopher, hailed the Chinese Empire in the 1700's as "the finest administered country in the world." For 100 years law and order were upheld throughout the Qing empire. Travelers could move about freely without fear of encountering bandits. Equally important to the country's well being was the absence of destructive rebellions and war. Unlike certain parts of Europe, which were ripped by repeated conflict during the eighteenth century, China enjoyed long periods of peace. A few minor border disturbances far to the west were quickly suppressed.

Improving the Peasants' Lives

In China's past history, when new dynasties had been founded, they had usually taken steps to repair the damage caused by the struggle for power. By taking steps to repair damage, new dynasties hoped to relieve the discontent of the peasants. The early Qing emperors understood this lesson of Chinese history. As a result of their encouragement and support, dikes along the rivers were strengthened, irrigation canals were dug, and roads and bridges were repaired and maintained. These public works not only were good for the country's economy, but they also reduced discontent among the peasants.

As China's population increased, more land was brought under the plow. Abandoned fields were once again farmed, swampy areas were drained and planted, and hitherto unused tracts were settled. Land-hungry peasants surged into the sparsely settled border regions in the north and northwest. Still others migrated to the offshore islands, such as Taiwan. Between 1650 and 1850, land under cultivation in China increased by a third. Also, land was more intensively farmed. That is, a greater amount of human labor was applied to the land in order to grow more food and non-food crops.

New Crops from Foreign Lands

Probably China's most important contribution to the world's collection of useful agricultural products is tea. The orange tree also originated in China. In fact, the German and Russian words for orange can be translated as "Chinese apple" in English. The soybean is a plant that is also native to China. The Chinese have grown this extremely useful crop for some 5,000 years. But other than these, few of China's native plants have been introduced in other lands. Since early times, however, many useful agricultural products were brought to China from other regions. Rice, for example, was probably carried to China from Southeast Asia in prehistoric times. In later centuries grapes, walnuts, carrots, alfalfa, sorghum, and cotton were transplanted to the Middle Kingdom.

Many other agricultural products were introduced to China and East Asia from the Americas. The Spanish and the Portuguese carried many valuable products including tobacco, corn, sweet potatoes, white potatoes, peanuts, and pineapples, from their colonies in the Americas across the Pacific Ocean. By the mid–1700's many Chinese peasants were raising these useful crops. Potatoes, peanuts, and corn were especially welcome, for they could be grown on lands unsuitable for rice. Sorghum was also introduced into North China about this time. (See map, page 7.) These new agricultural products greatly increased China's food supply.

Peasant Dissatisfaction

For thousands of years, poverty had been the fate of most of the Chinese peasants. The rapid expansion of the population during the 1700's and 1800's further impoverished the Chinese peasantry. Although China raised more food than it ever had before, the number of people who needed to be fed rose even more rapidly. When the demand for tillable land began to exceed the supply of available farmland, land prices rose sharply. Many peasants could not afford to buy even the smallest plots of land. More and more peasants were reduced to scratching out a meager living on tiny plots that they rented at high cost. After the peasants paid their expenses, their profits were often too small to support their families. Then the peasants would have to go to work for low wages on the fields of wealthy landlords. By the early nineteenth century, few peasants were able to escape from lifelong poverty.

Corruption in Government

The plight of the peasants was made worse by an increase in official corruption in the government. Many officials pocketed government revenues and squeezed the already impoverished peasants for higher taxes. In disputes between the peasants and wealthy landlords, bribes to officials often resulted in decisions favoring the landlords. The peasants became convinced that they could not expect justice from those who governed. "Heaven is high," they grimly remarked, "and the capital is far." Adding to the peasant discontent was the neglect of public works because the funds for these projects were often stolen by greedy government officials. By selfishly promoting their own interests, corrupt officials aroused the majority of peasants to deep anger against the Qing dynasty.

The tremendous burdens of poverty and resentment due to corruption and neglect of public works finally drove many Chinese peasants to rebel against the government. The first outbreaks took place in the closing years of the reign of Qian Long. (See page 104.) The revolt of the White Lotus Society, a secret **brotherhood,** raged for several years before the government suppressed it in 1804. The peasants' grievances were not relieved, however, and new rebellions soon broke out. These rebellions are discussed in the next chapter.

Check Your Understanding

1. What were the causes of the rapid population growth that took place in the early centuries of the Qing Empire?
2. **a.** What group did the Qing try hardest to satisfy?
   b. Why was this group singled out for satisfaction?
   c. How did the Manchus try to improve the lot of this group?
3. *Thinking Critically:* Why did the lot of the peasants worsen? What was the result for the Qing? For the peasants?

3. The Qing Domain

Almost every state adjacent to China eventually fell under Qing political and military influence. (See map, page 103.) Qing claims to sovereignty extended as far northward as the icy waters of the Sea of Okhotsk (oh-KAHTSK). The entire basin of the Amur (ah-MOOR) River, today the boundary between Manchuria and the USSR in eastern Siberia, was under the control of the Qing dynasty. In the south the empire bordered the monarchy of Tonking (today part of Vietnam). The Qing rulers added such offshore islands as Taiwan to their domain. But what made the realm of the Qing so huge was its success in gaining control over the great arc of borderlands. Mongolia, Xinjiang, and Tibet all came under Qing rule. With some exaggeration, the Qing claimed that their dominions included all lands "under Heaven," all regions "within the Four Seas."

The Tributary System

Long before the Manchus conquered China Proper, they had become familiar with the tributary system, the Chinese system of controlling neighboring states. The Manchus themselves had been, at least in theory, a subject people under this system. Once in control of the Chinese government, the Manchus adopted the tributary system and continued its use in China's relations with surrounding states. The tribute payments served as an acknowledgment of the Qing emperor's superiority and as a form of taxation.

The tributary system was based on the Confucian ideal that a family could have only one head. In a family of states, as in

In the painting above, a Mongol envoy kowtows as he presents a valuable white horse to Emperor Qian Long. Thus a tributary state acknowledged the overlordship of the Qing emperor of China.

a family of people, there could be only one undisputed head. That head was the Chinese emperor, who was thus regarded as first among the many rulers of the world. According to this view, all other monarchs and princes owed filial respect to the emperor. Therefore, the relationship between the emperor and foreign states had to be that between a superior and inferiors.

Keeping Peace

The system of tributary states gave the emperor tremendous prestige. More important, however, it helped to keep down turmoil in the frontier regions of the empire. Long experience had taught the rulers of China that dynasties endured only when peace prevailed at home and abroad. But keeping the peace was difficult. A rebellion within China Proper often compelled an emperor to relax his vigilance in border areas, a move that allowed non-Chinese to harass these outlying regions. Then, to restore order to the border areas, the emperor had to neglect outbreaks of trouble in China Proper. When all rulers of tributary states behaved in a proper manner—that is, when they acknowledged their position of inferiority—peace and harmony reigned. In return, the Chinese emperor never interfered in the affairs of these inferior states.

After the Qing dynasty was founded, almost all neighboring rulers accepted a tributary relationship with the Middle Kingdom. When their territories were attacked, these states relied on Chinese help against the aggressors. Korea, Okinawa, the states of Indochina, Siam (presently Thailand), and Burma were among the empire's many tributary states. Japan was one of the few countries that refused to join the system. For that reason, the Chinese regarded the Japanese as "barbarians."

In practice, the tributary system amounted to a system of international diplomacy because China dealt with foreigners only through the tributary system. The Europeans who carried on trade with Chinese merchants in the 1600's and 1700's did not participate in the tributary system. Like the Japanese, therefore, they were classified as outsiders and foreigners.

Welcoming Ceremonies

A mission sent by the ruler of a tributary state was welcomed at the frontier by emissaries of the emperor. The delegation was then escorted to the imperial capital. There, elaborate ceremonies marked the ties that existed between the emperor and the tributary states. The members of the mission presented their ruler's tribute, and the emperor bestowed gifts upon the tributary rulers and their emissaries. All this was done with great pomp and ceremony, and the emperor was always the center of the show.

The most impressive display of respect to the emperor was the **kowtow.** This ritual was described by Father Ripa, an Italian missionary of the eighteenth century. "When the dinner was over," Father Ripa reported,

> we were presented to his Majesty in his private apartments. He was seated . . . on a divan covered with velvet and had before him a small table, upon which were placed some books and writing materials. Upon his right and left were some European missionaries. . . . They had their feet close together and their arms were hanging down, which in China is a sign of modesty and respect. Following the instructions received from the mandarins [officials], as soon as we were within sight of the Emperor, we hastened our steps to the divan . . . and there we stood a few moments, with closed feet and arms hanging down. Then, at a signal given by the master of ceremonies lowering his hand, we bent our knees [to the ground]. After remaining a short time in this position, at another signal we inclined our heads slowly till we touched the ground with the forehead. This was repeated a second and third time. After these three prostrations we arose to our feet, and then we again repeated them in the same manner, till they amounted to nine. This homage is called . . . the great or solemn ceremony. [*Memories of Father Ripa*, trans. by Fortunato Prandi.]

The kowtow was considered the height of proper behavior on the part of an inferior toward a superior. Every Chinese performed the kowtow on one occasion or another. Even the emperors performed it before their parents on special occasions or when they prayed.

Check Your Understanding

1. Describe the extent of the Qing Empire.
2. What ceremonies made clear the relationship of the tributary states to the emperor?
3. *Thinking Critically:* What was the tributary system? What benefits did the tributary system have for the empire? For the tributary states? For the foreign countries that were not part of the empire?

4. European Pressures on Qing China

The Portuguese in the 1500's and then other Europeans in the next century established direct trade relations with China. (See pages 93–96.) These trading contacts were made by the Europeans, not by the Chinese. The people of the Middle Kingdom thought that everything needed by them was produced within their realm. Regarding their empire as self-sufficient, they made no effort to import food or other commodities. The minor role of foreign trade in the economy of the Middle Kingdom was made clear in 1795 by Emperor Qian Long in a letter to the king of Great Britain. "There is nothing that we do not possess," he wrote, "and the products of the foreign barbarians are really not needed to balance supply and demand."

Lack of Diplomatic Relations

The Chinese rulers sent no **ambassadors** to the distant capitals of European nations, and received no diplomatic officials as representatives of the European governments at the imperial court in Beijing. China also had no commercial treaties regulating its trade with these countries. The only exception among the European nations was Russia, whose Siberian possessions made it China's neighbor. By the Treaty of Nerchinsk (1689), the Russians were allowed to trade at special towns along the Mongolian frontier. They were also permitted to maintain a **diplomatic mission** in Beijing. All other Europeans carried on trade at the

Tea ranked high among Chinese exports, especially after the English became tea drinkers in the 1700's. Here we see various stages of tea production, starting with cultivation in the fields (top left). After picking, the leaves were dried, roasted, weighed, and packed (top right). They were then sold to the top-hatted Western purchasers (bottom left) and loaded on ships (bottom right).

pleasure of the Chinese. There was no discussion of conditions of trade. Unless Westerners met the Chinese requirements, no business was carried on.

Foreign Trade Restrictions

The Qing Empire placed many restrictions on Chinese trade with foreigners. Like Europeans of the seventeenth and eighteenth centuries, the Qing were unwilling to allow foreign merchants to trade freely at their ports and markets. During the early years of the Qing dynasty, traders from other parts of Asia and from Europe had been permitted to carry on their business along the China coast. In 1757, however, the government reversed this policy. Thereafter these traders had to confine their business to Quangzhou.

The Portuguese pioneers in the China trades came into competition with English, French, and Dutch merchants. The commerce of these latecomers was conducted by trading firms known as East India Companies. These companies enjoyed a monopoly in trade between their own countries and Asia. They were interested primarily in making profits and not in improving relations between their home governments and the countries of

113

East Asia. These companies often complained to Chinese officials about the many regulations restricting their business. Yet, realizing that the Qing government was too strong to be intimidated, the Europeans at first did not protest very forcefully.

China's European Trade

Chinese silks and porcelain found ready markets in Europe during the 1600's and 1700's. The cargoes shipped to such European ports as Lisbon and London also included silk brocades, sugar, rhubarb, other fruits and vegetables, and ginger. About 1666, enterprising merchants introduced tea to English customers, who soon came to value it highly as a tonic for various ailments. Before long, the English and their colonists in North America had adopted tea as an everyday drink. By the beginning of the 1800's, the aromatic leaves, tightly packed in special wooden chests, were China's chief export. In England duties on imports of tea became a major source of government revenue.

Although Chinese goods were profitably sold in Europe, there was little demand for European products in China. Western textiles, for example, compared with Eastern goods, were too expensive and of inferior quality. To trade with China, therefore, European merchants had to ship large amounts of silver **bullion** (uncoined metal) to China. Until about 1825 China enjoyed a favorable **balance of trade.** That is, the goods it *exported* were of far greater value than the small amount of goods it *imported.* At this time China had no complaint about the state of its foreign trade.

A Changing Balance of Trade

The sale of opium eventually gave European merchants an advantage in their trade with China. First the Portuguese and then the British began to buy opium in India and sell it to the Chinese. As the demand for Indian opium steadily rose in China, the flow of silver bullion gradually reversed. Instead of receiving silver, the Chinese began to pay it out. Thus, the opium trade tilted the balance of trade in favor of European merchants.

Opium is a narcotic that is made from the seed pod of certain kinds of poppy plants. The Chinese had grown opium poppies for hundreds of years, but they had used the product mainly for medicinal purposes. In the 1600's and 1700's, however, many Chinese began to smoke opium. Increasing numbers of people became addicted to the drug. By the early 1800's the "foreign mud," as opium came to be known in China, had become a curse.

Chinese and Western vessels anchored in the harbor at Guangzhou, long the only Chinese port open to foreign trade. National flags flew in front of the warehouses and offices of European and American merchants.

The Chinese government vainly tried to stamp out the traffic in opium. Laws were passed forbidding the import of opium into China and the smoking of opium. But these imperial edicts were not enforced. Moreover, the opium traders had little difficulty in smuggling the narcotic into China. Swift ships easily evaded the government's patrol boats and corrupt officials permitted the transfer of opium cargoes from ship to shore.

British Protests and the Opium War

China's resentment over the opium trade was matched by British irritation over the Chinese restrictions on commerce. Since the early 1800's British textile manufacturers had resented the monopoly on the China trade that their government had granted to the English East India Company, a firm that was interested only in the trade in tea. In 1834 British factory owners were successful in having the Company's monopoly on the China trade abolished. Shortly after that, the British demanded that their merchants be allowed to trade freely and on an equal basis with the Chinese. The Qing, however, refused to modify their tributary system, which placed China in a superior position to the Westerners. Neither government would compromise; and no trade agreements acceptable to both sides were reached.

The failure of the two countries to reach an agreement led to war. Fighting began in 1839 when the Chinese government made a real effort to wipe out the opium trade. After the Chinese confiscated and destroyed British stocks of opium at Guangzhou, Britain dispatched warships and troops to China. This Opium War raged on and off for three years before superior British firepower prevailed and the Qing asked for peace terms.

China's Changing Relations with the West

The Qing government had to pay dearly for peace. The Treaty of Nanjing, signed in 1842, ended the war. In this treaty, the Chinese agreed to open five **treaty ports** to trade, surrender the island of Hong Kong to Great Britain, and pay the British government a small **indemnity**. Also, foreign merchants were to be permitted to reside in the treaty ports, and their interests would be looked after by consuls appointed by their governments. Thus, the old system of trade was drastically revised in favor of Westerners. Most important, the Chinese government was no longer permitted to determine by itself the conditions of its commercial relations with foreign states. Henceforth, these important matters were to be decided by treaties between the governments involved.

The prestige of the Qing Empire was badly damaged. But the Chinese had little time in which to lament their defeat. Only seven years after the conclusion of the Treaty of Nanjing, rebellion broke out in China. This was the beginning of the end for the Qing dynasty, a subject that is treated in the next chapter.

Check Your Understanding

1. Why did the Chinese not have diplomatic relations with European nations?
2. How did the Chinese restrict their trade with other nations?
3. **a.** How did the demand for Chinese products result in a favorable balance of trade? **b.** How did the Chinese demand for opium change China's balance of trade?
4. **Thinking Critically:** Why did the Opium War start? How did it end? How did the outcome of the war change China's relations with the West?

CHAPTER REVIEW

■ **Chapter Summary**

Section 1. The Manchus gained control of China and ruled it for three centuries with remarkably few soldiers. They managed to preserve many aspects of their own way of life while respecting and encouraging Chinese culture. By continuing the traditional civil service examinations, they permitted Chinese scholar-officials to participate in the administration of the empire. By retaining the use of Chinese scholar-officials, the Manchus gained strong support for the Qing dynasty, which they founded. The Qing shrewdly placed Manchu officials in high positions to act as overseers. Village life, however, went on much as before because the Qing rarely interfered in village affairs.

Section 2. Once the Qing had consolidated their power, the Chinese Empire enjoyed long periods of peace that were characterized by good government, the maintenance of law and order, and the efficient operation of public works. New crops were introduced, and more land was cultivated. But the increased food supply also led to an increase in population. Tillable land became scarce and expensive, the government became more corrupt, and peasant rebellions began to break out.

Section 3. The Qing dynasty succeeded in extending the power and influence of the Chinese Empire throughout much of Asia. The Manchu rulers retained the tributary system in their relations with other states. This system, which assumed the superiority of the Chinese state and civilization, served the empire's need and desire for security and prestige, but it eventually outlived its purpose in dealings with Western nations.

Section 4. European pressures on China began to increase with demands for Chinese products. These demands led to protests over trade restrictions imposed by the Qing on foreign merchants. With the growth of the opium trade in China, however, European merchants eventually changed China's favorable balance of trade with the West into an unfavorable one. War with Great Britain over the opium trade resulted. The Treaty of Nanjing resulted in the opening of five treaty ports, giving the West the entrance into China that it had long sought.

- **Vocabulary Review**

    Define: banner, censor system, censor, queue, brotherhood, kowtow, ambassador, diplomatic mission, bullion, balance of trade, treaty port, indemnity

- **Places to Locate**

    Locate: Guangzhou, Japan, Taiwan, Mongolia, Tibet, Xinjiang, Tonking, Amur River, China Proper, Burma

- **People to Know**

    Identify: Manchus, Qing, Nurhachi, Kangxi, Qian Long

- **Thinking Critically**

    1. How did strong and shrewd Qing rulers shape a powerful Chinese state in the 1600's and 1700's? Compare their strengths and weaknesses with other forceful rulers that you have read about—Genghis Khan, for example.
    2. How does the tributary system differ from present-day relations between nations? Would the tributary system be effective today? Why or why not?
    3. Why did the problem of maintaining both internal and external peace continually trouble Chinese rulers?
    4. Could the Chinese have avoided the Opium War? Why or why not?

- **Extending and Applying Your Knowledge**

    1. On an outline map of Asia, use different colors to show the Qing Empire and the areas conquered by the Qing. Use symbols to indicate those states that were part of the tributary system. You might also locate the cities that became treaty ports for European nations.
    2. Research information on the emperors of the Qing dynasty. Indicate the accomplishments of each. Share your information with the class in the form of a chart or a report.

6

The End of the Chinese Empire

Crises mounted for the Qing Empire after the Opium War. The empire suffered from all the ills that had hastened the end of earlier dynasties. The growing discontent of the peasants was matched by increased corruption on the part of government officials. Defiance of the dynasty by provincial bureaucrats and wealthy landlords was even more menacing to Qing rule. No longer, moreover, could non-Chinese along the frontiers and from beyond the seas be held in check. But political giants like the Qing Empire were not easily laid low. Every symptom of dynastic decline was visible in China from the mid–1800's on. Nevertheless, the empire survived repeated attacks from its enemies for well over half a century.

The Qing rulers realized that some reforms were necessary if they were to retain power. But the Chinese scholar-officials were slow in awakening to the danger. Smug in the conviction that their way of life was superior to all others, they regarded any attempt at reform as a betrayal of their ancestral heritage and were slow to respond to the need for change.

Even sweeping reforms, however, could not have saved China's Confucian society. By the late 1800's the outside world, from which China had long sought to remain aloof, was undergoing great change. The Chinese, while they knew how to cope with invading armies, were thrown off balance by the effects of advances in science and technology and other new ideas from the West that began to filter into their land. China found that it could no longer ignore Western civilization.

1. Revolts in the Mid-1800's

The Chinese have a long history of rebellion. From the earliest times there have been uprisings against established authority in China. Many of these upheavals aimed at unseating rulers in whom the people had lost confidence. In other outbreaks, the people tried to overthrow foreign dynasties whose rule had never been completely accepted by the "Sons of Han." Still other rebellions were staged by minority peoples seeking to escape Chinese domination. Peasant uprisings began to break out around 1800. (See page 108.) Then, beginning in 1844, the empire was engulfed by several different uprisings. For 25 years the Qing dynasty found itself waging a struggle for survival.

The Taiping Rebellion

The leader of the most serious of these rebellions was a disgruntled scholar named Hong Xiuquan (HOONG SHOO-CHOO-AHN). Hong had failed to pass the civil service examinations and blamed the government for his failure. After reading about the teachings of Christianity in missionary booklets, Hong came to believe that he was destined to be the savior of the Chinese people. Hong persuaded his followers that his mission on earth was to establish a "Heavenly Kingdom of Great Peace." In Chinese, *taiping* (TY-PING) is the word for "Great Peace." Thus the rebellion started by Hong Xiuquan got its name.

In 1844 Hong's followers began to smash statuary in their village temples in southeast China. By 1850 Hong's followers numbered 10,000. In January 1851, on Hong's thirty-seventh birthday, the Taiping rebels issued a formal declaration of their revolution.

Neither the Taiping leaders nor the recruits in the rebel army were professional soldiers. The recruits were impoverished peasants who saw no hope of improving their lives as long as the Qing remained in power. Although the rebels' skill in warfare increased with experience, the greatest asset of the Taiping warriors was high morale. Most of them fervently believed in their cause, and they fought with fury on the battlefield.

By 1853 Hong's growing army had fought its way from southeast China to Nanjing near the mouth of the Chang Jiang. In the course of this advance, opposing forces—including Manchu banner-men and pro-Manchu Chinese troops—were easily defeated. Hong had proclaimed a new dynasty, the Taiping, with himself as emperor. But before he could make the new dynasty a reality, he had to destroy the Qing dynasty.

TIMETABLE

The Closing Years of Manchu Rule

1842–1844	First Treaty Settlement
1850–1864	Taiping Rebellion
1860	Second Treaty Settlement
1879	Okinawa annexed by Japan
1894–1895	China defeated in First Sino–Japanese War (Treaty of Shimonoseki)
1898	Failure of Hundred Days' Reform
1900	Boxer Uprising
1905	Civil service examination system ended
1911	Revolution
1912	Abdication of the last Manchu emperor

Hong's views however, sharply conflicted with many traditional beliefs, habits, and customs of the Chinese people. While his radical views attracted a horde of followers, they also attracted a number of enemies. These enemies were determined to destroy him before he could wreck traditional Chinese society.

The End of the Taiping Rebellion

Wealthy Chinese landowners and government officials rallied behind the Qing dynasty. They realized that they had much to lose if the Taiping Rebellion were successful. Some of them even raised peasant armies to fight the rebel forces. Well-trained and equipped with superior Western arms, these military units were soon able to stand up to Hong's troops. Gradually they forced the Taiping army to fall back on its capital at Nanjing. Because the government had to cope with major rebellions in other parts of the empire as well, the Taiping insurgents held out until imperial forces stormed Hong's capital in 1864. The first and only emperor of the Taiping dynasty then committed suicide, and the rebellion that had caused so much destruction and the loss of so many lives was over.

Foreign Intervention

The huge armies organized by the Chinese officials and landlords actually won the war against Taiping. They waged the principal battles and crushed the rebel forces. The exploits of

SIDELIGHT TO HISTORY

The Taiping Rebel Army

In the 1840's there were thousands of discontented people in southeastern China who became attracted to the teachings of Hong Xiuquan. Organized into a militant army by one of Hong's followers, the Taiping Rebels probably numbered more than one million by the time they took Nanjing in 1853. It has been estimated that about 20 million people lost their lives in the Taiping Rebellion's attempt to oust the Manchu rulers of the Qing dynasty.

Hong's teachings stressed a unique combination of ideas about morality and equality that the discontented peasants at first found attractive. The use of opium, tobacco, and alcohol were forbidden, as were gambling and sexual misconduct. Hong taught that women were the equals of men, and many of his reforms were aimed at making equality a reality. He promised every family five hens and two sows. He ordered the same amount of land to be distributed to each member of a family, thereby giving larger families more land than smaller families. He abolished arranged marriages and other practices that degraded women. He also allowed women to serve alongside men in the army. About 25 percent of the soldiers in the Taiping army were women, and some of them served as officers.

The rebels' downfall began, however, when they began to adopt some of the practices they had originally condemned. As the gap between their promises and their performance widened, more and more Chinese began to realize the threat to their traditional way of life that the Taiping rebels posed. In the end, the Chinese preferred to be ruled by the Qing, who had proved themselves to be more "civilized" than the rebels.

---

two foreign **mercenaries** in the service of the Chinese government, however, deserve to be mentioned.

Frederick Townsend Ward, an American, was a soldier of fortune who had been hired by Chinese merchants and officials to defend the port of Shanghai. Ward quickly organized and trained a small military force. For almost two years he fought the Taiping rebels in the outskirts of Shanghai. Winning battle after battle, the American adventurer soon became a legend among the Chinese. His apparently unbeatable troops were called the "Ever Victorious Army." But Ward's luck ran out, and in 1862 he was killed. His success at forging Chinese soldiers into Western-style fighting units, using Western arms and tactics, convinced the Chinese of the superiority of Western arms.

The Western-style army then came under the command of a British army officer, Major Charles George Gordon, who came to be known as "Chinese" Gordon even before the Taiping Rebellion was put down. Major Gordon was as skillful a commander as Ward. By preventing Shanghai and its rich revenues from falling into the hands of the Taiping forces, both men gave valuable service to the Chinese government and received Chinese military rank.

Other Uprisings

While the imperial government was fighting the Taiping forces, still other uprisings were taking place. The most serious outbreak occurred in the region between the Huai and Huang rivers in northeast China. Here Nien (NEE-EHN), bands of rebels, successfully defied imperial authority for 15 years (1853–1868). Composed largely of bandits and idlers, the Nien were masters of guerrilla warfare. Mounted on horses and moving with startling speed, these rebels baffled the imperial generals for years. In 1868, however, Qing imperial forces finally crushed the Nien uprising.

Rebellions against imperial rule were also started by Muslims in Yunnan in the southwest and in Xinjiang in the northwest. Followers of Islam had lived in these regions since the Tang era. By the time of the Qing, many Muslims resented not being treated on a equal basis with the Chinese. In addition, many peasants in these areas had grievances against officials and landlords. Several years before the close of the Taiping Rebellion, Muslims rose in revolt. By 1864 Muslim rebellion was widespread in the northwest. In the southwest the Muslim revolt lasted from 1855 to 1873. The Qing could do little about these revolts, which were in such distant parts of the empire, until the Taiping and Nien rebellions had been wiped out. But in 1877 the imperial government succeeded in re-establishing its authority in the Muslim regions of the empire.

The defeat of the various rebellions had been achieved at a terrible cost. Millions of lives had been lost, and large parts of the empire had been ravaged. But the Qing rulers still made no serious effort to eliminate the causes of the widespread unrest. Poverty still plagued the peasants, and tax burdens became heavier than ever. Furthermore, corrupt government officials were still in power, dispensing their own brands of "justice." China continued to smolder with unrest.

Check Your Understanding

1. **a.** How did Hong Xiuquan try to overthrow the Qing dynasty? **b.** Why was his rebellion so attractive to many of China's peasants?
2. **a.** What other groups rebelled against the Qing about this time? **b.** What were the causes of these rebellions?
3. *Thinking Critically:* Why were the Qing able to put down the Taiping and other rebellions?

2. Foreign Pressures on China

While rebellions shook the Chinese Empire from within, the demands of Western nations added to the Qing rulers' troubles. During the 1800's the power of Western states had increased tremendously as a result of industrial and technological developments growing out of the Industrial Revolution. The military and economic might of these countries was felt in many parts of the world. It was inevitable that the West's military and economic strength would affect relations with the Chinese Empire. Europeans had long been eager to increase their trade with China. Furthermore, they were no longer willing to put up with China's claims to superiority. When neither China nor the West backed down, a clash followed. The first phase of this conflict had been the Opium War between China and Great Britain.

The First Treaty Settlement

The Opium War won for Great Britain far greater opportunities for profit than were provided by the opium trade itself. Indeed the opium trade, which had led to the conflict, was not even mentioned in the Treaty of Nanjing. The most valuable prize gained by the British was the opening of the five treaty ports.

Once the door was opened to Great Britain, other Western powers demanded the same privileges. In 1844 China signed commercial treaties with France and the United States. These agreements between China and the three Western powers are collectively known as the First Treaty Settlement.

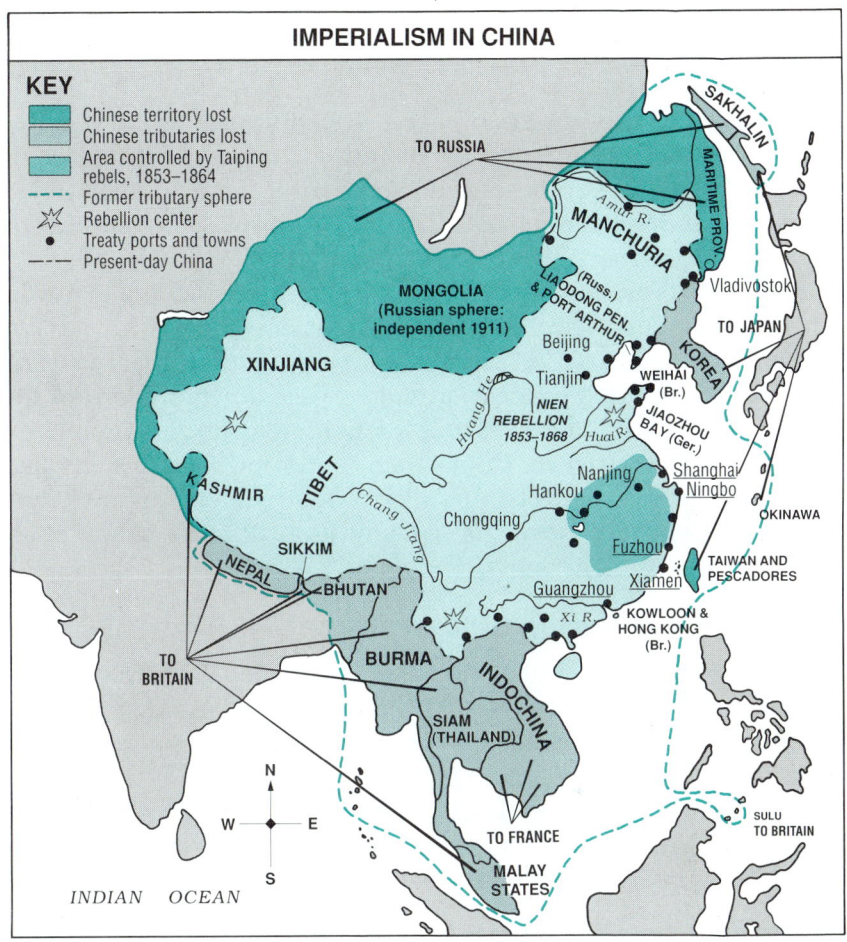

MOVEMENT: IMPERIALISM IN CHINA. The radiating lines show how foreign powers had destroyed China's tributary system by the end of the 1800's. These powers forced the Chinese to grant them special rights and to increase the number of treaty ports. (The names of the first five treaty ports granted by the Chinese are underlined.) Besides imperialist inroads, the Chinese also had to contend with internal rebellions.

To the Chinese the First Treaty Settlement was the beginning of a long series of **unequal treaties.** China's Confucian rulers had never accepted the Western idea that sovereign states were legally equal. The Chinese had long assumed that their empire was superior to all other states. Now the Qing had to give up this claim. Moreover, China was not even treated as an equal because circumstances forced China to sign treaties.

In more ways than one, China's **sovereign** rights were restricted by its agreements with the West. The unequal treaties also granted the Western powers the right of **extraterritoriality.**

This meant that foreigners charged with crimes in China were to be tried by officials of their own countries in special courts set up in the treaty ports. Furthermore, Western codes of law were to be followed in such cases. The purpose of extraterritoriality was to put an end to disputes that arose because of differences in the Chinese and Western legal and judicial systems. But the result was that China lost most of its control over the many foreigners living within its borders.

Another provision of the First Treaty Settlement had to do with **tariffs.** Tariffs were to be fixed by agreement with foreign states and could not be raised or lowered without the consent of these states. This concession did not seem very important for many years. Later, however, it severely handicapped China when it began to industrialize. China then found itself unable to raise tariffs on imports to protect its new industries. Like extraterritoriality, foreign **veto power** over Chinese tariffs was a limitation of China's sovereign rights.

Most-Favored-Nation Status

The First Treaty Settlement also gave the Western powers most-favored-nation status. If China granted certain privileges to one country within its territory, then it was obligated to extend the same rights to any other country that had a treaty with China calling for most-favored-nation status. This practice, which continued for many years, was the basis for the Open Door Policy later advocated by the United States. (See page 137.)

The Second Treaty Settlement

While the Taiping Rebellion was raging, the Western powers added to Qing woes by requesting additional privileges. When the Qing refused to enter into new treaty talks, an expedition of combined English and French forces invaded China. The imperial court fled as the European invaders marched on Beijing, and the capital was easily captured.

Peace was concluded in 1860 by an agreement that conferred many new rights on the Western powers. Additional ports were opened to trade, and foreigners were permitted to travel in China's interior. Moreover, arrangements were made for the opening of diplomatic relations between China and foreign states. The Western nations would now be permitted to send ambassadors to Beijing as their recognized representatives. These agreements were called the Second Treaty Settlement.

Western pressure on China relaxed following the Second Treaty Settlement. The Western powers realized that they might lose their new rights if the Taiping rebels were victorious. They saw, therefore, that the survival of the Qing dynasty was to their own advantage. Great Britain especially, with an eye to furthering its growing trade, favored stability in East Asia. Consequently, China was left in peace for several years after the Second Treaty Settlement.

The Qing had become more realistic in its relations with the Western nations, and slowly adjusted its policies to meet the changing international situation. In 1861 the Qing established a special government agency to handle foreign affairs. Foreign diplomats now could discuss problems directly with imperial officials. Not only were Western officials stationed in Beijing, but also representatives of China were sent to the capitals of the great powers.

Loss of Territory

During these years the leading powers of western Europe were carving out colonial empires for themselves in Africa, Asia, and the Pacific. But the empire-builders seized little land in China. In fact, until 1895, when the Qing empire was defeated in a war with Japan, the territorial losses of China were not serious. But there were a number of instances in which China did give up territory. (See map, page 125.)

As part of the Second Treaty Settlement, Britain in 1860 obtained the Kowloon Peninsula on the mainland opposite Hong Kong. Also in 1860 the Russians secured the transfer to the czar of a huge, largely unsettled tract of land north of the Amur River. The Amur then became the border between the Russian and Chinese empires. The Russians also obtained the territory north of Korea known as the Maritime Province. At its southern tip the Russian government built the naval base of Vladivostok. Finally, in 1879 Japan annexed the island of Okinawa in the western Pacific. Previously both China and Japan had claimed this island.

Destruction of the Chinese Tributary System

The Western powers refused to accept China's claims of overlordship in the tributary states lying beyond its frontiers. (See page 109.) Moreover, rulers in many of these outlying states had long since ceased to carry out their tributary obligations. The Western empire-builders saw no reason why they should stay out of these areas and felt no obligation to help China keep control of them. As a result, the Chinese tributary system vanished in the years after the Second Treaty Settlement. In the early 1880's the British completed their annexation of Burma and also brought the Malay States under their control. At the same time the French entrenched themselves in Indochina, now Vietnam, Cambodia (Kampuchea), and Laos. China's authority in lands beyond its borders had come to an end.

Check Your Understanding

1. How did demands from foreign nations add to the troubles of the Qing?
2. How were China's sovereign rights restricted by the First Treaty Settlement?
3. What gains were made by foreign powers through the Second Treaty Settlement?
4. *Thinking Critically:* How did the First and Second Treaty Settlements lead to the loss of Chinese territory and the end of China's tributary sphere?

3. The Empress Dowager and Reform

The rulers of China realized that their authority and prestige had been gravely weakened by internal revolts and the demands of Western nations. Unfortunately for the dynasty, however, the Qing failed to realize the need for reform in China until the closing years of the nineteenth century. When the Qing finally tried to make some badly needed changes, time had run out.

The Empress Dowager

About the time the empire started to crumble, a remarkable woman began to dominate the throne. She was Cixi (TSOO-SHEE), better known in history as the Empress Dowager. She has also been called the "Old Buddha." The intelligent and ambitious daughter of a Manchu official, Cixi entered the emperor's household in 1851 and bore him his only son a few years later. When the emperor died, his widow and Cixi became joint **regents.**

After Cixi's son, the emperor, died in 1875, she placed her four-year-old nephew Guangxu (GWAHNG-SHOO) upon the throne. Several years later Cixi became sole regent. Both Manchu and Chinese traditions forbade a woman to take the title of supreme ruler, but Cixi retained control of state affairs until the day of her death.

The Empress Dowager posed with the wives of Western diplomats in this photograph taken in 1903.

There is no doubt that the Empress Dowager was able and intelligent. But she was also crafty, vain, and unscrupulous. The "Old Buddha" has been described as follows:

> For thirty-seven . . . years she ruled the Palace and those nearest her with virtually absolute power, and for eleven years she ruled indirectly—a total of forty-eight years. Her outstanding endowments were an unquenchable ambition, a love of power, a love of money, and a physical vitality which almost never failed. She knew both the strength and weaknesses of men in high places; tactfully she used their talents to carry out great policies, and did not scruple to take advantage of their foibles [weaknesses] for ends both selfish and cruel. She was superstitious, but in matters of policy was realistic. Considering her limited advantages, she gained a broad view of Chinese literature and a good working knowledge of the Chinese documentary style. She was interested in music and art, and the theater owed much to her patronage. Her calligraphy was better than average and she could also paint. [Arthur W. Hummel (ed.), *Emminent Chinese of the Ch'ing [Qing] Period*]

Cixi lived most of her life in a court filled with intrigue and conspiracy. Intent on her struggle for personal power, she did little to promote the welfare of the Chinese people. At times she even lost sight of the interests of the empire. She was poorly informed about conditions in China and in the world at large and was suspicious of any change. Cixi's chief concern was to maintain the dynasty and her own power. In this aim she was opposed by many Manchu nobles who looked on her as an upstart who had violated imperial traditions. An even more serious threat to her power was the growing strength of the Chinese scholar-officials. Over time more and more Chinese had been appointed to positions of authority. By the end of the 1800's Chinese scholar-officials outnumbered their Manchu counterparts. During the great rebellions, moreover, many of these government officials had built up their military and financial power in the provinces.

Much as the imperial government feared these Chinese officials, it hesitated to provoke them by trying to curb their influence. Instead, Cixi tried to play off one scholar-official against another. This made it difficult to get agreement on government policy among rival officials. As a result, the efficiency of the administration declined.

Resistance to Change

Most government leaders were reluctant to tamper with China's time-honored ways of doing things. Continuing to insist on the superiority of Chinese civilization, imperial officials refused to admit that they had much to learn from the West. The general feeling was that the people from the West were clever in technical matters but not very wise in the arts of living. Many officials took the position that changes along Western lines would be an acknowledgment of Chinese cultural inferiority and weakness. They resisted any change, therefore, and even sabotaged reforms. "Defend the Chinese way!" was their slogan.

Some Chinese were willing to borrow from the West if only to strengthen China against foreign incursions. In the 1860's a "self-strengthening movement" began. It sought to adopt Western firearms and scientific knowledge and to train diplomats and language experts. Among the people in this movement was Li Hongzhang (LEE HOONG-JAHNG), who was most notable for his forward-looking views. He first became prominent during the period of the great rebellions. Armies that he built played a major part in suppressing both the Taiping and Nien rebels. Because of his power and prestige, Li was widely feared and

Li Hongzhang, a leading Chinese statesman of the late 1800's, urged the Chinese to study and use Western science and technology. Li made a world tour in 1896 and met leaders of the major Western countries.

respected. He enjoyed the confidence of the Empress Dowager and succeeded in introducing some changes in Chinese life.

Through his associations with Westerners, Li had learned to appreciate Western strength. He was particularly interested in munitions making and shipbuilding. One of Li's projects was to build a corps of specialists trained in the modern ways of the West. He hoped that this might help China solve its many problems. Beginning in 1872, he sent a small number of Chinese students to the United States to attend schools in New England. These first students to seek a Western education have been called "China's First Hundred." But Li waged a losing struggle against conservative officials, who argued that the project was a betrayal of Chinese culture. The students were finally recalled to China in 1881. Some of them, however, later became distinguished leaders in Chinese life.

Military and Naval Reforms

Efforts at military reform were more successful. Having seen the imperial armies destroyed by the Taiping rebels, the Qing recognized the need for military reform. They realized that without a reliable army their position as non-Chinese rulers of China was shaky. Moreover, Chinese officials were not contemptuous of Western military methods and weapons. After all, firearms, used so expertly by the Westerners, were originally a Chinese invention. The modernization of China's armed forces, therefore, was not blocked. In fact, the triumphant generals who had suppressed the rebellions of the mid-1800's had already equipped some of their troops with Western guns.

With the approval of the Empress Dowager, Western experts were employed to help build a modern fleet and military organization. Li Hongzhang was placed in charge of these projects. In the 1880's, under his direction, a strongly fortified naval base was constructed at the southern tip of Manchuria. Westerners called it Port Arthur (see map, page 125) in honor of an English naval officer who had visited its harbor in 1861. The Chinese called the base Lüshun.

Unfortunately Li Hongzhang had to work with many dishonest officials. While reporting progress, these officials actually did little except pocket government funds. Even the Empress Dowager dipped into the navy budget for money to build herself a new palace.

Efforts to Industrialize

In addition to military reforms, a small effort at industrialization was made in China during the late 1800's. Some industrial enterprises were launched and owned by the state, while others were privately sponsored. The first railroad in China was a short line built by foreigners near Shanghai in 1876. But it had a brief life. Chinese transportation workers violently objected to the railroad on the grounds that it "broke their rice bowls"; that is, it deprived them of the means of earning a living. Farmers complained that the railroad disrupted canals and took up valuable land. Chinese officials purchased the railroad and had it torn up a year after it was built. On the other hand, the establishment of a steamship line along the north China coast had

These engines were used on China's first railroad. Though its tracks were soon torn up, by 1894 a railroad system had been started in North China.

government support. Also, some coal mines were opened to produce fuel for Chinese and Western steamers. Nevertheless, the Chinese approach to technological development continued to be slow and wary.

The Hundred Days' Reform

Toward the end of the 1800's Guangxu, who had been reigning in the shadow of his overbearing aunt since 1875, decided to make a real effort at reform. Pushing aside the Empress Dowager and her advisers, Guangxu took over the government in 1898. Then, for over three months, daily edicts poured forth from the palace in Beijing. In what has been called the Hundred Days' Reform, Guangxu called for sweeping changes in many areas of Chinese life. He called for changes in education, administration, and foreign policy. He also asked for changes in agriculture, commerce, technology, and military affairs.

At first, prospects for Guangxu's reforms seemed bright. But unfortunately few of the imperial instructions were ever carried out. Many scholar-officials had no sympathy with Guangxu's tradition-breaking proposals. Furthermore, the scholar-officials were fearful of the Empress Dowager, who remained silently but ominously in the background. Before the summer of 1898 was over, the fears of the scholar-officials were realized. The Empress Dowager struck back, removing the emperor from power and arresting many of his reform-minded counselors. Most of the reforms were forgotten, and once again the Empress Dowager controlled the government.

For the last ten years of his life, Guangxu was confined to a small island in a lake within the imperial palace grounds. In 1908, by a strange coincidence, he died just one day before the death of the Empress Dowager. It has long been suspected that he was poisoned.

Check Your Understanding

1. **a.** How long was Cixi regent of China? **b.** Why was she able to stay in power so long?
2. How did Li Hongzhang help China move toward modernization?
3. Why was Guangxu unsuccessful in securing reform?
4. **Thinking Critically:** Why were the Chinese, especially the Empress Dowager, so reluctant to accept or introduce reform?

4. Japanese Inroads Against the Qing

Unlike China, Japan in the second half of the 1800's had begun to welcome Western ideas. The Japanese were impressed with the military strength and the modern industry of the Western European powers and the United States. Japan quickly adopted Western industrial methods and educational ideas. To a greater extent than the Qing, the Japanese government reorganized its army and navy and equipped it with modern weapons. Unfortunately for China, Japan made use of its growing strength to join the Western powers in making demands on the weakening Qing dynasty.

Contest for Korea

Since the days of the Han dynasty, China had regarded the Korean Peninsula as important to its security. Situated on the northeastern flank of the Chinese Empire, Korea was a natural base for would-be invaders of China. Both Mongol and Manchu conquerors had seized that peninsula before launching attacks against the Great Wall. The "Hermit Kingdom," as Korea was called, had refused for many centuries to have diplomatic relations with other countries. It had, however, paid regular tribute to the Qing emperors and was especially important to the Qing. Not only was it adjacent to Manchuria, the Mongol homeland, but its northern frontier was uncomfortably close to Beijing, the imperial capital. Korea, however, also lies very close to Japan. For that reason the Japanese, too, regarded Korea as important to their security. (See map, page 125.)

Hard-pressed as China's Qing rulers were in the late 1800's, they could not overlook a growing Japanese interest in Korea. Japan had no confidence in the ability of the weakened Qing rulers to keep Korea from falling into Western hands. In the 1870's, therefore, Japan began to interfere in the affairs of the Korean government. The unhappy Hermit Kingdom soon found itself caught in a rivalry between China and Japan.

The Sino-Japanese War

In 1894 the contest between China and Japan over Korea finally resulted in the First Sino-Japanese War. (*Sino* is a prefix meaning "Chinese.") The small kingdom of Japan easily defeated the great Chinese Empire. In less than a year, the Chinese asked for peace terms.

In the Treaty of Shimonoseki (SHEEM-oh-noh-SAY-kee), which ended the war in 1895, China paid a heavy price for its defeat.

It had to pay a large indemnity to Japan and to abandon its claims to a special position in Korea. China also extended most-favored-nation status to Japan. Furthermore, China surrendered to Japan the island of Taiwan and the nearby Pescadores (PEHS-kuh-DOHR-eez) Islands. In addition, China agreed to surrender the Liaodong (LYOW-DOONG) Peninsula in southern Manchuria, where Port Arthur was located. This transfer never took place, however, because the governments of Russia, France, and Germany warned Japan not to take possession. Japan heeded the warning, and China retained the peninsula.

The outcome of the Sino–Japanese War marked a turning point in the history of East Asia. For one thing, it gave the Western powers new respect for Japan. But, equally important, the weakness of the Chinese Empire was fully revealed. Both the Chinese people and the foreign powers now realized that the Qing dynasty was only a "paper tiger" and could not last long. Unwilling to wait for the end, some Western powers took action to hasten the dynasty's collapse.

The Rush for Spheres of Influence

Several European powers cast aside the restraint they had shown since the Second Treaty Settlement and demanded further rights and privileges in China. None of these nations wanted to share its gains with other governments. Instead, each of them sought to stake out a **sphere of influence** within China to exploit and manage.

Germany began the rush for special privileges in China. When two German missionaries were killed by Chinese bandits, the German government demanded that China make amends. In 1898 the Qing agreed to lease Jiaozhou (jih-OW-JOH) Bay to Germany for 99 years. (See map, page 125.) Here the Germans soon built a strong naval and commercial base. Hardly had this concession been granted, when Russia insisted on a similar concession at Port Arthur. Other European powers then demanded equal treatment. Afraid to refuse, China leased good harbors to Britain and France. These gains at China's expense encouraged the Western powers to ask for still more privileges.

Stemming the Breakup of China

The concessions granted to foreign nations led to talk about the breakup of China. Some of the Western powers looked on China as an overripe melon ready for carving into slices, or spheres of influence. Both Great Britain and the United States, however, opposed any further carving up of the Chinese Empire.

Besieged Westerners used this 40-year-old cannon to defend a Beijing legation from the Boxers. An Allied expedition finally rescued the Westerners, who at one point had been given up for dead.

It was the United States, however, that took the lead in seeking to check the threatened breakup of the Chinese Empire. In 1899 Secretary of State John Hay issued a proposal, or "note," on China. Hay called on the great powers to support the principle of an open door, or an equal trading opportunity for all, in China. But the nations had little chance to respond before the long-smoldering Chinese resentment over foreign disregard for China's sovereign rights erupted into violence.

The Boxer Uprising

The violence was started by a powerful secret society known to the Chinese as the Society of Harmonious Fists, and to the Westerners as Boxers. Westerners gave the society this name because the gymnastic exercise its members practiced resembled Western-style boxing. For years the Society of Harmonious Fists had blamed the Qing for China's many troubles. But after the Sino-Japanese War, the imperial government convinced the society's members that foreigners, not the Qing, were responsible for China's misfortunes.

At the outset of the uprising, bands of society members attacked foreigners in many parts of China and destroyed their property. Many Chinese provincial governors, fearing stern action by the foreign powers, acted quickly to crush the Boxer Uprising. In the north, however, Westerners had to flee to the safety of their **legations** in Beijing. Seeing the uprising as an opportunity to rid China of foreigners, the Empress Dowager sent imperial troops to help the Boxers. For 55 days the Westerners fought off the besieging Chinese. Finally an Allied Expeditionary Force, composed of soldiers from six nations, battled its way to Beijing and rescued the embattled Westerners.

The Open Door Policy

When the Boxer rioting broke out, the United States government feared that the European powers at last had an excuse to partition China, a belief that was hardly groundless. For example, Russia sent an army into Manchuria, stating that its purpose was to maintain law and order and to protect the area for the Qing dynasty. But other powers suspected that **annexation** of the region by Russia would soon follow.

Seeking to prevent a scramble for Chinese territory by the great powers, Secretary of State Hay in 1900 issued a second note on China. This document asked the powers to stop seeking special privileges at the expense of China and other East Asian nations. Had the United States stood alone, the two notes, which together became known as the Open Door Policy, would not have had much force. All the nations that had interests in China increasingly mistrusted one another's motives. Each suspected the others might turn their spheres of influence into outright colonies. Great Britain, strongly interested in preserving free trade and also suspicious of other nations, opposed the dismemberment of the Chinese Empire. With the most powerful naval fleet in the world, Great Britain gave strong backing to the Open Door Policy. The Chinese Empire never was carved up politically. It remained intact under its own government, but it paid a heavy price for the Boxer Uprising.

China's Heavy Price

Western governments were determined to punish China for the outrages that the Boxers had inflicted on foreign citizens. By a treaty negotiated in 1901, the Qing agreed to compensate for the loss of life and damage caused by the Boxers. The settlement amounted to several hundred million dollars and put the Chinese government deeply in debt. In addition, China agreed that the foreign governments could maintain troops at their legations in Beijing. The foreign powers were also given the right to patrol a railway that operated between the coast and Beijing. These last two concessions were to ensure the safety of foreigners in case of future disturbances.

China had one consolation in connection with the Boxer Uprising and its aftermath. The Qing government was spared the shame of admitting its guilt in furthering the assault on foreigners. The Western powers and China agreed that the episode would be called a "rebellion," implying that the Boxers had acted in defiance of the Qing government. For this reason, the episode has commonly been known as the Boxer Rebellion, although it is more accurate to call it the Boxer Uprising.

Check Your Understanding

1. How did Japan differ from China in its response to Western ideas?
2. **a.** What were the results of the Sino–Japanese War (1894–1895)? **b.** How did the war mark a turning point in the history of East Asia?
3. How did the Open Door Policy affect **a.** China? **b.** the Western Powers?
4. *Thinking Critically:* What caused the Boxer Uprising? How did the Western powers use it as an excuse to intervene in China? What effects did the Boxer Uprising have on China?

5. Attempts at Reform in China

Once the dust had settled following the Boxer Uprising, no one, not even the conservative Empress Dowager, could deny that China and the Qing dynasty faced enormous problems. The Western powers had gained more influence and control. China's defeat in the Sino–Japanese War and its inability to stand up to the Allied Expeditionary Force during the Boxer Uprising pointed up China's military weaknesses, including the lack of properly trained officers and inadequate weaponry. The humiliations inflicted on China following the Boxer Uprising convinced the Qing that reforms were badly needed. The broad program of reforms that was subsequently initiated was reminiscent of the Hundred Days of 1898, which the Empress Dowager had decisively opposed. The reform offered a program of sweeping institutional and social change, affecting the military, education, government, and politics.

Military Reform

The Qing began to reform the army. The Chinese armies were led by officers who had been chosen by an outdated military examination system. To strengthen military leadership, the Qing in 1901 abolished this examination system and established more military academies throughout the empire. They also encouraged provincial governors to raise and drill new military units. Foreign advisers, usually Germans, were employed, and modern weapons were purchased abroad. Several first-rate units were organized. One of these was led by the powerful Yuan Shikai (YOO-AHN SHUR-KY), a disciple of Li Hongzhang. Yuan's troops were well-trained and equipped with modern weapons. Moreover, they were personally loyal to him, probably because, unlike other Chinese armies, they were well-fed, well-housed, and—most important—paid on time.

Changes in Education

Like the military examination system, the ancient system of civil service examinations had become outdated. In 1905 it was final-

Mathematics was among the subjects studied in Western-style schools opened in China during the early 1900's. This student found his queue useful in analyzing a geometry problem. Note that the class was conducted in English.

ly abolished, and the government announced that appointments to official positions would be made on the basis of merit. New schools were opened to train students for government service. Furthermore, the Qing at last began to realize that to keep up with the West, China would have to advance technologically. As a start, schools were opened to give students technical training.

Many Chinese students had gone to Japan and Western nations after the Sino–Japanese War, hoping to acquire skills that would be useful in the modernization of their country. Now, with government support, students began to go abroad in much greater numbers. By 1911 thousands of Chinese students were enrolled in the universities of Japan, the United States, and Europe. Moreover, in 1908 the United States had returned to China about two thirds of the indemnity it had received after the Boxer Uprising. In 1924 the balance of the indemnity was returned. The Chinese used the initial money to establish a college in Beijing. Beginning in 1911, a steady flow of graduates from this college entered American universities for further education. They were supported by Boxer Fellowships, which were also paid for out of the money that the United States had returned to China.

Other Changes

For years students, officials, and some other Chinese had called for a reduction of the powers held by the emperor and his advisers. These reformers thought it wrong that the imperial court should be able to make and enforce laws as it saw fit. The reformers proposed the adoption of a national **constitution,** the creation of a national **parliament,** and a system of provincial legislatures.

The Qing rulers at first resisted proposals for changes in government. The example of Japan, however, finally led them to change their attitude. In 1890 the Japanese had adopted parliamentary government, but without reducing the power of their emperor. The Qing saw that the Japanese had been able to adopt political reforms and at the same time increase the country's military power. The rulers of China had been impressed by Japanese victories in wars with their own empire and with Russia. In 1908, therefore, the Empress Dowager announced that constitutional parliamentary government would be established in China after nine years. As a first step the dynasty agreed to permit the formation of legislatures in the provinces.

The constitutional issue sharpened the struggle between the central and provincial governments. The Qing dynasty had no intention of permitting the reins of power to slip from its grasp. Rather it hoped to use the new constitution and the national parliament to reinforce the power of the imperial state. Provincial leaders, however, were determined to limit the authority of the monarchy. Their hope was that a national parliament and the provincial legislatures would be able to dominate the dynasty. Thus, competition for political power increased, becoming even more bitter after the Empress Dowager died in 1908.

But the issue was never resolved. Many Chinese believed that the dynasty had outlived its usefulness. They held the Qing responsible for China's troubles. Furthermore, they were skeptical of any reform program advanced by the Qing dynasty. In the years following the First Sino–Japanese War, a growing number of revolutionaries dedicated themselves to the overthrow of the dynasty and the establishment of a **republic.** In 1911 revolt again erupted in China, and the tottering Qing dynasty fell. The Imperial Age in China had come to an end. This event is discussed in the next chapter.

Check Your Understanding

1. What events convinced the Qing that reforms in China were needed?
2. Why did China abolish the military and civil service examination systems?
3. How did China finance the education of students abroad?
4. **Thinking Critically:** How did the constitutional issue sharpen the struggle for power between the central government and the provincial governments?

CHAPTER REVIEW

■ **Chapter Summary**

Section 1. Beginning in the mid–1800's the Chinese Empire was severely shaken by peasant uprisings. One that nearly succeeded was the Taiping Rebellion. Begun by Hong Xiuquan, the rebellion had wide appeal among peasants, especially women, who were attracted by promises of social and political equality (that never really materialized). The Taiping program of reform, however, angered the scholar-officials, wealthy landlords, and others threatened by changes in China's traditional way of life. With the help of these groups, the Qing crushed the Taiping Rebellion. It also survived rebellions by Muslim groups and by the Nien.

Section 2. Foreign pressures greatly added to China's internal troubles. Western influence in China increased after the Opium War and the opening of the first five treaty ports granted to Great Britain with the Treaty of Nanjing. Other Western powers then wrested special privileges from the Chinese in a series of negotiations called Treaty Settlements. With the First Treaty Settlement, Western nations gained extraterritoriality, veto power over China's tariff rates, and most-favored-nation status. After the Second Treaty Settlement, additional treaty ports were opened and diplomatic relations were begun with China in an exchange of ambassadors. More important to China's prestige was the loss of territory it suffered and the destruction of its tributary system.

Section 3. Cixi, the Empress Dowager, rose to power in the mid–1800's as regent for emperors too young to rule. Able and intelligent, Cixi managed to keep the empire from crumbling for almost 50 years. Although she allowed some reforms to be made, her main interest was to preserve the Qing dynasty and her own power. Many efforts at modernization, especially in the military, were undertaken by Li Hongzhang, but these efforts were hampered by corruption in government and the imperial court and a failure to understand the need for railways and other technological developments.

Section 4. A revitalized Japan, strengthened by its own modernization efforts, took advantage of China's weakness and successfully gained special privileges from China, including the control of Korea, by defeating China in the First Sino–Japanese War (1894–1895). With the weakness of China revealed for all the world to see, Western powers rushed to extend their spheres of influence. But resentment over foreign intervention in China's affairs built up and resulted in the Boxer Uprising, which was put down by the Western powers in a further revelation of China's weakness. The United States, supported by Great Britain, took the lead in trying to prevent the partition of China. It issued a series of notes that resulted in the establishment of the Open Door Policy and a stemming of further partition.

Section 5. As the twentieth century opened, China again attempted reform and modernization. China's traditional military and civil service examinations were replaced by new systems of appointment and training. Promising students were encouraged to complete their education abroad, and the Empress Dowager gave permission for a new constitution and national parliament. But political reform became a struggle for power between the Qing who were determined to preserve their power and others who were determined to limit its power. But the dynasty fell before the power of a revolution that began in 1911 and finally brought China's 2,000-year-old empire to an end.

■ Vocabulary Review

Define: mercenary, unequal treaty, sovereign, extraterritoriality, tariff, veto power, regent, sphere of influence, legation, annexation, constitution, parliament, republic

■ Places to Locate

Locate: Shanghai, Kowloon Peninsula, Amur River, Maritime Province, Vladivostok, Okinawa, Burma, Malay States, Indochina, Korea, Liaodong Peninsula, Port Arthur

■ People to Know

Identify: Hong Xiuquan, Taiping Rebels, Frederick T. Ward, Charles Gordon, Nien, Cixi, Li Hongzhang, Guangxu, John Hay, Society of Harmonious Fists, Yuan Shikai

■ Thinking Critically

1. What might have happened to China if the Taiping Rebellion had been successful? Use as much evidence from the textbook as possible to support your answer.
2. How did foreign powers violate China's sovereign rights from the 1850's onward?
3. How did circumstances combine to keep the Qing dynasty in power until after 1900?
4. Why do you think it is nearly impossible for any traditional nation to resist modernization for very long? What is likely to happen to any present-day nation that resists modernization? Explain.

■ Extending and Applying Your Knowledge

1. Do further research on either the Taiping Rebellion or the Boxer Uprising. Prepare a report to share with the

class that focuses on causes, goals, outcome, and personalities involved.
2. Prepare a mock panel discussion of nations involved in China at the time of the Open Door notes. Ask classmates to assume the roles of diplomats representing each of the nations to which the notes were sent. Have each diplomat present his or her country's viewpoint, discussing the kind of reaction the policy received, both by those who favored it and by those who opposed it.

7

The Struggling Republic

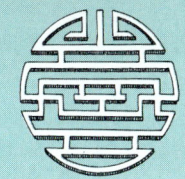

Edmund Burke, a British statesman and thinker of the eighteenth century, analyzed the French Revolution of 1789 in these words: "When ancient opinions and rules of life are taken away, the loss cannot possibly be estimated. From that moment we have no compass to govern us; nor can we know distinctly to what port we steer."

Burke's observation could also apply to the Chinese Revolution of 1911. The opponents of imperial rule found it easy to overthrow the Qing dynasty and establish a republic in China. But, even before the smoke of battle cleared away, it was evident that the new republic was headed for serious trouble.

For more than 2,000 years the Middle Kingdom had been ruled by emperors—some wise and capable, others foolish and grasping. The Chinese people themselves had usually been wary of government and public officials. Although they realized the need for both a government and an administrative staff of officials, they avoided contact with them as much as possible.

Few Chinese shed tears at the ouster of the Manchus and the passing of the Qing dynasty. But many Chinese would have been satisfied to see a new dynasty appear. Imperial government was familiar, and a new dynasty might improve the conditions that had led to the fall of the Qing rulers. But, instead, the Chinese saw a republic formed, a constitution proclaimed, and a parliament organized. Most Chinese were puzzled by talk of elections and a bill of rights—political ideas from Europe and the United States that were strange to a people who had no experience with democratic government.

145

1. The Republic's Shaky Foundation

The leader of the revolutionary movement in China was Sun Yat-sen (SOON YAT-SEN). Born in 1866 near Guangzhou, Sun migrated at the age of 13 to Hawaii, where his older brother had settled some years before. In Honolulu, Sun studied at an English missionary school and learned about Western civilization. With the advantage of distance, he could clearly see the continuing decline of his homeland. Sun later attended a medical school in Hong Kong, and on graduation in 1894 he became a doctor. But he did not practice his profession very long. After China's humiliating defeat by Japan in 1895, Sun decided to devote his life to the salvation of his country. He never wavered from his course to the day of his death 30 years later.

The Kuomintang

In 1895 Sun launched the first of his many efforts to overthrow the Qing dynasty. It ended in failure. As a result of Sun's activities, the Manchus placed a price on his head. Sun fled to Japan where he lived as an exile, not daring to set foot in his homeland. But he visited the overseas Chinese communities in Japan, Hawaii, Southeast Asia, Canada, the United States, and Europe. From the Chinese in these communities, Sun recruited followers and secured financial support. He succeeded in establishing a **revolutionary** organization. After several changes of names it finally became known as the Kuomintang (GWOH-min-DAHNG), or the Nation–People–Party, and so is translated as the Nationalist Party.

The End of Qing Rule

In 1911 Sun and his followers were planning another attempt to overthrow the Qing dynasty. For his part, Sun was to make a tour of Chinese communities in Canada and the United States to raise funds. One morning in October, Sun left his hotel in Denver, Colorado, and went to a restaurant for breakfast. On his way he bought a newspaper. To his astonishment the headlines announced that a revolution had broken out in China.

"Wuchang Occupied by Revolutionaries," the bold print stated. Sun correctly guessed that the capture of key cities, like Wuchang in Central China, heralded the downfall of the Qing. Looking ahead to the establishment of a Chinese republic, he went on to Europe to obtain support for the new government. By the time Sun returned to his homeland in December 1911, the end of Qing rule was certain.

Sun Yat-sen, "Father of the Chinese Revolution," became provisional president of the republic that was founded after the Wuchang uprising. He soon resigned in order to win the support of General Yuan Shikai for the republic. Sun spent much of the rest of his life in exile. His one aim was to see the unification of China under a republican government.

In preparing for their attack on the Qing regime, the revolutionaries had manufactured crude bombs in their secret headquarters at Hankou. (This is one of three adjoining cities in Central China collectively known as Wuhan. The other Wuhan cities are Hanyang and Wuchang.) On October 9, 1911, one of the bombs accidentally exploded. Fearing the arrival of the police, the conspirators had fled in a panic. The quick arrest of a few revolutionaries and the seizure of their secret records threatened to expose the entire plot.

Sun's comrades in Hankou acted in desperation. Rather than be captured and executed, they vowed to die fighting. On October 10, 1911, a day that became celebrated as the "double ten" (tenth day of the tenth month), the Chinese patriots made their move. Mutinous troops of the local army garrison, who were persuaded to cast their lot with the revolutionaries, even forced their commander to support them. By the following day much of Wuchang had fallen into the hands of the rebels. For the first time, the revolutionaries had a strong base.

The spark ignited at Hankou kindled a revolutionary bonfire. Many political and military leaders in the provinces needed little encouragement to defy the Qing government. The country had long been seething with discontent. Emboldened by the success of the revolutionaries in Wuhan, people throughout China turned against the imperial rulers. The Qing realized with dismay that few of their subjects were willing to support the

TIMETABLE

The Early Republic

1911–1912	Revolution and abdication of last Qing emperor
	Beginning of republican government
1912–1916	Presidency of Yuan Shikai
1915	Japan's Twenty-one Demands
1916–1928	Warlord period
1919	Beijing demonstrations against Versailles Treaty
	Beginning of May Fourth Movement
1921	Founding of Chinese Communist Party
1923	Sun–Joffe Agreement
	Reorganization of revolutionary government
1925	Death of Sun Yat-sen
1926–1927	Northern Expedition
1927	Expulsion of Communists from Kuomintang
	Government's move to Nanjing

throne. The authority of the dynasty in Central and South China crumbled with astonishing speed.

Lack of Unity and Direction

The country-wide uprisings were largely spontaneous. With Sun Yat-sen abroad, the movement had no central leader, and his revolutionary organization could not coordinate the many local upheavals. Furthermore, Sun was not even known in many sections of China. Consequently, the many uprisings against the imperial government were led and directed by local leaders.

These leaders were not agreed on the aims and purposes of the revolution. Some preferred a powerful central government. Others, pointing out that the Qing dynasty had too often interfered in local affairs, wanted to keep power in local hands. Some of the revolutionaries favored a strong chief executive or president. But others thought there should be a strong parliament. Such differences of opinion had not been settled before the revolution broke out, and it was unlikely that they could be settled during its course.

The Role of Yuan Shikai

The Qing rulers in Beijing realized that only drastic action could prevent disaster. In desperation they turned to Yuan Shikai, the retired general who had organized the national army. Yuan was granted broad powers to deal with the crisis, and the imperial army was hurled against the revolutionaries. Unable to withstand Yuan's well-trained and well-equipped regiments, the rebels were defeated in less than two weeks. But Yuan was in no hurry to destroy these enemies of the throne. He had no intention of bailing the dynasty out of its difficulties. Instead, he cleverly exploited the crisis to further his personal ambition.

Holding his armies in check, Yuan abandoned the emperor and entered into discussions with the revolutionary leaders. Both Yuan and the revolutionary leaders knew that the anti-Qing forces had little hope of defeating the imperial army. So they struck a bargain.

Soon after the October uprising the revolutionaries had proclaimed a republic and elected Sun Yat-sen its temporary president. Sun, who had returned to China, now agreed to resign to allow Yuan to become head of the new government. Yuan, in turn, agreed to support the republic. He also promised to persuade the Qing emperor to abdicate. Abandoned by his strongest supporter, Emperor Xuan Tong (shoo-AHN TOONG)—his given name was Pu Yi—had to comply. On February 12, 1912, the last of the Qing emperors officially declared his dynasty at an end. Because the emperor was only five years old, the edict of abdication was signed by his mother. Xuan Tong was a nephew of Guangxu, the emperor who had died in 1908. (See page 133.) By the terms of the abdication the child emperor was permitted to retain his title and to live in a palace in Beijing.

Conflict in the Republic

Only their conviction that a republic must be established whatever the cost drove the revolutionaries to join forces with Yuan Shikai. They knew his long record of double-dealing, and they must have realized that this former Manchu official had little sympathy for the new government. It soon became clear that personal power was Yuan's goal. From the moment a parliament was established in 1912, a struggle for control began. Yuan's supporters competed with Sun's supporters to gain the upper hand in the new government. Quarrels over political appointments and control of the national budget seriously weakened the republican government. As fears and distrust mounted, chances for **compromise** between the conflicting parties faded.

President Yuan spared no effort to strengthen his authority. He even ordered the assassination of those who protested too strongly against his highhanded actions. Realizing that the republic would fail if Yuan were not stopped, Sun Yat-sen and his followers tried to overthrow him in 1913. But Yuan quickly suppressed the uprising; and Sun, "Father of the Chinese Revolution," again had to flee to Japan. Not long afterward, Yuan took steps to destroy the parliament. Removing his political enemies by force, he also deprived the legislative body of what little power it had enjoyed. Thereafter he completely ignored it. Parliamentary government ceased, and Yuan became a **dictator.**

Imperial Restoration Plans

Yuan plotted to restore the empire. Actually the republican form of government had been favored by only a very small minority of the Chinese people. These few included the revolutionaries themselves, young people who had studied abroad, and some modern-minded business people. But the great mass of people knew nothing about constitutions, parliaments, elections, and political rights. They had little interest in the democratic system that Sun and his followers wanted to introduce in China.

Yuan Shikai, of course, had never concealed his dislike for the republican government of which he was president. In 1915 it became apparent that he was plotting to restore the empire. Newspapers began publishing proposals that the republic be abolished and the empire re-established. These news reports also urged Yuan himself to found a new imperial dynasty. Telegrams poured into Yuan's office, supporting the idea.

Few were deceived by this show of support for Yuan. Many people realized that Yuan himself was behind the campaign to destroy the republic and restore the imperial government to power. The would-be emperor encountered firm opposition from military leaders in southern and western China. Yuan Shikai abandoned his imperial ambitions early in 1916, just two months before he died.

The leaders who had blocked the restoration of the empire were by no means devoted to the republic. Yuan's opponents had been chiefly interested in preserving their own power. They knew that a weak central government struggling for survival could not seriously challenge their authority in the provinces. These self-seeking military leaders, or **warlords** as they were called, had opposed Yuan Shikai because they feared a strong imperial state. They preferred to have a weak and ineffective government in Beijing.

Some of the Chinese warlords, among them Feng Yuxiang, won the respect of foreign powers. Feng had been converted to Christianity and became known as "the Christian general." He insisted on strict discipline among his troops. Unlike most of the warlord armies, Feng's troops were generally respected for their good behavior.

The Warlord Period

Warlords disrupting the countryside were nothing new in Chinese history. Many times in the past lawless strongmen had organized armed bands, usually for their own profit, when government authority was undermined by rebellion or invasion. Selfish and brutal, these men preyed on the helpless people. The collapse of the Qing dynasty paved the way for the emergence of a new warlord period. Former officers of the imperial army, chieftains of robber bands, and bold and ambitious peasants began to organize independent military forces in many parts of the country. The most successful warlords gained control over whole provinces or even larger areas of China.

Thus, Yuan Shikai's death brought chaos to China. As long as he was alive, the warlords showed some restraint in ravaging the countryside, but after Yuan's death, the ability of the central government to exercise its authority and keep the warlords restrained rapidly disappeared. The area around the capital city of Beijing became the grand prize sought by the warlords of North China. Whatever warlord held Beijing was recognized as the official government of China by foreign countries. Official positions—even the office of president—were sold to the highest bidders. China had rarely been so politically corrupt as it was during the decade after the death of Yuan Shikai.

Check Your Understanding

1. **a.** Who was the leader of the revolution against the Qing rulers? **b.** How did the revolution begin? **c.** How did it spread?
2. **a.** How did the Qing try to suppress the revolution? **b.** How did their plan backfire?
3. **a.** Why did the revolutionaries make an alliance with Yuan Shikai? **b.** What was Sun Yat-sen's role in the alliance? **c.** What happened to the Chinese parliament? **d.** What was Yuan's ultimate goal?
4. **a.** Who were the warlords? **b.** How did they affect the revolution?
5. **Thinking Critically:** Did Sun Yat-sen make the right decision in stepping down from the presidency in favor of Yuan Shikai? Explain your answer.

2. Increased Friction Between China and Foreign Nations

By the terms of the unequal treaties, the Western powers and Japan were permitted to station troops and gunboats in certain parts of China. With the rise of the warlords, these foreign governments became concerned about the safety of their citizens and the security of their property in China. Consequently, the foreign powers strengthened their military garrisons in Chinese cities and sent more war vessels to patrol the rivers and coastal waters. The foreigners living in China welcomed the measures taken by their governments to protect them, but the Chinese understandably were resentful. The presence in their country of privileged foreigners supported by soldiers and ships was humiliating. Many of the younger Chinese waited impatiently for the day when the foreigners would have to leave.

Resentment Toward Great Britain and Japan

The British were especially resented in China because of their power and wealth. Britain's stake in China's foreign trade was larger than that of all other nations combined. The British invested heavily in the construction of railroads and the opening of mines, and they owned and operated many factories in the treaty ports along the coast. Also, they had made loans to China's impoverished government. The British were always careful to remind the Chinese of the many privileges guaranteed the Westerners by treaty.

The Chinese also regarded Japan as a menace. In 1905 Japan had made significant gains after defeating Russia in the Russo–Japanese War. As a result of the peace terms, Japan took over Russia's rights in Port Arthur and made Korea a protectorate. In 1910 Japan annexed Korea. This expansion of Japanese power so close to the Chinese borders naturally alarmed China. Relations with Japan worsened after the Revolution of 1911. The Japanese, whose government was a monarchy, were not happy to see a republic established in China. In fact, Japan was the last major power to recognize the new republic. During World War I the tension between the two Asian countries further increased. When war broke out in Europe in 1914, the government of China decided to remain neutral. Japan, which had a defensive alliance with Great Britain, entered the war on the side of the Allies.

Japanese Gains in Power

Soon after the war began in Europe, the Japanese sent an expedition to seize the German base at Qingdao (CHING-DOW). This was the headquarters of the territory at Jiaozhou Bay, which China had leased to Germany during the scramble for concessions in 1898. (See map, page 125.) The Japanese quickly captured this base and held it for the rest of the war. Other German rights in Shandong province, where Qingdao was located, were also taken over by the island empire. In 1917 Japan made a secret agreement with Great Britain, France, and Italy. These four countries agreed that German possessions and rights in China would be transferred to Japan after the war.

In 1915 Japan made its most serious attempt to gain power over China. Realizing that the European powers were too busy to interfere, Japan secretly made demands on the government of Yuan Shikai for special privileges in China. These included the right to send officials to help supervise China's government and police force. Acceptance of the Twenty-one Demands, as they were called, would have made China a Japanese protectorate. Japan warned the Chinese government not to make the demands public.

Despite the warning, Yuan let the world know about the Twenty-one Demands. He hoped that some of the great powers would come to China's rescue. Several countries did protest, especially the United States, and the Japanese government withdrew its more extreme demands. But the remainder were granted in a treaty. Naturally the Chinese were deeply angered by Japan's aggressive action.

China finally joined the Allies in World War I at the urging of President Woodrow Wilson of the United States. He pointed out that the Allies were certain to win and that it would be advantageous for the Chinese republic to be on the victorious side when the war ended. After the war was won, China's representatives would have an opportunity at the peace conference to voice China's many grievances against Japan and the unequal treaty system in general.

In 1917 China did declare war against Germany and the other Central Powers. Although China sent no troops to the battlefronts in Europe, it sent labor battalions to Europe. In France and the Middle East these labor battalions performed a valuable service in the war effort. Their work made it possible to release Europeans for the battlefront, thus increasing Allied troops in the final war campaigns.

Peace Negotiations

After World War I, delegates from China were invited to participate in the lengthy peace negotiations held at Versailles in France. China's hope was to recover for itself the special rights originally granted to Germany and later transferred to Japan. The Shandong Question, as the issue was called, became one of the most troublesome controversies of the Versailles Conference. Determined to keep the fruits of its victory, Japan revealed to the world its secret agreement with Great Britain, France, and Italy. The other members of the conference finally decided to let China and Japan settle the problem themselves. Asking China to negotiate with Japan was like asking a kitten to deal with a tiger, for Japan was much more powerful than China. Recognizing the insult, the furious Chinese delegates left the conference and refused to sign the Treaty of Versailles at this time. Later, China signed a separate peace treaty with Germany.

The treatment of China's representatives at Versailles led to demonstrations in China. The Chinese people felt that justice for China through the securing of its sovereign rights had been sacrificed on the altar of **imperialism.** Demonstrations were organized by professors and students at Beijing University to protest the decision reached on the Shandong Question.

The protests by the Beijing professors and students on May 4, 1919, were quickly followed by demonstrations at other schools throughout China. In what became known as the May Fourth Movement, demonstrators condemned the betrayal of

In 1919 Chinese nationalism exploded in demonstrations and refusals to buy Japanese goods. These demonstrators in Shanghai carried banners reading "Down with the traitors—don't buy Japanese goods."

China, denounced Japanese imperialism, and in some cities staged a **boycott** of Japanese goods. The spectacle of an aroused nation was startling to people in the West. The demonstrations signaled a change of attitude on the part of the Chinese people. No longer would they accept humiliation by foreign powers in silent anger nor passively stand by when their government failed to serve the national interest.

Check Your Understanding

1. Why did the Chinese especially resent Great Britain and Japan?
2. What gains in power were made by Japan during World War I?
3. Why did China finally join the war on the side of the Allies?
4. How did the May Fourth Movement begin?
5. *Thinking Critically:* In what ways was the increased friction between the Chinese and foreign powers an advantage for China's movement toward democratic government?

3. Changes in Chinese Life Following World War I

China, like other lands in Asia, was cut off from its regular sources of manufactured goods during World War I. The factories of industrial nations like Great Britain and Germany were converted to the production of military supplies. Thus, there were fewer articles for export to Asia. As goods became scarce in China, prices of **consumer** items rose. This made foreign industrialists think it might be worthwhile to open factories in China. Japanese and British businessmen found it increasingly profitable to start textile mills and other plants in the **treaty ports**. Chinese businessmen also helped to develop new industrial centers in Shanghai, Guangzhou, Hong Kong, and Tianjin (tee-ENT-SIN). The number of factory workers in the cities steadily grew.

Working Conditions

Because people eagerly competed for jobs in the new Chinese factories, employers had no difficulty finding workers to run the machines. Wages were pitifully low, and the hours of work were very long. Working conditions were much the same as they had been during the early years of the Industrial Revolution in Western Europe. The safety and health of the workers were disregarded. Moreover, workers were caught in a squeeze because wages did not keep pace with the rising cost of living.

As unrest among factory workers increased, **trade unions** were slowly but steadily organized in China. The unions persuaded workers to join by promising to secure higher wages and better working conditions. When employers rejected the unions' demands, workers sometimes went out on strike. These strikes usually ended in failure, however, because the unions were small and weak. Moreover, there were no labor laws to protect the workers. The warlord government in Beijing was indifferent to the plight of industrial workers and had no power to interfere with the factories in the treaty ports. In these industrial centers foreign employers ran their businesses much as they wished.

Demonstrations Against Foreign Employers

Foreign factory owners were resented by the Chinese because they imposed harsh working conditions on their workers while enjoying special privileges for themselves. Actually, conditions in Chinese-owned factories were no better. In the area of Shanghai known as the International Settlement, the government was dominated by foreigners. Here and elsewhere foreign nations maintained military garrisons and had their own courts and police forces. Although the foreigners were few in number, they were protected by the power of their governments. It is little wonder that many Chinese believed they were really second-class citizens in their own country.

The growing anger of the workers finally exploded. In 1925 workers and students paraded in the International Settlement in Shanghai to protest the murder of a Chinese laborer in a Japanese-owned factory. A clash with British-led police led to shooting, and 100 Chinese demonstrators were killed or wounded. The Chinese retaliated by calling a general strike that paralyzed the great city of Shanghai for weeks. Violent clashes broke out in other cities as well. The greatest demonstration took place in the British colony of Hong Kong, where thousands of Chinese workers left their jobs to protest the shooting. Trade in this usually busy port was brought to a standstill for 15 months. These events were a clear warning that Chinese patience was coming to an end.

Efforts to Modernize Education

During the years after World War I, new ideas in education also began to circulate in China. Many Chinese scholars and teachers returned to their homeland after years of study abroad. Some became instructors in colleges and high schools. They were eager to modernize China's educational system, which was still based on Confucian traditions. They hoped to introduce new methods of teaching and modern subjects.

These reform-minded educators realized that one of the most critical problems in China was widespread **illiteracy.** For centuries only a small minority of Chinese had ever learned to read and write. As late as 1919 this state of affairs showed few signs of change.

One method of fighting illiteracy was devised by James Y.C. Yen, a Young Men's Christian Association (YMCA) worker who had studied in the United States. While serving with Chinese labor troops in France during the war, Yen had often written letters to the families of men who could not write. He noticed that their language was simple and direct. It occurred to him that it would not be difficult to teach them the Chinese characters for the words they most frequently used. Yen compiled a list of 1,000 Chinese characters that were most common. In France, and later in China, he patiently taught many Chinese to read and write these characters. His methods were widely adopted and are still used today in the People's Republic of China and in Taiwan.

The Literacy Movement

The father of another successful literacy movement was Hu Shi (HOO SHIR). While studying at the American universities of Cornell and Columbia, Hu Shi and other Chinese students became interested in the need to overhaul their nation's system of writing. The major problem was that almost all serious writing in Chinese was dominated by the language of Confucius.

Any spoken language, of course, constantly changes with the passage of time. New words are introduced, some old ones die out, and pronunciations change. In China the spoken tongues had slowly altered over the centuries. By the 1900's the spoken languages were very different from the language of Confucian times. Most people could not understand classical Chinese when they heard it spoken. Yet this was the language in which most Chinese books had been written for more than 2,000 years. Hu Shi and his comrades were determined to find a way to make written Chinese understandable when it was read aloud.

After Dr. Hu's return to China, he wrote many literary and scholarly articles in the language of the people instead of in classical Chinese. In lectures before college professors and students he urged the use of common language, or *baihua* (BY-HWAH). Many were impressed by his sensible proposals and decided to join in the movement. Students in colleges all over China started newspapers and magazines written in *baihua*. The articles printed in these publications could be read with ease by literate people. More important, when they were read aloud in homes and teahouses and on street corners, they could be understood by the illiterate. For the first time in centuries the written word became intelligible to the great mass of people in China.

Effects of Language Reform

Intellectuals, students, and politicians began to use the common language in their writings. They realized that with this weapon new ideas could be spread rapidly and effectively among the people. Forward-looking leaders could now tell the people about their dreams for China's future. They could now wage large-scale propaganda campaigns against foreign domination and the ravages of the warlords. Chinese nationalists looked ahead to the unification of their land and to the end of humiliations suffered at the hands of foreign powers.

The literacy movements also made possible the wider circulation of Western ideas. Before World War I, Western political and social ideas were scarcely known in China. Only a few scholars had any acquaintance with European and American thought. But once the literacy movements got under way, Chinese scholars and students began to study Western theories of democracy, socialism, and communism. During the 1920's China was swept by a number of competing political movements and parties. Their programs were usually strongly influenced by these newly discovered political theories. Thereafter no political party in China could afford to ignore the political and social ideas of the Western world.

Check Your Understanding

1. **a.** How was Chinese industry stimulated after World War I? **b.** What effect did trade unions have on labor unrest?
2. **a.** Compare working conditions in foreign-owned factories with working conditions in Chinese-owned factories. **b.** Why did Chinese workers demonstrate against foreign employers?
3. **a.** How did the work of James Y.C. Yen fight illiteracy in China? **b.** What differences existed between the written language of the ancient classics and contemporary spoken Chinese?
4. *Thinking Critically:* How did the changes that took place in Chinese life after World War I stimulate Chinese nationalism?

4. Sun Yat-sen—Founder of the Chinese Nationalist Revolution

The revolutionary ferment in China after World War I encouraged Sun Yat-sen to return and resume his political activities. But the leader of the Kuomintang found that he could not act freely in a China ruled by hostile warlords. Sun decided to settle down in Guangzhou, where he was very popular. Although he organized several revolutionary governments, all were undermined by warlords whose help he had tried to secure because his own military power was very weak. These warlords had been willing to support Sun's revolutionary plans only so long as such activities served their own ambitions. For more than five years Sun Yat-sen tried in vain to set up a strong and permanent headquarters for his revolutionary movement.

Sun's Nationalist Goals

Under Sun's direction, the aims of the Kuomintang were spread by newspapers, leaflets, lectures, and street-corner speeches. In all of these efforts, the Nationalists stated their goal briefly and simply—to end the chaos that had existed since 1911 and to unify China under an effective government. The Nationalists hoped to reach this goal in two steps. First, they would overthrow the warlords. Second, they would end the interference of foreign powers. Only by following these steps could China regain its self-respect and its rights as a sovereign nation.

Repressed and distrusted at home, Sun and his followers sought help abroad. After World War I had come to an end, Sun, outlining his proposals for the economic development of China, appealed to the Allied nations for financial assistance, but with little success.

Then, in 1923 Sun Yat-sen went to Shanghai for a fateful conference with Adolf Joffe (YOH-fuh), a Russian diplomat. Joffe represented the Communist International, also known as the Comintern. This association was founded by the Bolsheviks, who in 1917 had seized power in Russia and in 1922 set up the Soviet Union as a Communist state. The Comintern had as its purpose the stirring up of Communist revolutions all over the world. At their meeting Joffe promised Sun that the Comintern would help the Kuomintang in working for a united China. They agreed, however, that the Communist system would not be introduced in China. The understanding reached by the two men became known as the Sun–Joffe Agreement.

Sun was a revolutionary, but he was not a Communist. His decision to accept Communist help showed how desperate he felt his cause had become. At this stage Sun was prepared to accept the help of anyone who would help him unite China. Sun may have suspected that the Comintern was not primarily interested in the aims of the Kuomintang. He probably knew too that the Communists were seeking to use the Chinese revolutionary movement for their own purposes. But Sun, realizing that his time was running out, wanted victory before he died.

Strengthening of the Nationalist Revolution

With Russian assistance, Sun's Nationalist movement grew stronger. In 1923 a new revolutionary government was set up in Guangzhou by Sun and the Kuomintang. Michael Borodin, a veteran Bolshevik, became one of Sun's most important advisers. He helped reorganize the Kuomintang and shape it into a powerful revolutionary party. The Russians also helped the Na-

THE NATIONALIST ARMY. Chiang Kai-shek (left) had been a cadet in the imperial army before the Revolution of 1911 and had also received military training in Japan. After meeting Sun Yat-sen, Chiang became a staunch supporter of the Nationalist leader. When the Kuomintang founded a military academy at Whampoa, Chiang was named its first commandant. Troops of the Nationalist army (below) drill to prepare for leadership in a new China.

tionalists establish a military academy at Whampoa, near Guangzhou. Here officers devoted to the ideals of the Chinese revolution were trained for a new national revolutionary army. No longer would the Kuomintang have to ask warlords for military support. Chiang Kai-shek (JYAHNG ky-SHEK), a professional soldier and a long-time friend of Sun, was placed in command of Whampoa.

Sun now had hopes of building a strong political party and a trusted army for his movement. In the closing years of his life, Sun Yat-sen presented his ideas on revolution in a series of lectures. These talks were collected as a book, *San-min chu-i* (SAHN-MIN JOO-EE), or *Three Principles of the People*. *San-min chu-i* became the manual of the Nationalist Revolution.

Nationalism—the First Principle

Sun believed that the Chinese people had been held together over the centuries by a common culture and way of life. They shared a common history, traditions, ideals, and customs, but they had never developed a sense of country and nation. Whatever loyalties they had were directed toward their families and relatives. Sun stated:

> We have never had national unity. Have we had any other kind of unity? . . . China has had exceedingly compact family and clan groups, and the family and clan sentiment of the Chinese is very deep-rooted. For instance, when two Chinese meet each other on the road, they will chat together and ask each other's "honorable surname" and "given name." If they happen to find they are of the same clan, they become wonderfully intimate and cordial and look upon each other as uncle or brother of the same family. . . . If this worthy clan sentiment could be expanded, we might develop nationalism out of clanism. If we are to recover our lost nationalism, we must have some kind of . . . large group unity. [Sun Yat-sen, *San-min chu-i: The Three Principles of the People*.]

Sun thought that it was necessary for the Chinese people to acquire a sense of **nationalism** if they were to survive in the modern world.

Democracy—the Second Principle

The leader of the Kuomintang believed that **democracy** was not a completely new idea in Chinese civilization. It had, according to Sun, been discussed in theory as early as the times of Confucius, but it had never been put into practice in China. "Now if we are going to advocate democracy for China," said Sun,

> we should understand very clearly what it means. China from the beginning of her history has never put democracy into practice. Even in the last thirteen years [since the Revolution of 1911] we have not had democracy. In all these four thousand years, through periods of order and of disorder, China has seen nothing but autocracy [government by an absolute monarch]. If we ask history whether autocracy has really been a good thing for China or not, we find that its effects have been about half advantageous and half disadvantageous. But if we base our judgment upon the intelligence and the ability of the Chinese people, we come to the conclusion that the sovereignty of the people would be far more suitable for us. . . .
>
> Now that Europe and America have founded republics and have applied democracy for one hundred and fifty years, we whose ancients have dreamed of these things should certainly follow the tide of world events if we expect

our state to rule long and peacefully and our people to enjoy happiness. [Sun Yat-sen, *San-min chu-i.*]

Sun Yat-sen knew that China could not be transformed into a democracy overnight. He wisely understood that time was needed to change the political thinking and behavior of the Chinese. In line with this understanding, Sun Yat-sen proposed that the goal of democracy might be reached in three phases. The first phase in Sun's proposal called for the unification of China. Sun recognized that putting this first step into action would undoubtedly involve force. The warlords would never willingly give up their power and Sun Yat-sen knew that force would be needed to unite China. Once China was united by military means, Sun advocated a period of "political tutelage," or guardianship. During these years of political tutelage, constitutional government would be gradually introduced, and the people would be taught how to govern themselves and guided in the practice of democracy. In the final phase, constitutional government and democracy would be fully and independently practiced by the Chinese people.

The People's Livelihood—the Third Principle

Sun Yat-sen himself was never completely clear about the meaning of his last principle. Yet there was never any question about his purpose in presenting the people's livelihood as one of his three principles. Sun felt strongly that something needed to be done about the extreme poverty of the Chinese people. He was deeply stirred by their patient suffering and by their daily struggle to make a living. Moreover, he looked with disapproval on the great wealth that was possessed by a small number of Chinese. He proposed, by government action and taxation, to reduce these great differences in wealth that were a part of Chinese life. Sun was especially interested in seeing that every person in China was able to secure the basic necessities of life. The principle of the people's livelihood was therefore a kind of **socialism.**

By early 1925 the Nationalist movement centered at Guangzhou was rapidly gaining strength. Even so, Sun sought to avoid plunging the country into war. He traveled to Beijing to negotiate for political unity with the warlords who controlled the capital city. By the time he arrived, he was seriously ill. Sun died on March 12, 1925, but his spirit and dream lived on. The founder of the Kuomintang soon became the very symbol of the Chinese Nationalist Revolution.

Check Your Understanding

1. **a.** What was the major goal of the Kuomintang when Sun Yat-sen returned to China? **b.** Why did Sun Yat-sen need the help of warlords in securing this goal? **c.** What were the two steps by which the Nationalists hoped to reach their goal?
2. **a.** Why did Sun Yat-sen agree to take help from the Communists? **b.** What was achieved by accepting help from the Communists?
3. *Thinking Critically:* Describe the three main principles around which Sun Yat-sen's ideas of revolution rested. How did Sun hope to put the three principles into action? Was Sun correct in thinking that the Chinese people needed time to make democracy work? Why or why not?

5. Chiang Kai-shek's Leadership of the Kuomintang

The death of Sun Yat-sen plunged the Kuomintang into a crisis. As long as Sun lived, the Nationalists had been a unified force. But after his death, rivalries for leadership and disputes over policies split the ranks of the Kuomintang. As a result, the Nationalists were weakened at the very time when it seemed the drive for national unification had a chance of success.

The Chinese Communist Party

How to deal with the Chinese Communists was the most troublesome question facing the Nationalists. The Chinese branch of the Communist movement had been founded in 1921. One of the original members of the Chinese Communist Party was Mao Zedong. Mao had been born to a prosperous peasant family in Hunan Province in 1893. He attended local schools and then worked as an assistant to the librarian at Beijing University. While at the university, Mao became interested in the teachings of Karl Marx and was converted to **communism.** Mao played a major part in organizing the Chinese Communist Party, but he did not become its undisputed leader until many years later.

At first, the Chinese Communist Party had made little headway. Its big chance had come when the Sun–Joffe Agreement was concluded. The Comintern then ordered the Chinese Communists to help the Kuomintang work for the political unification of China. Consequently, a number of Communists enrolled as members in the Kuomintang. They were ordered to remain under the Kuomintang's authority until the time was ripe to seize control of the national revolutionary movement. Sun Yat-sen decided to accept the help of the Chinese Communists. But Chiang Kai-shek and many other members of the Kuomintang were disturbed by this decision. They were suspicious of Borodin and Sun's other Russian advisers and wanted to curb the Communist's power in the revolutionary movement. After Sun's death in 1925 it looked as if the movement might be torn apart over this issue.

The Northern Expedition

The men who followed Sun in the leadership of the Kuomintang hoped that a campaign against the warlords might postpone a split within their movement. Early in 1926, therefore, troops of the National Revolutionary Army set out from southeast China on a long march to the north. This march was called the Northern Expedition and was led by Chiang Kai-shek. The aim of the Northern Expedition was to overthrow the warlords along the way and to capture the capital city, Beijing. The morale, discipline, and training of the National Revolutionary Army were too much for its opponents. By the winter of 1926–1927, Chiang's soldiers had plunged deep into central China and seized the city of Hankou. The Kuomintang government was transferred from Guangzhou to Hankou. General Chiang then led an army through the valley of the Chang Jiang toward Shanghai. The city fell in March. At this point the elated Nationalists believed that nothing could stop them from capturing Beijing.

Chiang Kai-shek's Raid Against the Communists

The rivalries and suspicions within the Nationalist ranks, however, could no longer be held in check. The Communists held several important positions in the government at Hankou. Furthermore, Chiang Kai-shek and his followers believed, perhaps incorrectly, that the Communists were stirring up unrest among the workers in Shanghai. Chiang became convinced that the Communists were planning to seize control of the revolutionary movement. In April 1927, Chiang decided to strike first. Nationalist soldiers and police in Shanghai quickly rounded up Communists, labor leaders, and others suspected of being radicals. Some were immediately executed. Many others were arrested and imprisoned.

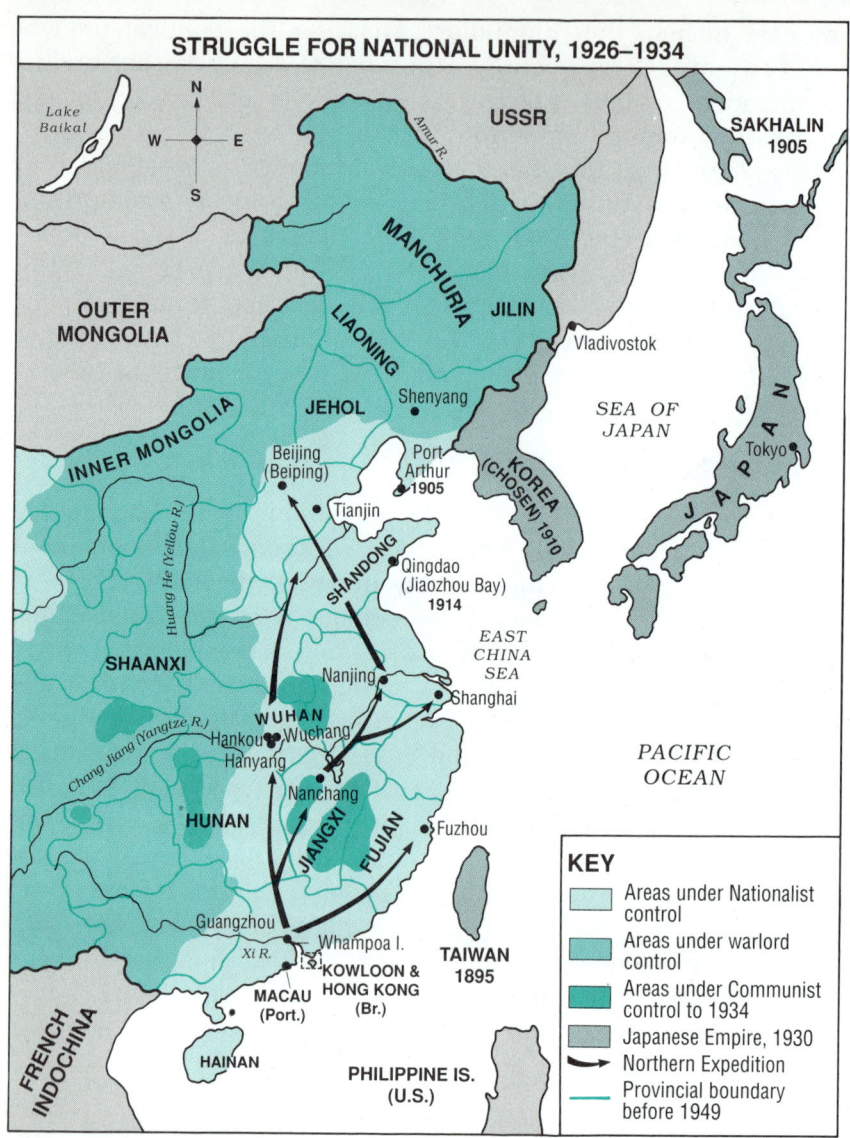

MOVEMENT: CHINA, 1926–1934. This is the first of three maps that document the two decades of war that racked China after 1930. Following the Northern Expedition, Chiang Kai-shek's Nationalist forces controlled much of China Proper. But Japanese expansionism and a Communist recovery in southeast China were signs of trouble for the Kuomintang. The maps on pages 183 and 194 in Chapter 8 show later stages in the struggle for control of China. In the map above, what group appears in control of eastern China? In what years did Japan expand into areas shown on the map?

Chiang's raids against the Communists and their sympathizers meant an open split in the revolutionary movement. The Northern Expedition came to a halt while the two rival factions struggled for control. The struggle between the Nationalists and Communists, centering on Hankou, ended in August when the leaders of the Hankou government joined with Chiang and turned against the Communists. The Hankou leaders then carried out their own **purge.** The Communists were ousted, and Borodin and other Russian advisers were ordered to leave the country.

Kuomintang Control

The Kuomintang government had become China's strongest since the overthrow of the Qing. Chiang moved the Nationalist headquarters to Nanjing closer to the mouth of the Chang Jiang. Nanjing was more centrally located than the former revolutionary center at Guangzhou in the deep south. Beijing came under Chiang's control early in 1928. To mark the completion of the Northern Expedition, the old imperial capital was renamed Beiping, a word that means "peace." The people of North China never liked the new name. When the Chinese Communists came to power in 1949, they restored the traditional name of Beijing, meaning "northern capital," and made it their capital.

The Kuomintang now controlled the east central region, the richest and most heavily populated part of China. The Kuomintang government also enjoyed the advantage of official recognition by foreign powers. Its leadership had the right to speak for

An early photograph of Communist leaders shows three who survived the struggles of the 1930's and the 1940's to hold top positions in the People's Republic. Mao Zedong is on the right; in the middle are Zhou Enlai and Zhu De. Chinese press reports of the 1930's spoke so much of "Zhou-Mao" that many people thought the name referred to one man. On the left is Bo Gu, a Communist leader who died in an air crash in the early 1940's.

China and to direct its international affairs. The head of the Nanjing government and the chief of the Kuomintang was General Chiang.

Continuing Troubles

The National Revolutionary Army had destroyed many local warlords during the Northern Expedition, but some of the stronger warlords had been left alone. These warlords paid lip service to the Nationalist government at Nanjing, but in fact they remained semi-independent. Many of them would not even permit Kuomintang officials to set foot in the territories under their rule. Such warlords still dominated areas in the north, west, and south. They were also powerful in the border regions of Manchuria, Mongolia, and Xinjiang. The continued existence of these warlords meant that the Nationalist goal of a politically unified country had not yet been achieved.

The Comintern's followers in China had been badly mauled by Chiang in 1927, but a considerable number escaped the purge and went into hiding. The Communists were more determined than ever to eliminate Chiang and to gain control over China. They knew that their plans for a Communist China could not be achieved until the Nationalist government was overthrown.

Mao Zedong was one of those Communists who had escaped. He found refuge from Chiang's troops in the rugged mountains of southeast China. Here he and others organized a revolutionary base that slowly grew in strength after 1928. A Communist government was set up. The Communists rallied many poverty-stricken peasants to their side by confiscating land from wealthy landlords and redistributing it. A military force with high morale was created, and guerrilla raids were directed against nearby territories held by warlords. Two of Mao's lieutenants were Zhou Enlai (JOH EN-LEYE) and Zhu De (JOO DUH). Zhou, a shrewd politician, was one of the founders of the Chinese Communist movement. Zhu De was a highly capable professional soldier. During the next few years these revolutionaries caused the Nationalists endless trouble.

Successes of the Nanjing Government

Although their country was not yet united, under Chiang's leadership many Chinese people were inspired with hope for the future. One of the most promising developments was the government's success in reducing the privileges enjoyed by foreign powers. During and immediately after the Northern Expedition,

Chiang Kai-shek and other Kuomintang leaders insisted that the old unequal treaties must be renegotiated. The foreign states, impressed with the swelling tide of Chinese nationalism, reluctantly agreed. Thus, many of the privileges enjoyed by foreigners since the 1800's were swept aside. For example, during the mid–1800's the British had imposed restrictions on the size of the tariffs that the Chinese could levy on imported goods. But in 1929 the Chinese recovered control over tariffs. Thereafter China's government was free to set tariffs on imported goods. These achievements filled patriotic Chinese with pride and made them hopeful of further gains for their country.

Check Your Understanding

1. **a.** How did the Communists hope to gain control of China? **b.** What did Chiang Kai-shek hope to achieve through the Northern Expedition? **c.** How successful was the expedition?
2. **a.** Why were some Nationalists suspicious of the Communists? **b.** How did Chiang deal with the Communists?
3. What advantages did the Nationalists enjoy after the ouster of the Communists from the Kuomintang?
4. *Thinking Critically:* Discuss the pros and cons of Chiang's move in ousting the Communists from the Kuomintang. Did Chiang sacrifice long-term gains for short-term gains in making the move?

CHAPTER REVIEW

■ Chapter Summary

Section 1. The leader of the revolutionary movement in China was Sun Yat-sen. So dedicated was he to the establishment of a Chinese republic that he resigned as president in order to assure its survival. Replacing Sun was Yuan Shikai, a leader mainly interested in his own imperial ambitions. When Yuan died, the central government in China was replaced by warlords who divided the country among themselves and preyed on the helpless people.

Section 2. With affairs in China in chaos, friction increased between the Chinese and foreign powers, especially Great

Britain and Japan. The Japanese expanded their sphere of influence, forcing the Twenty-one Demands on the Chinese. But disappointment over lack of foreign support against the Japanese led to protests and demonstrations called the May Fourth Movement.

Section 3. Foreign investments in China increased after World War I, leading to renewed protests over harsh working conditions. Advances were made in education, and successful attacks on the centuries-old problem of mass illiteracy made it easier to read and write Chinese. The literacy movements had the important effect of increasing Chinese pride in their country and of spreading Western political and social ideas.

Section 4. After World War I Sun Yat-sen returned to China, making the unity of China his chief goal. To this end Sun accepted the assistance of the newly formed Chinese Communist Party, which had its own dreams of establishing a Communist state in China. Sun also educated the people in his three main principles—nationalism, democracy, and the people's livelihood. But Sun died in 1925 before his dream of a united and independent China was realized.

Section 5. Chiang Kai-shek assumed leadership of the Kuomintang. In 1927 he forced the Communists out of the Kuomintang and continued the drive to unify China. After undertaking the Northern Expedition, he wrested control of the east central part of China from warlords and established Nanjing as the republic's capital. But Chiang was just as unsuccessful as Sun in uniting the whole country.

■ Vocabulary Review

Define: revolutionary, compromise, dictator, warlord, imperialism, boycott, consumer, treaty port, trade union, illiteracy, nationalism, democracy, socialism, communism, purge

■ Places to Locate

Locate: Guangzhou, Wuchang, Hankou, Wuhan, Japan, Qingdao, Jiaozhou Bay, Shandong, Shanghai, Hong Kong, Nanjing, Beiping

■ People to Know

Identify: Sun Yat-sen, Yuan Shikai, Xuan Tong, Feng Yuxiang, Woodrow Wilson, James Y.C. Yen, Hu Shi, Adolf Joffe, Michael Borodin, Chiang Kai-shek, Mao Zedong, Zhou Enlai, Zhu De

■ **Thinking Critically**

1. Why was Yuan Shikai a poor choice to lead the republic of China?
2. Why did World War I increase friction between China and its treaty powers? Why were the Chinese disappointed over the results of the Versailles Conference?
3. How did changes in working conditions and education increase the spirit of nationalism in China after World War I?
4. Why is Sun Yat-sen called the "Father of China's Revolution"?
5. Why was Chiang Kai-shek unable to unify China at this time?

■ **Extending and Applying Your Knowledge**

1. Research more about the thoughts of Sun Yat-sen. Prepare a list of three to five sayings that might have inspired the Chinese to become followers and revolutionaries.
2. Using the card catalog at your local library as well as encyclopedias and other reference books, investigate the lives of the Soong sisters. Qingling became the wife of Sun Yat-sen while Meiling married Chiang Kai-shek. Write a brief report on their influence in China's political affairs.

8

China—From Nationalist to Communist

When Chiang Kai-shek founded his government in Nanjing in 1928, the task of unification was only half-achieved. In his drive to achieve the other half, Chiang found himself battling three rivals—the warlords, the Communists, and the Japanese.

Against these three rivals, Chiang waged almost constant war for 20 years. Increasingly he postponed seeking solutions to China's domestic problems. Pressing needs for reforms were allowed to slip into the background, to be dealt with after national unity and security had been achieved. When war with Japan broke out in 1937, all social and economic problems were put aside. All efforts were put into strengthening the Nationalist army because the very existence of an independent China was at stake.

As life became more and more of a struggle for survival, the people of China became increasingly disenchanted with the Nationalist government. They blamed the Nationalists for the hardships they had to endure. They also accused many Nationalist officials of dishonesty and corruption. At the war's end, Chiang's Nationalist government had lost much of the popularity it had once enjoyed. Meanwhile the Chinese Communists had increased their power and won much popular support. By 1949 the Communists had defeated the Nationalists, who fled to the island of Taiwan, where Chiang's government continued to exist as the Republic of China. Mainland China became the People's Republic of China under the leadership of Mao Zedong.

1. The Conflict Between Chinese Nationalism and Japanese Imperialism

In the late 1920's the Nationalist government at Nanjing demanded foreign respect for China's sovereign rights. It won back tariff autonomy and the return to Chinese control of some of the foreign concessions granted in the late 1800's. China's policy of self-assertion surprised and disturbed some countries. Japan was especially concerned, for it had important political and business interests in China. Some Japanese leaders urged their government to accept China's rebirth and make the necessary changes in Japan's political and economic policies. But other Japanese leaders were disturbed by the thought that Japan's gains in China since the war of 1894–1895 might be lost. It was obvious that Chinese nationalism and Japanese imperialism would eventually clash. In 1931 an incident in Manchuria finally touched off the conflict.

Japan's Manchurian Takeover

Japan had special interests in Manchuria. Many Japanese subjects had settled there. The region had rich natural resources, Japanese investments (including an important railroad) were heavy, and Japan had already been granted special rights in Manchuria by China. Moreover, this northern borderland served as a useful **buffer** between Japan and Russia, who were rivals in the area since the Russo–Japanese War of 1905. Since 1911 a warlord had ruled in Manchuria, but a Japanese force stationed in the region held a great deal of power. The officers of this army were determined to protect Japanese interests.

One night in September 1931, Japanese soldiers exploded a bomb on the tracks of the Japanese railroad near the Manchurian city of Shenyang. The bomb explosion was intended to justify an attack on Chinese military forces in the area. Japanese officers sent their troops into action against the Manchurian warlord, Zhang Xueliang (JAHNG SHOO-EH-LEE-AHNG), popularly called the "Young Marshal." Although he was not hostile to the Nationalist government, Zhang had insisted on maintaining his rule in Manchuria. Now his troops had to face the advancing Japanese. Zhang's forces fought stubbornly, but they were easily swept aside by the enemy. At the outset the Japanese objective had been to occupy strategic places in southern Manchuria. Their quick victories, however, inspired the Japanese commanders to enlarge the area of military operations. Within the next six months the Japanese army swept over all of Manchuria.

TIMETABLE

China Under the Kuomintang

1931	Japanese invasion of Manchuria
1931–1934	Purge of Communists
1934–1935	Communist Long March
1936	Manchurian kidnapping of Chiang Kai-shek
	Formation of Nationalist–Communist united front against Japan
1937	Japanese invasion of China Proper
1941	Entry of United States into World War II
1945	Japan's defeat and surrender
1947–1949	Civil war between Nationalists and Communists
1949	Communist victory and withdrawal of Nationalists to Taiwan
	Proclamation of People's Republic of China

Chinese Protests

China sent a protest to the League of Nations, an organization set up after World War I to deal with international disputes. The League sent a committee of representatives from five nations to investigate the situation in Manchuria. After a careful study, this committee, called the Lytton Commission, drew up a report that held Japan guilty of an unjustified attack on China. The League members were unwilling, however, to take any effective action against Japan. The Chinese were unhappy, but the Japanese were also displeased. Calling the decision one-sided and prejudiced, Japan in 1933 withdrew from the League.

Manchukuo

After their conquest, the Japanese set up a **puppet government** in Manchuria and gave the area the name of Manchukuo (MAHN-CHOO-KWOH), meaning "Land of the Manchus." The Japanese transformed Manchuria into a vast military base. They also began to build a huge iron and steel industry near Shenyang. This industrial base proved to be of great help in building up the Japanese war machine.

JAPAN'S EARLY MOVES IN CHINA. Japanese soldiers (above) celebrate after capturing the railroad system in Manchuria in 1931. The Japanese government promised to halt the armies in Manchuria, but it was uanble to control the Japanese army officers and stop the military advance. What action did the League of Nations take against Japan? When the Japanese set up the state of Manchukuo, they installed the last Qing monarch, Pu Yi, as its emperor (below). Here the 27-year-old emperor (middle figure) is shown in ceremonial robes after his enthronement. Why did so few governments recognize Manchukuo?

In 1934 Xuan Tong (Pu Yi), the last emperor of the Qing dynasty, who had abdicated 22 years before, was installed as the Emperor of Manchukuo. But everyone knew that the emperor was powerless. Manchukuo remained under Japanese rule until 1945 and the end of World War II.

United States Secretary of State Henry Stimson took the lead in protesting the conquest of Manchuria. But the United States was no more eager than the European powers to antagonize Japan. Suffering from the effects of a worldwide economic depression that had begun in 1929, these nations feared involvement in an East Asian war.

In 1932 when the United States refused to recognize the new state of Manchukuo, other governments also refused to recognize the puppet state. During its existence Manchukuo was recognized by fewer than a dozen governments.

Further Assaults on China

The loss of Manchuria was a serious blow to the Nanjing government. In addition to being rich in coal and iron ore, Manchuria was a large and fertile region. As a sparsely populated area, it also provided an outlet for China's growing population.

To demonstrate their anger over the invasion of Manchuria, the Chinese began to boycott Japanese goods. The boycott proved effective, and Japanese trade with China dropped off sharply. Irritated by this counterblow, the Japanese extended their area of military operations. In early 1932 Japan dispatched a naval expedition to Shanghai, a center of the boycott, but Chinese troops put up a spirited defense of the city. Only by bringing in heavy reinforcements did the Japanese manage to avoid a major setback. Large parts of Shanghai were destroyed in the attack. Although the Chinese defenders finally were forced to withdraw, their gallant fight stirred the entire nation. The Japanese captured the city, except for the International Settlement. They soon evacuated their military forces, but only after Chiang and the Kuomintang agreed to the establishment of a neutral zone around Shanghai.

China suffered also from Japanese attacks on Inner Mongolia and North China. The inability of Chiang Kai-shek's government to fight off these attacks revealed its military weakness. The Japanese assaults hinted at the directions of possible future attacks. They also taught the Chinese not to expect help from the League of Nations or any individual country in opposing Japanese aggression. Above all, these military actions made clear the need to prepare for an ultimate showdown with Japan.

Check Your Understanding

1. **a.** Why was Japan interested in Manchuria? **b.** How did the Japanese provoke a crisis in Manchuria?
2. **a.** How did Chiang Kai-shek respond to the Japanese takeover? **b.** Why did so few nations recognize Manchukuo?
3. **a.** What response did the Japanese make to the Chinese trade boycott? **b.** How was the Japanese attack on Shanghai resolved?
4. *Thinking Critically:* Why was the loss of Manchuria a serious blow to the Nationalists? How did the Japanese make use of Manchuria? What lessons did the Chinese learn from the assaults on their country by Japan at this time?

2. Revival of the Chinese Communist Movement

Although the number of Chinese Communists had been greatly reduced by Chiang's purge beginning in 1927, some had escaped. Going into hiding in scattered areas across the country, they waged **guerrilla warfare** against the Nanjing government. The Communists were more determined than ever to destroy the Kuomintang and seize power in China. They also had a bitter hatred for Chiang. They realized that their dream of a Communist China would require a long struggle to overthrow Chiang and the Nationalist government.

Rebuilding the Communist Movement

During Chiang's purge of Communists, Mao Zedong and other Communist leaders fled to the mountains of Jiangxi and Hunan. (See map, page 183.) In organizing a new Communist base there, Mao learned many useful political and military lessons that he would put to good use in later years. Before his flight Mao had had to follow orthodox Communist doctrines while at the same time working within the Kuomintang. In his mountain stronghold Mao developed his own revolutionary ideas.

The Communists had always believed that their revolution would have to be spearheaded by oppressed factory workers in the cities. Supposedly these workers were the only people desperate enough to rise against the existing society and replace it with a Communist system. But Mao Zedong and other leaders within the Communist Party showed that a revolutionary base could be established in a region far from cities and towns. After their flight their only alternative was to seek the support of downtrodden peasants. They began to stir up the peasants' resentment against a government that seemed to be indifferent to their misery. From these peasants Mao and other leaders recruited members for the Chinese Communist Party and troops for a military force called the Red Army. By raiding the forces of nearby warlords, Mao and his supporters obtained needed military supplies. Also, they learned how to fight against more numerous and better-equipped troops. After years of experience they became masters of guerrilla warfare. In the areas under their control, Mao and others established a Communist-style government called the Chinese Soviet Republic.

Moves Against the Communists

In 1931 Chiang Kai-shek decided to eliminate the Communist threat once and for all. Over the next three years he launched five military expeditions against the Communists in southeast China. These offensives were called Bandit Extermination Campaigns. At first Chiang made use of warlord armies near the Communist refuge for these operations. Chiang hoped that the Communists and warlords would destroy one another. But when the Red Army easily routed the warlords and captured their forces and military equipment, Chiang finally sent his Nationalist troops against the Communists.

Chiang subjected the Communist-held zone to a crushing **blockade.** The Nationalist troops constructed rings of small concrete fortresses called pillboxes to encircle and isolate the Communists. As the rings of fortified points gradually closed, the Communists were caught in a giant squeeze. The Communists realized that they would be destroyed if they tried to hold their ground. The whole Communist community—about 80,000 in all—broke through the Nationalist lines and fled for their lives.

The Long March

The flight of Mao's revolutionary force from southeastern China in 1934–1935 was an agonizing ordeal. The Communists call this episode the **Long March.** The route led westward to the edges of eastern Tibet and then turned northward across barren and uninhabited regions. The Communists finally ended their year-long trek in the mountains of northwest China, where they joined forces with other Communist groups at Yan'an in Shaanxi province. (See map, page 183.)

Throughout the more than 5,000 miles of the Long March, Mao and his comrades were harassed by Nationalist forces as well as those of local warlords. The fleeing Communists were bombed and strafed by Nationalist airplanes. Many marchers died of starvation and disease. It has been estimated that only about 20,000 survived. These survivors of the Long March became the iron core of both the Chinese Communist Party and the Red Army. To have taken part in the grueling march was considered a mark of distinction and a badge of honor. For years many top-ranking leaders of the Communist regime were veterans of the Long March.

Action Against the Communists

The Nationalists continued to attack the battered Communist forces. The Nationalist government planned to corner the Communists in their new base and to wipe out the remnants of the Red Army. This task was entrusted to the "Young Marshal," Zhang Xueliang, the Manchurian warlord who had stubbornly opposed the Japanese advance into his land in 1931. After the Japanese conquest of Manchuria, Zhang and his remaining troops had withdrawn to North China. They were now ordered to wipe out the Communists in the northwest, a mission Zhang reluctantly undertook.

Disturbing reports trickled into Chiang Kai-shek's Nanjing headquarters, indicating that Marshal Zhang's soldiers were making friends with the Communists. For their part, the Communists made known their unwillingness to fight the Manchurians. The Chinese Communists urged all Chinese people not to fight one another but to unite and defend China against Japanese aggression. This argument impressed the Manchurians, who naturally wanted to recover their homeland from the Japanese. The Manchurians felt they had no quarrel with the Chinese Communists.

The Kidnaping of Chiang Kai-shek

Chiang Kai-shek was disturbed by Zhang's failure to crush the Red Army. To get a firsthand view of the situation, Chiang flew to Shaanxi province late in 1936. Soon after Chiang's arrival in the city of Xi'an (SHEE-AHN), Marshal Zhang's officers placed Chiang under arrest. The news of Chiang's kidnapping caused a sensation all over the world.

Much of what happened during Chiang's imprisonment is still unknown. Marshall Zhang's officers were furious with the Nationalist government for refusing to declare war against the

Japanese. Apparently they now urged Chiang Kai-shek to call off the war against the Communists. Zhang's officers insisted that all Chinese should unite in waging war against Japan. For days Chiang stubbornly refused to accept his captors' terms. Chiang argued that the political unification of China under Kuomintang leadership should have top priority. Unification, he declared, could not be achieved until the Chinese Communists were destroyed. He also questioned the wisdom of a divided nation waging war against so formidable and powerful an enemy as Japan. Angered by Chiang's unyielding stand, some of his captors proposed that he be executed.

Rescue by the Communists

The Chinese Communists had no personal sympathy for Chiang, but they feared that Chiang's execution would further divide China and pave the way for more Japanese aggressions. This concern was shared by Joseph Stalin, the dictator of the Soviet Union. It was the Soviet Union that dominated Communist parties in other countries.

The Soviet dictator Joseph Stalin ordered the Communist parties in various countries to suspend their efforts to overthrow existing governments. Fearing that the aggressive tactics of Germany, Italy, and Japan would threaten Soviet interests, Stalin believed that the Communist parties should establish united fronts against their common enemy. This meant that the Communists were to cooperate with any governments that were opposed to the dictators that ruled Germany and Italy and the Japanese militarists.

The Chinese Communists did not overestimate their own power. They were aware that only an **alliance** led by the head of the Kuomintang had any chance of being successful in uniting China against Japan. To have allowed the execution of Chiang Kai-shek would have upset the Chinese Communist strategy of forming an alliance against Japan. The Chinese Communist leaders, therefore, persuaded Marshal Zhang's troops to spare the Nationalist leader's life. For his part, Chiang Kai-shek evidently agreed to consider the formation of a united front against Japan.

After returning to Nanjing, Chiang was true to his word. He relaxed his opposition to the Chinese Communist movement and permitted greater freedom in the regions under Kuomintang control. Although China remained weak economically and militarily, political unity was greatly furthered during the early months of 1937.

Check Your Understanding

1. How did the Communists rebuild their strength in China after Chiang's 1927 purge?
2. How did Chiang's plan to eliminate the Communist threat result in the Communist's Long March?
3. **Thinking Critically:** How did Chiang's plan to use Marshal Zhang's Manchurian forces in the fight against the Communists result in a Nationalist–Communist united front against the Japanese?

3. The Kuomintang Attempts at Reform

In addition to the problems posed by the warlords, the Communists, and the Japanese, the Kuomintang faced staggering tasks in governing China. Problems that had worsened for well over 100 years weighed heavily on China by the time the Nationalists came to power. The country was politically divided, and honest and efficient government had yet to be achieved. Reforms in agriculture were overdue. Industrial development was lagging, and the transportation network was totally inadequate. Few modern schools or hospitals existed, and competent scientists and engineers were in short supply. Resources that might have improved living conditions were used up in the Nationalist campaigns against the warlords, the Communists, and the Japanese. Chiang drew on his country's scanty assets to hire foreign military advisers and to buy modern equipment for the army. By mid–1937, Chiang had built up a strong modern army, but this had been achieved at the expense of much-needed improvements in other areas of Chinese life.

Agricultural Reform

Probably the most serious problem that faced the Kuomintang was the extreme poverty that the Chinese people had suffered for centuries. In the 1930's they continued to be desperately poor. The average Chinese peasant perhaps earned as much in a year as an American worker made in one week. If drought or floods destroyed their crops, the Chinese peasants went hungry and some even starved. The payment of even the smallest tax was a heavy burden for these poor Chinese farmers. Yet most of the government's income came from taxes on the land. Thus, painful sacrifices were demanded from people who already had suffered too much. From the record of Chinese history, it could have been predicted that the Nanjing government was headed for serious trouble unless it could provide relief for the millions of peasants.

During the past century, China's most basic problem had been the growing population pressure on the land. During the early years of Kuomintang rule, millions of peasants cultivated land they did not own. They leased tiny plots of land for high rentals and were never certain that their leases would be extended from one year to the next. Rural areas had few banks, forcing the peasants to go to local moneylenders who charged extremely high interest rates. Very few peasants were free of heavy debt. Furthermore, those peasants who were fortunate enough to own land were mercilessly squeezed for taxes by local governments and warlords.

Chiang Kai-shek's government placed ceilings on land rentals, but these were rarely enforced. Peasant banks were established that were supposed to extend loans at reasonable rates. Unfortunately these banks usually lacked the necessary capital to be effective. The government also encouraged the formation of cooperative groups for purchasing farm equipment and marketing crops. These cooperatives, however, encountered strong opposition from large landlords and influential city merchants. By 1938, 10 years after the Nationalists had taken control, the government had made only a slight dent in reforms intended to help the peasants.

The Nationalists' failure to solve the farm problem had unfortunate results. The inability of the peasants to increase crop production meant hunger throughout the land. Lack of farm surpluses to use in trade limited China's ability to purchase machinery abroad. Furthermore, the suffering of the peasants furnished the Communists with a powerful weapon to use against the Nanjing government. The Kuomintang was blamed for all of China's troubles.

Attempts to Improve Transportation and Education

Over the centuries, China's network of roads had become sadly inadequate. During the turbulent period following the Revolution of 1911, the nation's roads had been completely neglected. The Kuomintang tried to do something about this situation. Despite the cost, Chiang's government repaired roads and built new highways. It also made some effort to extend the railroad system. Still, by the end of 1935 there were only about 8,200 miles of railway in China Proper.

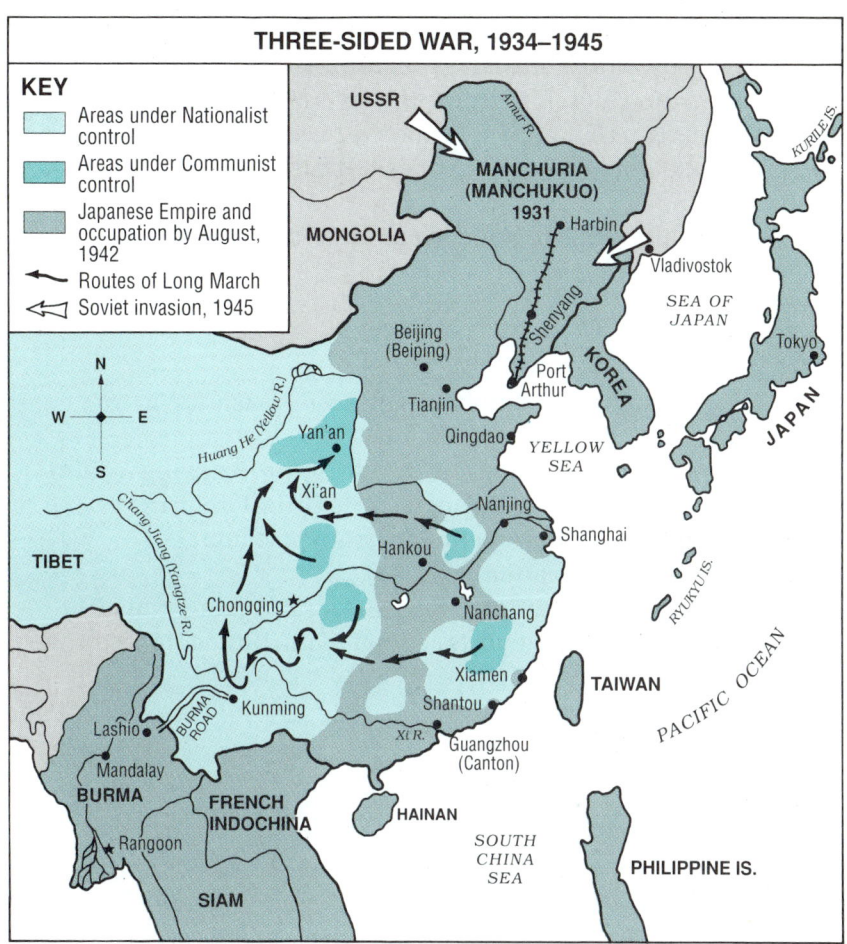

MOVEMENT: CHINA, 1934–1945. The Communists, eluding the Nationalists and their Extermination Campaign, made the Long March to Yan'an, where they prepared to battle the Kuomintang's forces for control of all China. But with the Japanese invasion, the Communists and Nationalists put aside their differences to offer the invading Japanese a united front and as much resistance as possible. But the Japanese forces moved relentlessly through China and East Asia until the armed forces of the United States began to push back the lines of the Japanese Empire.

China's school system had been gradually introduced after World War I. Many leaders of the Kuomintang had been educated in the modern schools established by the government and by foreign missionaries. Hundreds of vocational training schools, technical institutes, and universities had been founded. Yet far greater efforts were necessary to keep up with the growing need for education. In 1937, for example, China had at least 40 million children of elementary school age, but schools existed for no more than 15 million students. And few of these schools were equipped to provide a modern program of education. Given time and money, the Kuomintang might have been able to use education to modernize China. But China's resources were scarce and the need for military preparedness drained away the bulk of available funds. The outbreak of war shattered any hope that China might be able to modernize quickly.

Check Your Understanding

1. Why was the condition of Chinese peasants in urgent need of improvement?
2. How did the Kuomintang try to improve living conditions in China: **a.** through agricultural reform? **b.** through improvements in transportation? **c.** through education?
3. **Thinking Critically:** How successful were the Kuomintang's reform efforts? What contributed to their success or lack of it?

4. War with Japan

On July 7, 1937, Nationalist soldiers clashed with Japanese troops near the Marco Polo Bridge outside Beiping, where a Japanese force had been stationed since the Boxer Uprising in 1900. This fighting spread and became known as the China Incident. Actually the incident, or event, became the first skirmish in a long and cruel war.

After the China Incident, Japan began a determined invasion of the Chinese mainland. This Second Sino–Japanese War is generally regarded as the beginning of World War II. The war in Europe did not officially begin until Nazi Germany invaded Poland in 1939, although Adolf Hitler, the Nazi dictator, had begun the first of his warlike moves in Europe several years before. Germany, Italy, and Japan reached agreements that brought them together as the Axis Powers. China was one of the Allies, together with Great Britain and the Soviet Union. In December 1941, when the Japanese bombed Pearl Harbor in Hawaii, the United States joined the Allies in the war against the Axis. After the attack on Pearl Harbor, China officially declared war on Japan, although actually the two countries had been fighting since 1937.

The Japanese Push

After the clash near Beiping, fighting had continued. While the soldiers fought, the diplomats bargained, but neither government was willing to accept the demands of the other. As hopes for a settlement dimmed, the conflict spread through eastern China. The cities of Beiping and Tianjin quickly fell to the attacking Japanese forces. In the battle for control of Shanghai, however, the Japanese encountered stubborn resistance from the Nationalist army. In the defense of Shanghai, Chiang Kai-shek proved to the world that his troops could stand up and fight. Yet in so doing he sacrificed many of his best divisions. After his stand at Shanghai, Chiang was compelled to conserve his remaining forces and fight a defensive war.

Nanjing, the Nationalist capital, was captured by the advancing Japanese in December 1937. During the next year the Japanese occupied Guangzhou and other coastal cities in southern China. The Japanese navy then set up a blockade that cut off Nationalist China from the rest of the world. Pursuing the retreating Nationalists into central China, the Japanese armies next captured Hankou, which had become the Chinese capital after the fall of Nanjing.

China's Struggle

Chiang, continuing to fall back, established his headquarters at Chongqing in southwestern China. Situated on a plateau encircled by rugged mountains, this city had natural defenses against attack. Chongqing became the capital of Free China, as unoccupied China was called, and remained so until after World War II. (See map, page 194.)

To continue resistance against the Japanese, great numbers of Chinese people made their way westward to Chongqing. Whatever material and equipment they could transport was carried away, a step ahead of the invaders. Machines in factories were taken apart and carried piece by piece on the backs of volunteers. Hospital equipment and medical supplies also were borne into Free China. Despite heroic efforts to salvage munitions and other war equipment, Nationalist China was badly handicapped by shortages. But it continued to fight.

Failure to force the Nationalist government to its knees led the Japanese to redouble their attacks. Whenever the Nationalist Army risked battle, its casualties were appallingly heavy. Many of the sick and wounded died because of inadequate medical treatment. Nor did civilians escape the ravages of war. Japanese military authorities seized the crops of helpless peasants. Their

WAR–TORN CHINA. As Japanese forces overran eastern China, the civilian population fled before them. Above, Japanese soldiers patrolled occupied Guangzhou. They had not yet torn down a huge banner bearing Chiang Kai-shek's portrait. Below, Chinese refugees swarmed into the International Settlement at Shanghai, hoping to find safety. Why did they expect to find safety there?

SIDELIGHT TO HISTORY

Support for Free China

The United States government, concerned that the government of the Chinese Nationalists might collapse before Japan could be defeated, managed to send supplies into Free China to offset the effects of Japan's blockade of the Chinese coast.

Perhaps the most famous route into China was the Burma Road. (See map, page 183.) A crude but usable highway, the Burma Road was built by thousands of Chinese men, women, and children with the help of many technical advisers and equipment from Britain and the United States. Although its two end points were only 360 miles apart by air, the road wound through 700 miles of rugged mountainous terrain in northern Burma and southwest China.

When the Japanese cut the Burma Road shortly after Pearl Harbor, the United States established an air route to China over the "Hump," or the Himalayas. The United States was thus able to ferry in desperately needed supplies to Chiang's forces. The United States was not just being a good friend to China. Japanese troops tied down on the China mainland could not be used against the advancing American forces in the Pacific.

The United States dispatched few combat troops to China. China, with its great population, always had enough troops. But training them to be efficient soldiers, as well as keeping them supplied with ammunition and other equipment, was another matter. The United States also sent military advisers and technicians to help China in its fight against Japan. Under General "Vinegar Joe" Stilwell, new Nationalist divisions were trained and equipped. An American volunteer air group called the Flying Tigers had fought for Nationalist China even before the entry of the United States into World War II. This force, commanded by General Claire Chennault (sheh-NAWLT), defended Nationalist China against Japanese air attacks. In 1942 the Flying Tigers became part of the American armed forces, continuing their efforts to defend East Asia against the Japanese.

airplanes bombed towns and cities in the Nationalist areas until they were reduced to rubble. Some Japanese soldiers committed atrocities. Yet Free China miraculously managed to hold out against the Japanese forces.

United States Support

In the United States, concern over Japanese expansion in the Far East had steadily mounted after the China Incident in 1937. By 1941 relations between the United States and the Japanese Empire were severely strained. Representatives of the two governments held discussions but could find no basis for a settlement of differences. Japan refused to withdraw from China or to cease its aggression.

Japan's military leaders finally decided to break off negotiations with the United States and to extend their conquests into Southeast Asia. Hoping to remove the threat of American intervention, Japanese forces in December 1941 bombed naval and military bases at Pearl Harbor in Hawaii. This attack brought the United States into World War II. At last, China had the ally it had been seeking since the invasion of Manchuria.

The United States took steps to strengthen the morale of the Chinese people. One such action concerned the special rights in China that had been granted to the United States almost a century earlier. In the late 1920's the Nationalist government had begun a campaign to end foreign privileges in China. In 1943 the United States voluntarily surrendered the rest of its special rights, an example that was quickly followed by Great Britain. In addition, Nationalist China was treated as an equal by the leading Allied nations. President Franklin D. Roosevelt and Prime Minister Winston Churchill invited Chiang Kai-shek to the conference of Allied leaders at Cairo, Egypt, in 1943. More significant, when the United Nations was organized in 1945, Nationalist China was included in the Security Council as one of its five permanent members.

Dwindling Support for the Kuomintang

The Nationalist regime had many corrupt and dishonest officials. Army officers often abused their troops, neglected to pay them, and sold military supplies for personal profit. Moreover, living conditions in China were miserable, and prices of food and other basic commodities increased almost daily. Soaring inflation threatened to make Chinese money worthless. For these reasons the Nationalist government became increasingly unpopular with the war-weary people.

ALLIED SUPPORT. American army engineers built the Ledo Road (right) through jungles and over mountains to connect a railroad in India with the Burma Road. As a result, desperately needed supplies could reach wartime China.

In the photograph below, Chiang Kai-shek (far left) sits next to President Franklin D. Roosevelt of the United States. Madame Chiang (far right) sits next to Prime Minister Winston Churchill of Great Britain. Chiang's meeting with Roosevelt and Churchill in Cairo in 1943 meant that China's government was recognized as an important member of the Allies.

Many of the conditions that existed in wartime China stemmed from China's poverty, which was made worse by the war and the Japanese blockade, and were not the fault of Chiang's regime. Nevertheless, the Nationalist government was responsible for part of the trouble. Although the United States prodded Chiang to rid his government and military forces of dishonest officials, the Generalissimo, as Chiang was called, which meant commander-in-chief, took no such action. He was careful not to offend politicians, military officers, landlords, and business people because his control of the Nationalist movement was based on their support. Chiang never forgot that he would have to fight for control of China after Japan was defeated. He never lost sight of the threat presented by the Chinese Communist Party and its Red Army.

The Communists' Long-Range Goals

When war broke out in 1937, the Chinese Communists and Nationalists cooperated in fighting the enemy. This joint action continued until 1940 when the alliance began to crack. Mutual suspicion between the Nationalists and Communists was too great to be dispelled even by the Japanese attack. During the last half of the war, both Nationalists and Communists acted more to advance their own interests than to fight the common enemy. Chiang Kai-shek used some of his divisions to blockade the Communist-held regions in the northwest. The Communists, in turn, struck back at the Nationalists from time to time. As a result, China was torn by a three-sided war among Nationalists, Communists, and Japanese until the end of World War II in 1945.

During the war with Japan, Mao Zedong never abandoned his main goal—to establish Communist control over all China. He made use of the war to further this aim. Like Nationalist leader Chiang Kai-shek, he was cautious in committing his troops to fight the stronger Japanese forces. He was aware that the success or failure of his Red Army would determine the future of the Communist movement in China. Mao stated his strategy in this way: "Because our enemies are so powerful, our revolutionary forces can only be strengthened and accumulated over a long period of time, so that it may become an invincible force in achieving ultimate victory. . . . Our revolutionary force must be persistent and strong in guarding its own camp. . . ." Mao, therefore, concentrated on strengthening the Chinese Communist Army for the showdown that lay ahead with the Nationalist regime.

COMMUNIST POWER.

Yan'an, a village in the arid northwest, became the Communist center of power after the Long March of 1934–1935. Note the caves in the picture of Yan'an above. From this rugged base, Mao directed guerrilla assaults on the Japanese. Peasant soldiers (right) took up spears to join the "Eighth Route Army," as the Communist forces were called. To get more modern weapons, the Communists captured enemy supplies.

Winning Popular Support

The policy of the united front had demanded that Mao suspend his revolutionary program. Although the Communists for years had advocated the use of force to overthrow the government, they now posed as champions of peaceful reform. Badly needed improvements were carried out in the areas under their control.

Landlords were persuaded to reduce excessively high rentals on land. Moneylenders were induced to lower their exorbitant interest rates. Red Army soldiers helped in community projects and on many peasant farms. As a result, the Communists were welcomed wherever they went.

The Red Army soldiers also gained many recruits among the peasants. Now as never before, Mao and other Communist leaders demonstrated their considerable skill at guerrilla warfare. They directed swift strikes against Japanese outposts, cutting again and again the enemy's lines of communication. In these raids the Communists not only harassed the enemy but secured weapons and other supplies. The guerrilla warfare of the Communist forces annoyed the Japanese but did not seriously threaten their occupation of major cities and towns throughout the war. But many of the Chinese in the enemy-held areas were inspired by what they heard of the Communist resistance. By the end of the war the ranks of the Red Army had swelled to a million men and women.

In August 1945, after the United States had dropped two atomic bombs on Japanese cities, the Emperor of Japan accepted the terms of surrender offered him by the Allies. World War II, perhaps the bloodiest conflict in history, came to a close. China was utterly exhausted. Chiang's government was more than ever held responsible for the nation's plight and so was extremely unpopular. Mao and the Communist movement, on the other hand, were stronger and bolder than ever before. The Kuomintang soon faced its most critical challenge for leadership of China.

Check Your Understanding

1. **a.** When did China declare war against Japan? **b.** How long had the two countries been fighting before war was formally declared? **c.** Why did China wait so long to declare war formally against Japan?
2. **a.** Describe China's struggle against the advancing Japanese. **b.** How did the United States help the Chinese in their fight against the Japanese?
3. **Thinking Critically:** What effects did the war have on the Nationalist–Communist rivalry? Why did support for the Nationalists dwindle while support for the Communists increased?

5. Communist Control of China

At the war's end China was a gutted land. Cities and towns were pockmarked with craters and strewn with the ruins of homes and other buildings. Most of the roads had deteriorated, and few trains were running. Refugees—especially children, elderly people, the sick, and the wounded—were in desperate need. Food and other essential goods were in scarce supply, and prices skyrocketed. **Black marketeers** squeezed out as much profit as they could from the few people who had the means to buy. Factory owners, unable to secure raw materials, had to suspend production, thus adding to the unemployment that was already widespread in the cities. Not even in the worst of the pre-war years had China been so close to disaster.

The United States and the United Nations tried to provide relief for China. Great quantities of food, clothing, and medical supplies that were shipped to the suffering country prevented a complete breakdown. But a large part of these supplies never reached the people most in need. Inadequate transportation facilities hampered distribution. An even greater problem was widespread cheating and corruption. Many government officials, themselves engaged in a struggle for survival, took advantage of their positions. They often sold food and supplies intended for the needy, pocketing the profits.

Competition for Control

Both the Nationalists and the Communists were eager to win control of the areas in eastern and northern China that the Japanese had held for so long. The United States supported the Kuomintang government by airlifting its troops to key cities. The Communists, meanwhile, hurried to seize weapons and supplies turned over by the Japanese forces when they surrendered. As clashes between the rival Chinese forces increased, the shattered country was plunged into even greater chaos.

In an effort to prevent war between the Nationalists and the Communists, President Harry Truman of the United States sent General George C. Marshall to China in late 1945. Marshall's mission was to close the breach between Chiang and Mao. The United States believed that cooperation between the two leaders was urgently needed if China were to have a chance to heal the wounds of eight years of war.

The Marshall mission ended in failure. The American general spent 13 months trying to bring Chiang and Mao together, but the antagonisms of 20 years were too strong. When General

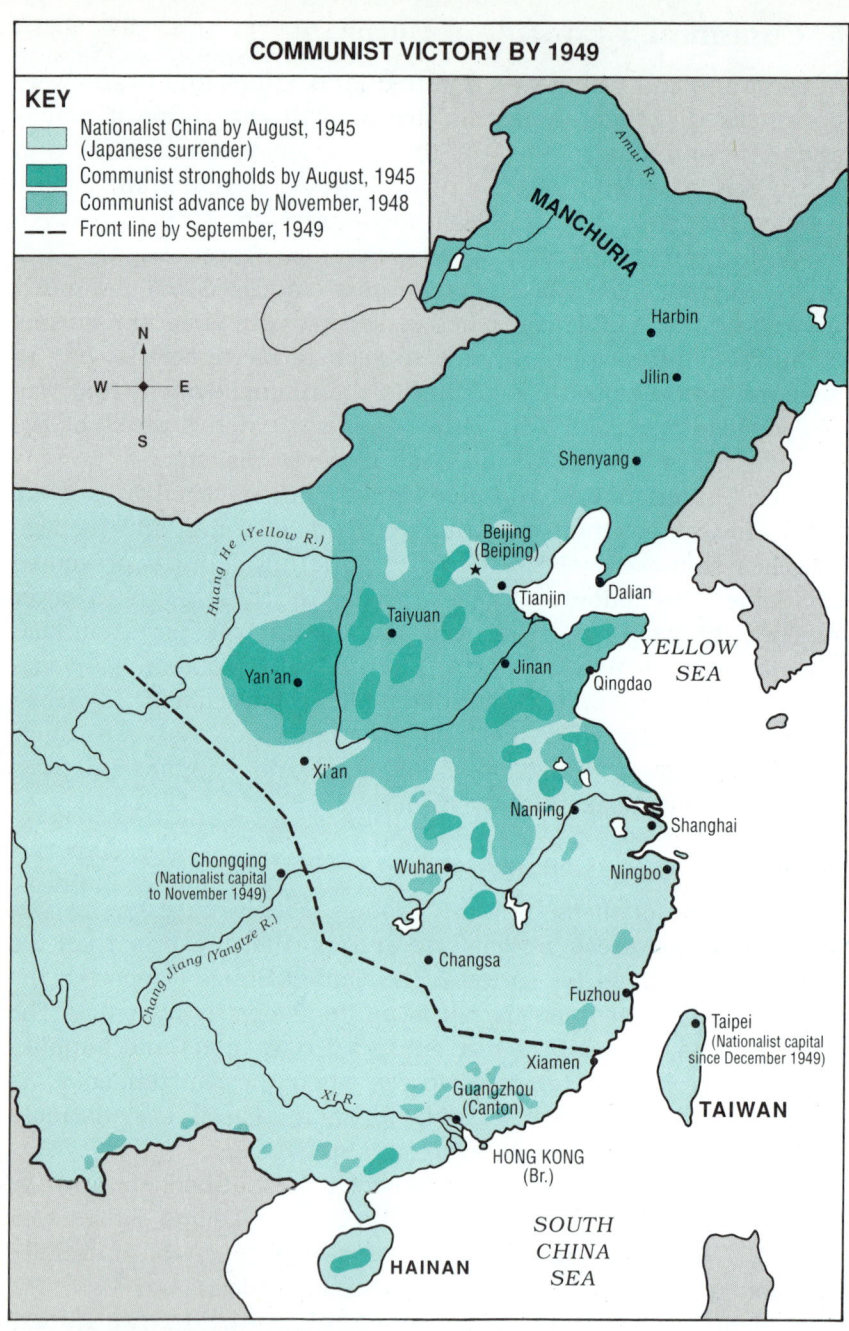

MOVEMENT: CHINA, 1945–1949. After the defeat of Japan, the battle for control of China continued between the Nationalists and the Communists. Although the Nationalists held out in many large cities, their surrounded garrisons eventually had to surrender. By the fall of 1949 the Communist victory was a certainty. Why was the Nationalist cause so unpopular?

Marshall left China in early 1947, the uneasy truce fell apart. The would-be peacemaker summed up the situation in his final report to President Truman:

> On the side of the National Government which is in effect the Kuomintang, there is a dominant group of reactionaries. They have been opposed, in my opinion, to almost every effort I have made to influence the formation of a genuine coalition government. . . . They were quite frank in publicly stating their belief that cooperation by the Chinese Communist Party in the Government was inconceivable and that only a policy of force could definitely settle the issue. . . . The dyed-in-the-wool Communists do not hesitate at the most drastic measures to gain their end as, for instance, the destruction of communication in order to wreck the economy. . . .They completely distrust the leaders of the Kuomintang and appear convinced that every Government proposal is designed to crush the Chinese Communist Party. [George C. Marshall, *United States Relations with China*.]

Disaster in Manchuria

The struggle between the Nationalists and Communists came to a focus in Manchuria. Chiang hoped to use the resources of Manchuria and the industries built there by Japan in the reconstruction of China. He was impatient, therefore, to regain control of the area. But Manchuria was far from the centers of nationalist strength, and troops could be transferred there only with great difficulty. Nationalist efforts were also obstructed by the Soviets, who had declared war on Japan and invaded Manchuria in the closing week of the war. Before withdrawing in 1946, the Soviets stripped the area of its industrial equipment. Meanwhile, the Communist seizure of arms and military supplies from Japanese arsenals and munitions depots greatly strengthened the Red Army.

A fierce struggle for control of Manchuria broke out in 1947. The Nationalist garrisons in the cities were gradually surrounded and finally isolated by the Red Army, which had little trouble in cutting Chiang's overextended supply lines. After a bitter siege, Shenyang, the metropolis of southern Manchuria, surrendered to Mao's forces in the fall of 1948. The loss of this base was a catastrophe for the Nationalists. The troops of many first-class divisions were captured. In addition, the Red Army seized valuable military equipment that the United States had furnished to Chiang's troops. After the surrender of Shenyang,

THE PEOPLE'S REPUBLIC. By 1949 the Red Army was well-equipped with military supplies captured from the Japanese and the Nationalists. Compare the Communist forces entering Guangzhou after the city's surrender (above) with the spear-carrying militia shown on page 191. Mao Zedong (below) and other top Communists in 1950 celebrated the first anniversary of their proclamation of the People's Republic of China.

there was no stopping the Communist advance. (See map, page 194.)

The Spread of Communist Control

With Manchuria securely in their grasp, the Communists opened a gigantic offensive for the conquest of China. The impressive power and combat efficiency of the Red Army amazed the Nationalists and the world. The days of guerrilla warfare were left behind. The onrushing Red Army occupied Beiping, where scarcely a shot was fired in defense. The old name of the capital, Beijing, was soon restored. The Communists then began a mighty push into the valley of the Chang Jiang. Shanghai, Nanjing, and Hankou fell into their hands in the spring of 1949.

Unable to check the Communist advance, Chiang and the Kuomintang government retreated to the island of Taiwan. On the mainland, the Communists proclaimed a new government, the People's Republic of China, on October 1, 1949.

Neither lack of troops nor inferior weapons caused the Nationalist defeat. Until near the end of the struggle for the control of China, Chiang's forces had outnumbered the Red Army. Nor were the Nationalists short of modern equipment. A crucial factor was spirit and morale. The Nationalist troops were war-weary. They had little faith in their cause and little confidence in their leaders. In battle after battle they either fought half-heartedly or surrendered by the thousands after offering token resistance. Chiang's forces melted away before the relentless assaults of the confident Red Army.

Tired of the wars and misery that had filled their lives for more than a decade, the Chinese people also had lost confidence in Kuomintang leadership. In the struggle between the Nationalists and Communists, the great majority of Chinese were probably neutral, desiring only peace. If most of them did not actively support the Communists, neither did they rally behind the sagging regime of the Nationalists. In the eyes of many Chinese, it seemed that the Communists might represent an improvement over the Kuomintang.

The Endless Debate

An explanation of the Communist conquest of China calls for an evaluation of many factors. Despite all the troubles that handicapped their government, Chiang and the Kuomintang must be charged with major responsibility. The Generalissimo could not or would not put an end to corruption on the part of his officials. In the end, the effect on public morale was devastating.

The United States had sought to buttress the collapsing Nationalist regime. Whether more military and economic aid would have turned the Communist tide is arguable. The United States could hardly have taken an active part in the conflict. Though the Soviet Union did not take part in the fighting either, it did have a hand in the downfall of the Kuomintang government. The ability of the Chinese Communist leaders, however, should not be overlooked. By his victory in China, Mao Zedong established himself as the foremost Communist revolutionary of the times. In the next chapter we shall read how China fared under Mao's leadership.

Check Your Understanding

1. **a.** What were conditions like in China at the end of World War II? **b.** How did the United States and the United Nations try to help? **c.** How effective was their help?
2. **a.** Where did an open struggle between the Chinese Nationalists and the Communists break out? **b.** What were the results?
3. *Thinking Critically:* How can the Nationalists' loss of China to the Communists be explained? What are the major factors to be considered? Can any one person, group, or nation be held solely responsible? Why or why not?

CHAPTER REVIEW

■ Chapter Summary

Section 1. The Japanese invasion of Manchuria in 1931 was a major blow to Chiang Kai-shek's struggling Nationalist government. Undeterred by Chinese resistance or by the condemnation of the League of Nations, Japan transformed Manchuria into an industrial and military base and set it up as the puppet government of Manchukuo. Further aggressions by Japan signaled the likelihood of an ultimate showdown between China and Japan.

Section 2. The Nationalists' difficulties with Japan gave the Chinese Communists a chance to recover from Chiang Kai-shek's Bandit Extermination Campaigns and the Long

March that resulted. Further troubles ensued when Chinese soldiers in Manchuria refused to fight against the Chinese Communists, arguing that their real battle was against the Japanese. After Chiang was arrested by Manchurian officers, he retreated from his plan to exterminate the Chinese Communists and formed a united front with them to drive out the Japanese invaders.

Section 3. In the years after 1927, the Nationalists fought a three-sided war against warlords, Communists, and the Japanese. At the same time, the Nationalists tried to reform China's social and economic life. Although some advances were made, land reform and relief of peasant poverty were sidetracked in favor of military and political needs. With the ravages of war adding to the already miserable conditions of their lives, peasant discontent increased.

Section 4. In July 1937 the China Incident at the Marco Polo Bridge began the Second Sino–Japanese War. It was a conflict for which China was poorly prepared. During the eight years of fighting, the Nationalist regime was severely battered and the morale of the people sank to an all-time low. Help from the United States enabled Chiang's government to survive the war. But Chiang was unable to cope with dishonesty and corruption in his government or to counter the Communists' clever exploitation of wartime conditions to increase their own political and military power.

Section 5. Immediately following World War II, the United States unsuccessfully tried to arrange a political settlement between Nationalists and Communists. Thereafter a full-scale struggle for control of China broke out between the Nationalist forces of Chiang Kai-shek and the Communist forces of Mao Zedong. Brilliant on the battlefield and masterful in political warfare, Mao led the Communists to victory in 1949. With the retreat of the Kuomintang to Taiwan, Mao proclaimed the beginning of the People's Republic of China.

■ **Vocabulary Review**

Define: buffer, puppet government, guerrilla warfare, blockade, Long March, alliance, black marketeers

■ **Places to Locate**

Locate: Manchuria, Shenyang, Manchukuo, Nanjing, Shanghai, Yan'an, Xi'an, Beiping, Hankou, Chongqing, Qingdao, Burma Road, Taipei

■ **People to Know**

Identify: Chiang Kai-shek, Mao Zedong, Zhang Xueliang, Xuan Tong, Henry Stimson, General Stilwell, General Chennault, George C. Marshall

■ **Thinking Critically**

1. Why were the nations of the world, including the League of Nations and the United States, reluctant to take a firm stand against Japanese aggression in Manchuria in 1931?
2. Why did the Chinese people eventually give their support to the Communist takeover of China?
3. Why was the Kuomintang unable to tackle directly the task of rebuilding China?
4. How did mistrust between Nationalists and Communists affect the so-called united front against Japanese aggression?

■ **Extending and Applying Your Knowledge**

1. Do research to find out more about the Flying Tigers and General Claire Chennault. Prepare an oral report for the class.
2. Using *The World Almanac of World War II*, published by Bison Books Corporation, prepare a chronology of World War II in China. Share the preparation of the chronology with other students. Put the chronology in the form of a timeline for the classroom.

9

China Under Mao Zedong

The rise of the People's Republic to power at first gave new strength to the world Communist movement, which up to this time had been directed by the Soviet Union. Together the two Communist giants had the capacity to shake the world. Instead friction between the two soon developed, and the two nations became rivals.

From the day that the new government was proclaimed, Mao Zedong and his comrades began to forge a new life for their country. The Chinese Communists announced that the humiliation of China at the hands of foreign nations was at an end. They demanded that China be treated with full respect by other governments. Captivated by the dream of building a better life for their children and grandchildren, the Chinese Communist leaders regarded no price too high to pay in working for their goals. Year after year, the Chinese Communists drove themselves and the Chinese people forward. They started an all-out drive to transform China into an industrial nation. They also shook up the Chinese agricultural system more drastically than at any time during the past 2,000 years.

The Chinese Communist leaders met many of their early goals. But they also experienced notable failures and crises. Moreover, after years of political unity, the leaders were drawn into a fierce rivalry for power—the Great Proletarian Cultural Revolution.

1. China as a Totalitarian State

Within a few years of their triumph in China, the Chinese Communists had succeeded in unifying the country and imposing the kind of authority and control over the people that the Chinese emperors had sought for centuries. Never before had Chinese life been so thoroughly centralized and regimented. The Communist Party's will touched every person and every aspect of life in China.

Rooting Out Opposition

In 1949 the Red Army easily wiped out the last resistance of the Nationalist forces. The only Nationalist troops that survived the mopping up operation were those who escaped to Taiwan. (See page 234.) Soldiers of the Red Army also eliminated the last of the warlords who had held out in isolated areas. With these missions accomplished, the wars that had racked China for decades came to an end.

The Communists then hunted down the supporters of the Kuomintang. Anyone who had been associated with the ousted Nationalist government was suspect. In the cities and villages, former officials of the Kuomintang and officers of its army were imprisoned or executed for their "crimes." Joining them were landlords in the countryside and city merchants accused of being spies or **counterrevolutionaries,** regardless of the fact. It is estimated that millions of people fell victim to the Communist bloodbath.

The new rulers of China made special efforts to win over the intellectuals and professionals, people who would be useful in the Party's program for rebuilding the country. This process of changing the thinking of the people was called **reeducation.** Pressure by relatives, friends, neighbors, and fellow workers was exerted on the person being brought into line with Party doctrine. Those singled out for reeducation were compelled to confess publicly the "errors" in their earlier thinking and behavior and to acknowledge that they had been "enemies of the people." As a final step in their reeducation, they had to admit the superiority of Communist ideas.

The Chinese Communist Party aimed to root out any opposition before it had a chance to become dangerous. Like other leaders governing under **totalitarianism,** the Chinese Communists organized a network of secret police whose mission was to spy on the people and uncover plots against the Party. Newspapers, books, and other forms of communication were placed

TIMETABLE

China Under Mao Zedong

1949	Communist takeover
1950–1953	Korean War
1953–1957	First Five-Year Plan
1954	Government reorganization
1956	Beginning of Sino-Soviet rift
	Hundred Flowers Campaign
1958–1962	Second Five-Year Plan
1959	China's takeover of Tibet
1962	Sino-Indian border conflict
1964	First Chinese nuclear test explosion
1966–1976	The Great Proletarian Cultural Revolution
1971	Admittance to the United Nations
1972	President Nixon's visit to China
1976	Deaths of Zhou Enlai and Mao Zedong

under **censorship.** Meetings were forbidden without official approval. Such controls were not new in China, where democratic practices had seldom been followed. However, no previous Chinese government had been so thorough in its control of the people.

The policy of suppression, however, did not stamp out all discontent and criticism. In 1956 Mao ordered a relaxation of state controls on speech, press, and thought. Citing a well-known quotation from the Confucian classics, Mao said, "Let a hundred flowers bloom, let a hundred schools of thought contend." Mao's purpose in initiating the Hundred Flowers Campaign, as it came to be called, was never made clear. Perhaps the objective of his policy shift was to soften opposition to the Communist government's totalitarian controls by permitting carefully guided criticism. But Communist Party leaders were shocked by the flood of criticism that followed the opening of the Hundred Flowers Campaign. It was apparent to the Communist leadership that many Chinese had not been converted to the Communists' vision of a new society. The Hundred Flowers Campaign was abruptly discontinued, and the policy of strict censorship was reestablished.

A New System of Government

From 1949 to 1954, China was ruled under a temporary system of government. A few non-Communists even held high posts in the government, but they exercised little authority. In 1954, however, Mao felt secure enough to establish a permanent system of administration. A constitution was adopted, and the political life of China was reorganized according to its provisions. Since 1954, China has revised its state constitution three times, adopting new constitutions in 1975, 1978, and 1982.

As in the Soviet Union, China has been ruled by two parallel institutions: the state and the Party. In theory, but not in actual practice, the National People's Congress has been the supreme organ of government in China. Its members have been elected by regional congresses in the provinces. These bodies in turn have been elected by political assemblies operating in smaller geographical units. The National People's Congress has been called into session infrequently, and so its authority between meetings has been exercised by a Standing Committee. The chairperson of the Standing Committee has been chief of state and President of the People's Republic. Mao Zedong held this office until resigning in 1959. The post was then taken by Liu Shaoqi (LOO SHAH-oh-CHEE), who was Mao's closest assistant.

The National People's Congress elected a State Council, which in turn directed the ministries, bureaus, and officers that carried on the administration of the government. Zhou Enlai, one of the top-ranking officers of the Party, was chairperson of the State Council and had the title of premier. In 1958 Zhou gave up the post of minister of foreign affairs, which he had held for many years, but continued as premier.

The Communist Party

Actual power in China has been exercised by the Communist Party. Only candidates approved by the Party have been permitted to stand for election. Only Party members hold key government posts whether on the national or local level. The Party has also dominated such institutions as schools, trade unions, community organizations, and cultural associations.

The Party structure has been similar to the governmental structure of Communist China. A large Party Congress which has met irregularly is supposedly the supreme organ of the Party. However, it has delegated authority to a much smaller Central Committee that has varied somewhat in size over the years. The Central Committee, in turn, has delegated authority to the Politburo, an organization of about 24 people.

COMMUNIST LEADERS. Mao Zedong (above, left), intellectual leader and director of the Chinese Communist revolution, ruled China from 1949 until his death in 1976. Jiang Qing (above, right), his wife, was an influential leader during the Cultural Revolution. Zhou Enlai (left) held a position of power in the Chinese Communist Party from its early days until his death in 1976. How was stability in leadership an advantage for China? How was it a disadvantage?

In theory, the Chinese Communist Party has been guided by the principle of **democratic centralism.** According to this principle, members at each level of authority decide who will serve at the next highest level. In theory, all members have the right to voice their opinions and vote as they see fit. Once a decision has been reached by majority vote, everyone is expected to back the Party's position. In practice, however, power in the Chinese Communist Party has always flowed from the top down. The Politburo has always made the decisions and the rest of the Party has followed.

INDOCTRINATION. The Communist government set out to supervise every aspect of the people's lives. Mass propaganda rallies (left) were staged for adults. Even children (below) were indoctrinated with Communist teachings. In this play, the children taunted "Uncle Sam," the child wearing the tall hat. What were such plays teaching the children?

Check Your Understanding

1. **a.** What was the purpose of the Hundred Flowers Campaign? **b.** Why was it canceled so quickly?
2. **a.** How were the government and the Communist Party connected? **b.** How much choice did the people have in selecting their rulers?
3. *Thinking Critically:* How did the Chinese Communist Party try to stamp out opposition to its rule? Why did the Communists feel that it was necessary to "reeducate" the people?

2. The Economic Transformation of China

The Chinese Communists saw rapid industrialization as a key to greater power for China, and they were determined to change the basic pattern of the country's economy. Their goal was to transform China from an agricultural country into an industrial giant as quickly as possible. Mao Zedong and other Party leaders boasted that they intended to overtake the Western industrial nations. Day after day their speeches and their writings were sprinkled with statistics of production, making China's annual industrial output the measure of the country's progress. But agriculture was not forgotten, and the Communists made grand plans for modernizing it and for reorganizing the landholding system.

Drive Toward Industrialization

When the Chinese Communists started out in 1949 to transform China, they recognized the many handicaps they had to overcome to make China into an industrial giant. China had not made much progress toward industrialization after it became a republic in 1912. Moreover, the war with Japan had left many factories, power plants, bridges, and railroad lines in ruins. The Communists recognized that their first task was to clear away the rubble and make repairs. Then they could tackle the problems causing China's low industrial output. After increasing production, they could modernize farming, strengthen the armed forces, and become a recognized and respected power in the world.

Soon after the Communists came to power, they made an inventory of the country's known resources and began a search for new locations of raw materials. China possessed many of the natural resources necessary for modern industry. (See map, page 212.) But the country was handicapped by an inadequate transportation system and critical shortages of raw materials. China was rich in coal with large deposits located in central Manchuria. Other valuable beds of coal were found between the Huang He and the Chang Jiang. Although iron ore of high quality was relatively scarce, known deposits were ample for China's immediate needs. Copper was in sufficient supply, but known deposits of tin were inadequate. China also had adequate reserves of tungsten, manganese, bauxite, and gold. China had modest deposits of petroleum, and the continuing search for new oil fields in subsequent years resulted in the discovery of several fields.

Two of China's most serious handicaps were a shortage of skilled workers and a lack of **capital.** For many projects, China made effective use of its enormous numbers of unskilled workers. But time was needed to develop educational institutions and teachers to train scientists, engineers, technicians, and the other specialists who were needed to build and maintain an industrial society.

Before the Communists came to power, it was often said that differences among the people were based not on differences in wealth but on different degrees of poverty. During the early 1950's China received a modest amount of aid from the Soviet Union, mainly loans that had to be repaid. China's leaders also seized the properties of landlords and business people. But even these actions failed to provide enough capital for the building up of industry. To provide the capital needed to get industrialization moving, the Party leaders turned to China's agricultural sector. Leaving the peasants only enough to live on, the government gathered agricultural surpluses and sold them in foreign markets. In turn it bought badly needed machinery and technical equipment.

The First Five-Year Plan

Shortly after coming to power the Communists began to seize industrial, banking, and transportation facilities throughout China. This process of **nationalization** was not completed until the winter of 1955-1956. Meanwhile, in 1953 the Chinese launched a crash industrialization program, which they called a Five-Year Plan, using as a model the experience of the Soviet Union two decades earlier. The Chinese Communist leaders created an enormous bureaucracy to oversee and direct the effort toward industrialization. This bureaucracy, and not managers on the spot, made the major decisions. In effect, China's economy was run from Beijing.

In this first Five-Year Plan, **heavy industry** was given priority. The country's slim resources were committed to the expansion of steel mills and the building of railways, power plants, and tractor and other machinery assembly lines. **Light industry** and the production of **consumer goods** received little attention.

Everyone was expected to make sacrifices for the success of the Five-Year Plan. The low standard of living was to be raised only to the extent that available food and goods were to be fairly distributed. No longer were there frenzied scrambles for foodstuffs and other basic necessities of life. A strict system of **rationing,** price controls, and the elimination of widespread

black markets put an end to many abuses that had been common under the Kuomintang.

The targets of the first Five-Year Plan were largely reached. The production of iron and steel tripled between 1952 and 1957. During the same period the output of coal soared from 65 million tons to 130 million tons. Railway mileage increased from 15,000 to 18,000 miles. (See map, page 212.) The construction of dams and power plants was also begun. Confident that China was on the right course, the Communist Party announced plans for a second Five-Year Plan that was even more ambitious than the first.

The Great Leap Forward

"If you plant trees in the morning," says an old Chinese proverb, "don't expect to cut planks by nightfall." Mao and his advisers, however, ignored this piece of wisdom in devising the Second Five-Year Plan. In the Second Five-Year Plan, everyone in the entire country was called on to make a Great Leap Forward. Elated by the success of the First Five-Year Plan, the government greatly overestimated China's capacity for industrialization and set staggeringly high goals. Again the emphasis was on heavy industry. Again the peasants were expected to sacrifice.

In an all-out effort to boost the production of iron and steel, almost everyone was encouraged to become an ironmonger. In backyards, in parks, in nearby fields, the government asked citizens to build small blast furnaces where they could turn out crude iron. But the government soon abandoned the project when the iron produced was so full of impurities that it was almost worthless. Glowing reports of success were given at the end of the Second Five-Year Plan, but production figures for this period were never fully disclosed.

Shortly after the end of the Great Leap Forward, China's drive toward industrialization was disrupted by divisions over economic policies and economic priorities among Mao and his advisers and by the turmoil caused by the Great Proletarian Cultural Revolution. (See pages 220-225.) Not until the last few years of the Fourth Five-Year Plan, which was completed in 1975, was Communist China able to devote its energies once again to industrialization.

Agricultural Cooperatives

During the drive toward industrialization, agriculture played a major role, supplying the food needs of a growing population and providing a surplus for export. When the Communists came

INDUSTRIALIZATION.
Increased production of steel and electric power were major goals in the Communist drive to industrialize. Steelworkers (above) operate control boards in a factory making steel by the oxygen process, a technique first developed in Western countries. At a hydroelectric power station (left) technicians work high above patchwork fields in Zhejiang. The campaign to make iron in small backyard furnaces (below) proved a failure.

to power in 1949, they confiscated farmland from wealthy landowners and turned the land over to the peasants. A few years later, the Party organized the peasants into many small farming **cooperatives** of 30 or 40 families each. But the production of these small-sized farming cooperatives was not able to keep pace with the rapidly growing needs of both industry and a rising population.

Reorganization into Communes

Disturbed by the lagging production of small-scale farming, Mao Zedong decided to organize the peasants into still larger agricultural units called **communes.** The government hoped that these large-sized communes would be able to make better use of labor, machines, and capital.

During the period of the Great Leap Forward (1958–1962), the small agricultural cooperatives were united into large communes. In about a year almost 25,000 of these communes had been established. Each commune, operating under a central management, had about 10,000 acres of tillable land and was worked by about 5,000 households. With the reorganization into communes, the peasants lost their remaining rights in the land. They also had to turn over all their work animals and farm equipment to the commune. In return, the peasants were paid wages for their labor and were housed and fed. The crops and livestock of these giant farms was owned and sold by the commune.

The hope for more efficient agricultural production, however, was not realized. Several reasons accounted for the disappointing progress. For one, the efficiency of the communes suffered from too much interference by Party officials. For another, the managers of the communes lacked sufficient machinery and the technical knowledge needed to run farming operations on a large scale. Still another reason was resentment on the part of some peasants toward the controls imposed on them by the commune system.

Agricultural Disasters

To make matters worse, China suffered a series of severe natural disasters in 1959, 1960, and 1961. Long periods of drought, devastating floods, and violent storms severely reduced farm harvests and reduced the amount of crops that were available for export. Some areas of the country were also plagued by swarms of locusts that devoured the crops before they could be harvested.

INDUSTRIAL RESOURCES OF CHINA

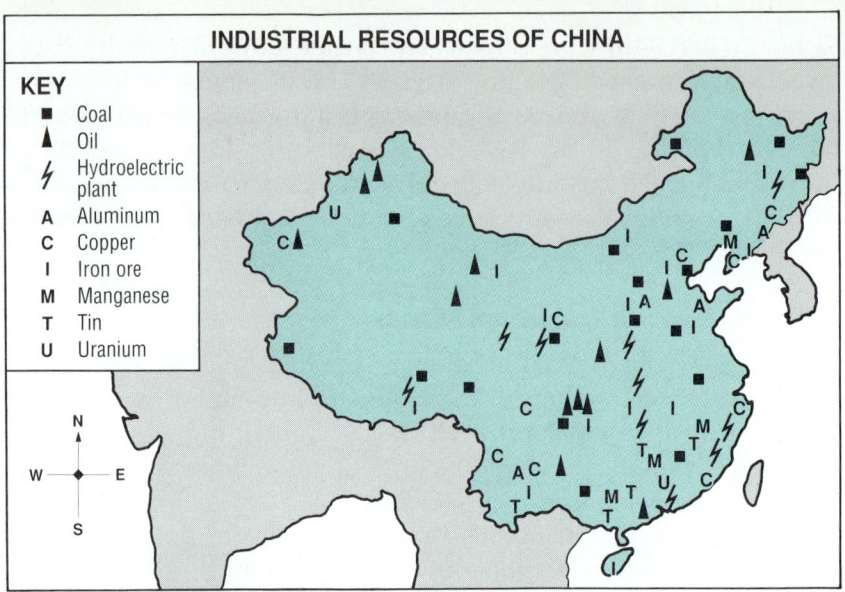

ENVIRONMENT: NATURAL RESOURCES AND TRANSPORTATION.

China's raw materials for use in manufacturing and other industries are found in many far-flung locations. Roads, railroads and waterways carry the raw materials to industrial sites in China proper. Airlines also link major cities.

TRANSPORTATION IN CHINA

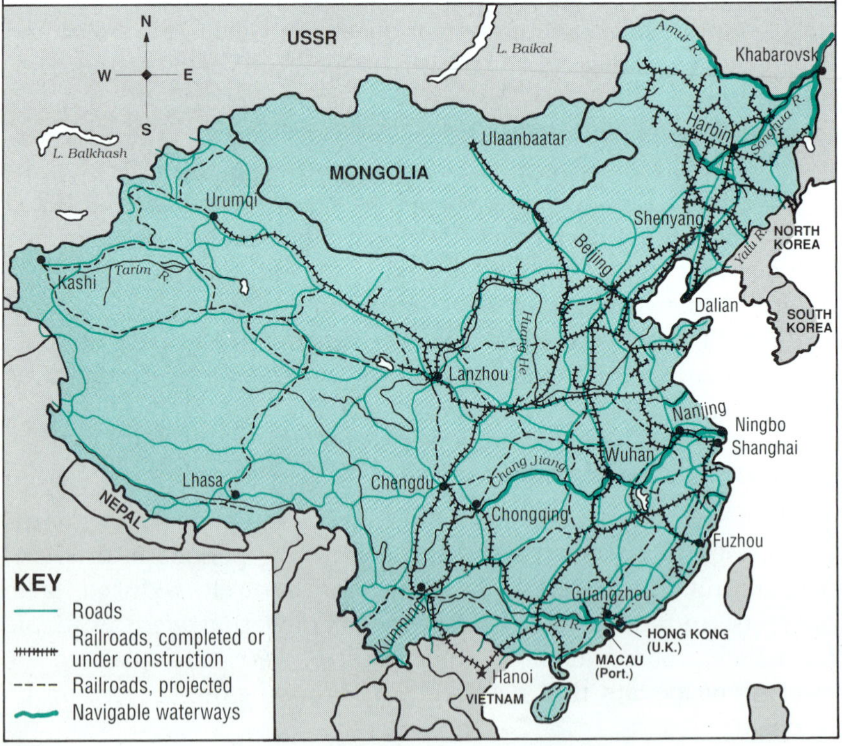

The combination of these natural disasters and the reorganization of agriculture into communes created a serious food shortage in China. The government found it necessary to spend millions of dollars buying grain from other countries. These grain purchases used up the funds that otherwise would have been spent for industrial equipment and for raw materials. Despite the government's efforts to supply food, starvation, malnutrition, and disease took the lives of about 16 million people between 1959 and 1961.

During the 1960's, with fewer natural disasters plaguing the nation, China's agricultural production began to improve. The Chinese were able to make more efficient use of labor and equipment and greater use of chemical fertilizers. In early 1975, Zhou Enlai boasted that since 1949 grain output had increased 140 percent. During those same years, however, China's population had expanded to 800 million. This was an increase of about 200 million—a number approximately equal to the total population of the United States in the mid-1970's. By the year 2000, it is estimated that mainland China's population will be more than 1.2 billion.

China's growing population made it difficult for China to meet its economic goals. On the one hand, its population was a tremendous asset, giving China a massive work force. On the other hand, uncontrolled population growth posed many problems for the country's economic well-being. Within a few years China's leaders began to make serious plans to stem the country's population growth. They launched a "one-child family" program. (See page 256.)

Check Your Understanding

1. How did the Communists intend to transform China economically?
2. **a.** What handicaps did the Chinese have to overcome in order to make the nation an industrial giant? **b.** What assets were in China's favor?
3. Describe and compare the First and Second Five-Year Plans.
4. How was agriculture reorganized?
5. **Thinking Critically:** Discuss the successes and failures of China's drive to transform itself economically from 1949 to 1975 in both the industrial and agricultural sectors.

3. Social Changes in Communist China

The Communists sought to build a new society in China through their programs of reeducation and indoctrination. In order to build a strong state, the Chinese Communists knew they had to win the complete allegiance of the people. But many traditional values and ways of doing things persisted, even among those people committed to the ideology of communism. This intermingling of traditional and Communist China became clearly evident in four key aspects of Communist Chinese society—the role of women, education, health care, and city life.

Women in Communist Society

For centuries the family had exercised a dominant influence on every Chinese. Generations of children had been taught from infancy to obey their parents, to advance the interests of their family, and to respect their elders. Women had been instructed to accept the higher position of men. The Communists claimed to be hostile to inequalities between men and women and boasted of their intention to emancipate women.

Soon after the Communists came to power they enacted new marriage and divorce laws that freed women from the long tyranny of the family and men. Arranged marriages, which gave

A scene from a modern Chinese ballet symbolizes the drastic change in the role of women under the Communist state.

daughters little or no voice in choosing their husbands, were discouraged. In traditional China a husband could easily divorce his wife, but not so the wife. In Communist China divorce laws favored neither sex, and a woman's rights over her children and property were protected.

To increase agricultural and industrial production, the Communists restructured family life and greatly reduced the traditional control of parents and elders over children. Women were urged to work in the fields and factories of the nation. In setting up communes, many homes were torn down and families resettled in dormitories. Meals were served in dining halls. Infants were cared for during the day in nurseries or in government-run kindergartens, and children of school age were sent to school.

Education

The Party regarded education as the key to rearing loyal and obedient citizens, but China's educational needs were staggering. With more than half of the population under the age of 20, providing for education put a tremendous demand on China's limited resources. China's adults also needed the opportunities to learn how to read and write that had been denied them.

The Chinese Communists tried to provide an elementary education for as many children as possible. Only a small percentage, however, went on to secondary schools, and admission to universities was reserved for students considered politically most reliable. For the Communists, work was also part of education. Many students spent part of the school day or year gaining work experience. In times of crisis, students and teachers were ordered to leave their classrooms and to work wherever help was needed.

Modernizing China's Cities

When they took power in 1949, the Communist leaders were sensitive about their country's rundown appearance, the result of many years of war and turmoil. As a result of their efforts, many of China's cities were transformed. Beijing became a city with well-paved streets. Slums were torn down and government buildings, hotels, stores, and offices were constructed in their place. The Great Hall of the People, a huge building used for political meetings and cultural purposes, was built in less than a year. The Communists also took care to maintain the many irreplaceable art treasures and architectural monuments of traditional China, which are regularly viewed and admired by streams of Chinese and foreign visitors.

EDUCATION. An important aspect of China's education program was a drive to end illiteracy. More children (top, left) were enrolled in primary schools, and adults of minority groups (top, right) were urged to learn to read and write Chinese. English (left) and other foreign languages were also studied. For peasants who had to spend most of their time at work (below), literacy classes were held outdoors. How would literacy help China in its drive to modernize its society?

HEALTH CARE. Under Mao Zedong traditional health practices were combined with new medical and educational techniques to improve health care. A health worker (above) taught commune members techniques in preventive medicine. "Barefoot" doctors (right) like the one on the island of Hainan had to ford streams to get from one place to another. Sometimes these doctors used acupuncture (below) to treat patients. Why was the use of "barefoot" doctors so important to China?

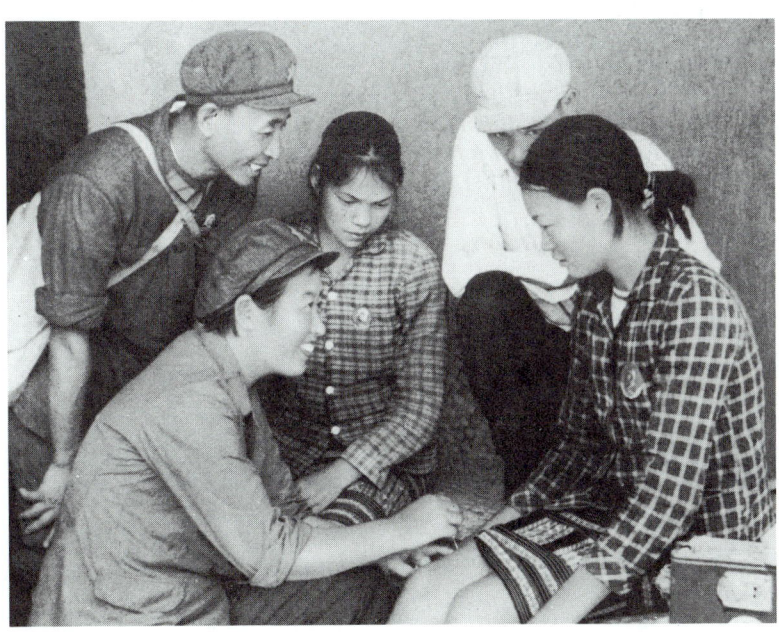

Sidelight to History

Village Doctors

Medicine and surgery have been practiced successfully by the Chinese for many hundreds of years. Acupunture, for example, is an ancient Chinese practice that has been used successfully to treat many ailments of the human body. This type of needle therapy has also been effective as a form of local anesthesia when surgery has been necessary.

Typically a Chinese doctor specializes in either traditional Chinese medical practices or in Western-style medicine, but knows something about the other. But China's shortage of medical personnel who are trained professionally has made it necessary for them to rely on traditionally trained peasants, who have been given several months of up-to-date medical training and then returned to their villages.

During the years when Mao was China's leader, these trained peasants were called "barefoot" doctors. In recent years the government has given its peasant medical personnel more extensive training. In the process, the term *barefoot doctor* has been replaced with the term *village doctor*. These village doctors are still the ones on whom most peasants rely for medical care.

Village doctors spend much of their time helping peasants learn how to prevent malnutrition, sickness, and disease. These village doctors handle emergencies and simple injuries and sicknesses, referring the more serious cases to physicians usually located in the nearest urban area. When seriously ill patients return to their villages to recuperate, the village doctors are the ones who apply the treatments prescribed by the medical personnel from the urban areas.

Without village doctors, Communist China would not have been able to improve health conditions to the extent that it has. By the mid-1980's China had nearly 60,000 hospitals and 1,413,000 doctors. Of these doctors, 336,000 specialized in the practice of Chinese traditional medicine.

Improvements in Public Health

A dramatic improvement in health care for the great numbers of Chinese peasants was one of the great accomplishments of the Chinese Communists. Mass campaigns were organized throughout all of China to teach the people about ways to prevent sickness from accidents and disease. But to safeguard the people's health, many more medical personnel were needed. When the Communists took over, there were not enough men and women trained in modern scientific medical practices. But the Chinese Communists made good use of the practitioners of traditional Chinese healing arts. Called *village doctors* and given additional training and instruction, these practitioners were able to deal effectively with basic health problems that stemmed from unsanitary conditions and malnutrition. They succeeded, for example, in drastically reducing the high death rate of mothers and the newborn.

In addition, the government waged campaigns to clean up the sources of disease and infection in both the countryside and the cities. Visitors to China noticed a startling change in the sanitary conditions of cities, many of which became sparkling examples of cleanliness, as main thoroughfares were regularly swept and baskets for disposal of trash were placed everywhere. By providing the Chinese people with an adequate diet, the Communists made a great effort to eradicate diseases caused by malnutrition. With these efforts to improve health, the death rate was further reduced, and life expectancy among the Chinese increased.

But even greater changes to China's social patterns were produced by the Great Proletarian Cultural Revolution, which you will read about in the next section.

Check Your Understanding

1. Why did the Communists attempt to form a new society?
2. How have the Communists sought to change the role of the family?
3. How have the Chinese Communists improved health care?
4. **Thinking Critically:** What evidence does the text present to support the Communists' belief that they have emancipated women?

4. The Great Proletarian Cultural Revolution

In 1966 Mao Zedong plunged China into a period of turmoil and virtual anarchy known as the Great Proletarian Cultural Revolution. The period finally came to a close in 1976 with the death of Mao and the arrest of several of his closest supporters. During the first phase of the Cultural Revolution, warfare raged in China's streets. Armed struggle largely ended in 1968–1969 and was followed by a bitter, although more peaceful, jockeying for power between two groups. The Maoists, or radicals, supported the Cultural Revolution's policies. They were opposed by the moderates, or rightists.

Political and Ideological Motives

Mao's precise motives in beginning the Cultural Revolution are not clear. He never explained his underlying thinking, at least not publicly. By examining what occurred, historians have tried to infer what Mao was trying to achieve. Whatever Mao's motives actually were, the Cultural Revolution remains one of the most bizarre episodes in Chinese history.

In part, Mao probably began the Cultural Revolution as a way to maintain his political power. For many years, Mao and a small group of his comrades had controlled the Communist Party. These comrades never challenged Mao's supremacy, nor did Mao find it necessary to root out anyone for disloyalty. But in the late 1950's, some leaders disagreed with Mao's economic policies. Others challenged his aggressive foreign policies. Uneasy because of China's economic and military weakness, they advocated policies of caution. During the next few years, the inner-Party split widened, and Mao lost some of his power. Of this period, Mao later said that he had been treated like a dead ancestor—worshiped but not consulted. By mid-1966 dissent within the Party leadership plunged Mao into a struggle for his political life. His response was a nationwide call to purge China of "capitalist" influences.

The Great Proletarian Cultural Revolution that Mao unleashed in 1966 involved more than just a struggle for power. By the mid-1960's, Mao had become greatly disturbed by the direction Chinese society seemed to be taking. The ultimate goal of the Revolution had been the creation of a classless society. Undeniably China had less social inequality under the Communists than under the Kuomintang. Considerable economic differences still persisted, however, between intellectuals and manual laborers and between urban workers and peasants. Mao argued that China's educational system actually reinforced the class divisions in Chinese society. He believed that a new elite was being created—an educated elite composed of skilled bureaucrats, professors, scientists, and engineers. Mao saw that these people lived far better than their less-educated comrades. Mao also disliked the special privileges that Party members received. He thought they had lost their dedication to communism's goal—a classless society.

China in Turmoil

The Great Proletarian Cultural Revolution of 1966–1976 began as an attempt to eliminate so-called "capitalist" influences in literature and art. Jiang Qing, Mao's wife, directed the reformation of the performing arts. Within months, the Cultural Revolution came to include every imagined "capitalist" influence among the intellectual class. A main target of the Revolution was Party officials who supposedly were following the "capitalist" road. All too often the "capitalist" charge was nothing more than a catch-all phrase designed to brand individuals as enemies of the people. Victims were subject to all kinds of arbitrary treatment, including mob violence. Few received even unfair trials.

A vital source of support for Chairman Mao was a group called the Red Guards. This civilian organization of several million teenagers and young adults had been formed in the spring and summer of 1966 to uphold the "purity" of Chairman Mao's revolutionary ideas. Mao urged the Red Guards, who were fanatically devoted to him, to travel throughout the country and to root out "capitalist" influences. Receiving free rail travel, the Red Guards went on a rampage, first in the cities and then in rural areas. The objects of their fury were "The Four Olds"—old thoughts, old culture, old customs, and old habits. The Red Guards interrogated professors, factory managers, and government and Party leaders. They beat people up and frequently killed these Party "enemies." The Red Guards closed schools and colleges and destroyed temples, books, and priceless art treasures. They took over factories and communes and sometimes even government and Party offices. They broke into homes, searching them for evidence of "capitalist" inclinations. The army and police were under orders from Mao not to restrain the Red Guards. Hoping to avoid trouble, many people placed pictures of Mao on their doors.

A primary aim of the Cultural Revolution was to change the system of higher education. Mao complained that the courses of study were too long and irrelevant to China's needs. The Red

RED GUARDS. Acting as Mao's shock troops in the Great Proletarian Cultural Revolution, the Red Guards showed enthusiasm and fervor (top, left) as they rampaged throughout China. They disrupted schools and colleges, invaded homes, and destroyed property and human lives. An army propaganda team (top, right) tours a provincial town, its mission to indoctrinate the people and to hand out "little red books" filled with Chairman Mao's sayings (left). When colleges reopened, emphasis was on work-study programs where students gained experience in a factory or other work environment (below). What other effects did the Red Guards have on education?

Guards virtually took over China's colleges and universities. Higher education fell into a state of complete chaos with Red Guard units battling one another and groups of students. The Red Guards harassed, humiliated, beat up, and murdered many professors. Rather than face further torment, some professors committed suicide. In July 1966, Mao closed down higher education completely so that his young followers could devote all of their attention to the Cultural Revolution. Schools did not reopen until 1969 or 1970.

In early 1967 Mao began urging the Red Guards to take control of the government. The Red Guards, acting with the military and various groups of workers and often aided and abetted by helpful government officials, began to seize control of city and provincial governments. They even seized a few of the ministries at the national level. Some of the officials who helped the Red Guards seize control were genuine supporters of the Cultural Revolution. Other helpful officials were seeking to advance their own careers or settle old scores.

Bringing the Turmoil to an End

The chaos created by the Red Guards finally led Mao to clamp down on them. In mid-1968, the army began to bring unruly youths under control. Thousands of young people were rounded up and ordered to perform "productive labor" on the nation's farms. Simultaneously, "revolutionary committees" composed of army officers, reliable Party members, and leaders of mass organizations were set up. By 1969 these revolutionary committees had succeeded in restoring a measure of order and a semblance of normality to Chinese life. The army's role as the guarantor of public order was reflected in the prominent places army representatives came to hold in the Party.

The army's leading role in Chinese politics began to decline in late 1971 following the Lin Biao (LIN BYOW) affair. As a military commander and Mao's designated heir apparent, Lin Biao worked closely with Mao during the course of the Cultural Revolution. But as the Cultural Revolution unfolded, Mao became concerned that Lin was becoming too powerful and decided to weaken his position. What happened next is not clear, but Lin probably died in September 1971. According to official Chinese reports, Lin had plotted to kill Mao. When the plot failed, Lin fled and died when his plane crashed in Mongolia. The official report, however, left important questions unanswered. To this day no one knows how or why the plane crashed or really what happened.

In the wake of the Lin Biao affair, Mao took steps to weaken the political power of the army. "The Party commands the gun," Mao had stated long ago, "and the gun must never be allowed to command the Party." Probably, too, Mao no longer needed the army to maintain order.

A Changing Mix of Leaders

With Lin Biao gone, Mao's leadership was once again undisputed. But Mao was in failing health and approaching 80. As Mao moved into semi-retirement, the reins of leadership fell to Zhou Enlai, clearly second in command in China. Like many people in the army, Zhou believed that China desperately needed the services of trained administrators, technicians, scientists, and engineers. These professionals, however, were the very people who had been purged during the Great Proletarian Cultural Revolution. From the late 1960's onward, many of these people were gradually restored to their former positions of power in government, industry, and education. By the early 1970's the Chinese power structure had become an incompatible mix of those who had favored the Cultural Revolution and those who had been its victims.

The first group of this incompatible mix, the radicals, controlled the performing arts, the media, and policy-making at the highest levels. Jiang Qing was one of the key leaders of the radical group. The second group, the moderates, controlled the implementation of policy. Their leader was Deng Xiaoping (DUNG SHEEOW-PING). Deng, a veteran of the Long March, had been badly treated during the Cultural Revolution. Although he had been a prominent Party leader for years with a reputation as a superb administrator, he had been placed under house arrest and forced to do manual labor in the outlying provinces. Zhou brought Deng back to power as vice premier in 1973. Zhou, who was somewhat younger than the 80-year-old Mao, had been diagnosed the preceding year as suffering from stomach cancer. China's leadership was nearing a major change, an event that took place in 1976 when first Zhou and than Mao died within nine months of each other.

Evaluating the Cultural Revolution

For China, the Great Proletarian Cultural Revolution was a disaster. Untold numbers of lives were ruined and thousands of people had died. The Party, the government, the professions, and industry had been stripped of much of their best talent. Millions of people had been shipped to the countryside to be reeducated in manual labor camps. The Cultural Revolution left China's education system in a shambles, and an entire generation of Chinese youths had been denied the benefits of a formal education. In addition, industrial production had fallen, and the Communist Party structure was in disarray. On an international level, China was diplomatically isolated.

It is an irony of history that this chaotic and cruel period of Chinese history had been dubbed the Great Proletarian Cultural Revolution. As one historian has explained, the names of history-making events sometimes endure no matter how badly they fit the facts:

> Great? Yes, if this is understood as a reference to the scope of devastation and ravages inflicted upon the Chinese. Proletarian? It is hardly fair to blame it on the working class, who had nothing to do with its initiation. Cultural? It is difficult to find another decade in modern Chinese history when so much damage was done to Chinese culture and its representatives. Revolution? By no stretch of the imagination could it be called a true revolution; it produced only 'great disorder under heaven,' the effects of which were more akin to those of a counter-revolution. [Witold Rodzinski, *The People's Republic of China: A Concise Political History*.]

Check Your Understanding

1. Why do historians think that Mao probably began the Cultural Revolution as a means of preserving his power?
2. Who were some of the main targets of the Cultural Revolution?
3. **a.** What part did the Red Guards play in the Cultural Revolution? **b.** What was the primary object of the Red Guards' fury?
4. For what reason does the historian quoted above think the Great Proletarian Cultural Revolution was misnamed?
5. *Thinking Critically:* What effect did the Cultural Revolution have on education in China? What were some other effects the Revolution had on China? How do you think it affected the Communists' aim of making China into a new society?

5. China's International Relations Under Mao

"Countries," the old saying goes, "have no permanent friends or foes, only permanent interests." The rulers of China, Communists and non-Communists alike, have all sought to create a ring of friendly and weak states along China's borders. Chinese rulers have also attempted, not always successfully, to prevent outside powers from establishing a position of influence in the nations bordering China.

In pursuing their foreign policy, the Communists' tactics have varied with the circumstances. When the situation permitted, Mao encouraged the creation of governments that would be neutral in the confrontation with "imperialist powers." When this technique did not suit China's purposes, China worked for the weakening or overthrow of nearby governments. China was also willing to demonstrate its military strength, as it did in the cases of Korea and India. Thus in foreign policy, Mao and his advisers were "broken-field runners," constantly shifting course but never losing sight of their main goal.

The Korean War

Not long after the Communist takeover of China, the Communist Army, which was called the People's Liberation Army (PLA), again went into action but this time in Korea, a neighboring country. In 1910, Korea had been annexed by Japan. After World War II Korea was occupied by American and Soviet troops. Soviet forces occupied that part of Korea that lay north of the 38th parallel. American troops were stationed in the area south of that boundary. In late 1948 the Soviet Union withdrew its forces from North Korea after a Communist government had been set up there. Meanwhile, elections in South Korea had established a government that had the support of the United States.

In June 1950, troops of the North Korean government invaded South Korea. Within a matter of days, military forces from the United States and from other member countries of the United Nations had been rushed to South Korea's defense. After a bloody struggle, South Korean and American troops drove as far north as the Yalu River, which separates Korea from China. It seemed at that moment that the conflict might soon end and that a divided Korea could be reunited. However, a new phase of the conflict suddenly began in the fall of 1950 when military troops of Communist China crossed the Yalu River into North Korea.

The United States and most members of the United Nations condemned China's entry into the Korean War as an act of aggression. Mao Zedong obviously thought differently. Like past leaders, he thought that protecting Manchuria, on the border between China and Korea, was vital to China's safety. Manchuria contained valuable natural resources and considerable heavy industry, and its loss would hamper China's industries. Probably from fear that an invasion of the People's Republic was about to take place, Mao sent the army into Korea.

After the People's Liberation Army entered the conflict, fighting seesawed up and down the Korean Peninsula until 1953. In that year the fighting ended with an armistice that left the country divided almost at the same place that the fighting began—the 38th parallel. Terms of the peace agreement called for the establishment of a **demilitarized zone** along the boundary between North and South Korea and a joint United Nations–Communist military armistice commission. At the beginning of the 1990's this commission was still operating, and peacekeeping forces still patrolled the demilitarized zone.

The Sino-Soviet Split

After Joseph Stalin's death in 1953, signs of a strain in relations between the Soviet Union and China began to appear. The struggle between the two nations was sharpened following the Twentieth Congress of the Communist Party of the Soviet Union, held in 1956. At this assembly, the Soviet leader Nikita Khrushchev delivered a scorching criticism of Stalin and his rule. The denunciation of the deceased dictator disturbed the Chinese Communists, who still supported many of Stalin's views. They were also angry because they had not been consulted on a matter of such crucial importance to Communists everywhere.

At the heart of the dispute were conflicting views on the methods of Communist expansion. Mao Zedong and his followers thought "wars of national liberation" should be encouraged in areas that had been under Western control as colonies. The Soviet leadership frowned on this approach because they thought it could set off a world war that would destroy communism. The Soviets favored a cautious approach based on economic competition with the capitalist nations of the West. Mao denounced the Soviet strategy as timid and cowardly.

Communist China's ideological challenge to the Soviet Union was sharpened by a territorial dispute along the extensive Sino–Soviet frontier. Beginning in 1958, Communist China charged that thousands of square miles of territory in Soviet Central Asia and eastern Siberia rightfully belonged to China. This territorial dispute triggered border clashes and massive concentrations of military forces on both sides of the Sino–Soviet frontier.

The dispute between China and the Soviet Union soon spilled over into other areas of policy, and the accusations made by each side grew more bitter. The Sino–Soviet dispute also divided Communist nations all over the world as both the Soviet Union and China sought their support. Sino–Soviet rivalry was especially strong in the newly independent nations of Asia and Africa where both countries sent aid and technical advisers.

Reestablishing a Hold on Tibet

The Chinese Communists believed that Tibet was part of their country. The borderland of Tibet had been loosely tied to China since the Qing period but had had its own government for a long time. Its hereditary rulers were lamas, who were monks of the Tibetan Buddhist faith. During the decades of confusion following the Chinese Revolution of 1911, Tibet had become practically independent. After declaring that Tibet was part of China, the Communists moved slowly to fasten their control over the mountainous land. But in 1959, clashes between the Tibetans and the Chinese broke out in Lhasa (LAH-suh), the capital of Tibet.

The Tibetan mountaineers fought desperately. But the Tibetans could not withstand the power of the Chinese army, and their resistance was soon broken. During the next few years, the Chinese Communists steadily absorbed the region and its inhabitants into the People's Republic of China. A steady stream of Chinese soon flowed into the area, with the result that by the 1970's the Tibetan people had become a minority in their homeland. Many changes were made in the traditional way of life of the Tibetans, as their economy was integrated into that of Communist China and their homeland became a part of China's security system.

China's Relations with India

During the early years of the People's Republic, the Chinese Communists sought friendly relations with India and the countries of Southeast Asia. They tried to convince these peoples that Western imperialism was their common enemy. This strategy was used with considerable success in 1955 at the Afro–Asian Conference held at Bandung, Indonesia, a gathering of representatives from the nations of Africa and Asia, many of them newly independent. Zhou Enlai sought to persuade the delegates that

China was dedicated to international peace. His efforts were not entirely in vain. Shortly after the Bandung Conference, China and India agreed to "Five Principles of Coexistence." In the agreement the two countries affirmed their desire for peace and their respect for each other's rights. The leaders of China and India also expressed their disapproval of imperialism and war. The pledge was enthusiastically hailed, especially in India, as a long step toward lasting peace.

For a number of years, Prime Minister Jawaharlal Nehru (jah-WAH-har-lahl NAY-roo) of India was a champion of Communist China. Nehru accepted Communist China's assurances that its foreign policy would be peaceful. Although India had its differences with China, Nehru was confident that these could be settled in a friendly way. In the fall of 1962, however, Nehru's confidence in China was badly shaken when the two countries fought a brief war over borders in the Himalayas. Chinese forces inflicted a humiliating defeat on the Indian border garrisons, but the Chinese forces then broke off the action and withdrew a short distance. The People's Republic of China has continued to retain possession of the occupied territory. Relations between China and India remained distant for many years. Only in the mid-1970's did relations slowly begin to improve.

Southeast Asia

Southeast Asia was another neighboring area in which mainland China sought to exert influence. In this vast and strategically important region, however, Communist China concentrated its attention on those areas that were closest to its own frontier. The politically unstable area of Indochina was of primary concern. This area had been swallowed up by France after the 1860's. But after World War II, nationalists and Communists in Indochina resisted France's efforts to reestablish its colonial rule. Following a hard-fought struggle, France was forced to withdraw and the peoples of Vietnam, Laos, and Cambodia achieved national independence.

Vietnam

In 1954, an international conference held in Geneva, Switzerland, decided that Vietnam would be divided along the 17th parallel. The northern half of the country, already held by the Vietnamese Communists, remained in their hands under the leadership of Ho Chi Minh (HOH CHEE MIN). In the southern half, a shaky anti-Communist government was in control. For about 10 years the badly managed and grossly corrupt South Vietnamese government staggered along, bolstered by aid and advisers from the United States. To add to South Vietnam's woes, Communist guerrillas called the Viet Cong used terrorism and sabotage to spread fear and disorder among the villagers.

In 1964 the United States retaliated against attacks on American warships in the Gulf of Tonkin by bombing North Vietnamese naval bases. The possibility that South Vietnam would fall to the Viet Cong led the American government to step up its dispatch of troops and equipment to the nation. At the same time, North Vietnamese military forces came to the support of the Viet Cong. To counter the massive aid furnished to South Vietnam by the United States, both Communist China and the Soviet Union steadily increased their assistance to the North Vietnamese and Viet Cong forces. In 1968 the fury of battle in South Vietnam reached its peak.

President Richard Nixon of the United States, after his election in 1968, launched a plan for the withdrawal of American forces from the Vietnamese war. To ease the way, he had his foreign policy advisor, Henry Kissinger, hold secret discussions with the governments of China and the Soviet Union. As a result of these talks, negotiations for a truce were undertaken by Kissinger with North Vietnamese and Viet Cong representatives. A truce was agreed to in 1973, and American military personnel and support was withdrawn from Vietnam. But the **truce** did not last long. In 1975 the Vietnamese Communist assault upon South Vietnam was renewed. Without American troop and air support, South Vietnamese defenses collapsed. After many years of bloody civil war, the two halves of Vietnam were reunited under a Communist government.

Laos and Cambodia

Not long after the close of World War II, the contest for political supremacy in Vietnam spilled over into Laos. In 1975 after years of warfare, the local Communists, who were called the Pathet Lao, captured control of the government and established the People's Democratic Republic of Laos.

Between 1954 and 1973, Cambodia tried to pursue a middle course between Communist and anti-Communist forces in Southeast Asia. The outcome was tragedy for Cambodia. Charging that Cambodia was being used as a base for Communist attacks upon South Vietnam, a combined American–South Vietnamese force carried the war into Cambodia in 1970. Shortly thereafter the Communist-supported government was overthrown and a new government was set up under Lon Nol, a strong anti-Communist. Cambodian Communists called the Khmer Rouge, who were backed by Communist China, waged a bitter armed struggle against the government of Lon Nol, and toppled it in 1975. In 1978 a Vietnamese army, backed by the Soviet Union, invaded Cambodia. The Khmer Rouge government was overthrown, and a leader friendly to Vietnam was installed. Since then Cambodia has continued to be torn by a struggle among China-backed Communist forces, Soviet-backed Communist forces, and anti-Communist forces. In late 1989 Vietnam removed its troops from Cambodia, but movement toward a peace treaty was slow.

The Issue of Taiwan

The existence of Chiang Kai-shek's Nationalist government on the island of Taiwan continued to anger the Chinese Communists. Mao Zedong could not consider his victory complete as long as the Nationalist leader held out on Taiwan. Mao probably intended to send the army against the island as soon as his grip on the mainland was secure. With the outbreak of the Korean War in 1950, however, Mao's plans suffered a setback. The United States, in a move aimed at preventing the war from spreading into East Asia, announced that its Seventh Fleet would patrol the channel that separates Taiwan from the mainland of China.

The Korean War also convinced the United States government to toughen its policy toward Communist China. An embattled South Korea, a disarmed Japan, and a weak Taiwan were unable to defend themselves against a militant China. Moreover, Communist movements were beginning to gain strength in parts of Southeast Asia. Lacking airpower and seapower, the Chinese did not dare attempt to invade Taiwan in the face of United States opposition.

The "Two Chinas" Impasse

In the years following the Nationalists' retreat from the mainland, the United States gave the government of the Republic of China generous amounts of aid. By 1965, when economic aid ended, the government on Taiwan had received aid amounting to $3.5 billion. American advisers and technicians also helped build up the Nationalist forces and economy. In addition, the United States signed a treaty of defense with the Republic of China. Furthermore the United States maintained its recognition of Nationalist China as the only representative of China in the United Nations.

THE REPUBLIC OF CHINA.

Chiang Kai-shek (above), who died in 1975, is shown inspecting graduates of a military academy. The government of the long-time Nationalist leader strongly emphasized military preparedness. The nation's economic prosperity is shown in this recent photo of Taipei, Taiwan's bustling, modern capital. Children perform a modern dance (below) in honor of Confucius, who lived in the fifth century B.C., illustrating Taiwan's intermingling of traditional beliefs and values with those of the modern world.

With these measures the United States showed the world that it stood firmly behind Taiwan. The American government made it clear that it would oppose an invasion of Taiwan. But the United States also indicated that it would not support a Nationalist attempt to recover the mainland by force. From this impasse emerged the problem of "two Chinas," which continued to agitate the post-World War II world for many years.

American policy toward Taiwan embittered Communist China. For Mao the Taiwan issue was more than a matter of politics. It also became an issue of national pride. The Chinese Communists felt that the continued existence of Chiang's government was a humiliation for China. The stance of the United States was a deep affront to the Communist leaders.

For the United States, the "two Chinas" impasse was also an important issue and was widely discussed. Many Americans supported the government policy that gave diplomatic recognition to the Republic of China on Taiwan and that withheld it from the People's Republic. Still other Americans argued that it was foolish to ignore the facts of international life and pretend that the People's Republic of China did not exist. Advocates of recognition claimed that American interests would be furthered if diplomatic relations were established with Communist China.

Nixon's Policy Shift

A major shift in the China policy of the United States occurred during the first presidential administration of Richard Nixon (1969–1973). Firm in his belief in a "generation of peace," Nixon set to work to decrease the international tensions that had long gripped the United States and the world. An immediate objective was realized when he pulled the United States out of the Vietnam War. Another objective was the relaxation of tensions with the USSR and with Communist China, which had successfully conducted its first nuclear test in 1964. When President Nixon announced in 1971 that he would visit both China and the USSR the next year, governments all over the world hastened to develop friendlier relations with China.

In the fall of 1971 at the annual meeting of the United Nations, a motion was made to admit the People's Republic of China as a member. The same motion had been made and defeated each of the previous 20 years. But this time it passed successfully. Not only was the Beijing government seated as the representative of China, but the Republic of China (Taiwan) was expelled from the United Nations. Moreover, the People's Repub-

(Continued on page 236)

SIDELIGHT TO HISTORY

The Republic of China on Taiwan

The Republic of China, with about 14,000 square miles and about 20 million people, ranks as one of the smaller nations of the world. It consists of the island of Taiwan and smaller islands that make up the surrounding archipelago. The capital of the republic is Taipei. It is located on the main island of Taiwan, which lies about 100 miles from the mainland of China. Taiwan's tropical climate, which in many ways is similar to that of South China, makes agriculture a year-round occupation.

The Republic is controlled by the remnants of the Nationalist government under Chiang Kai-shek that fled to the island in 1949. For many years after his flight, Chiang Kai-shek dreamed of returning to power on the mainland. To this end the Nationalist government gave top priority to military needs, maintaining Taiwan as an armed camp. With the passage of years, Chiang's dream began to fade, and by the beginning of the 1960's, the government started to press forward with programs of economic development. After Chiang Kai-shek's death in 1975, he was succeeded in the presidency by his son, Chiang Ching-Kuo, who died in 1988.

Before Taiwan become the Republic of China's home, the island's main and almost only source of wealth had been its agricultural harvests of rice, sugarcane, and tea. But once the Republic of China was settled on Taiwan, agriculture was improved and vast new areas were opened to cultivation. Even with the heavy demands made upon them, Taiwan's efficient farmers were able to feed a rapidly growing population.

More remarkable, though, was the mushrooming of industrial activity. Factories sprouted up in all parts of the island, turning out petroleum products, electronic equipment, chemical products, textiles, and processed foods for local consumption and for sale overseas. Taiwan's exports soared.

Today the Republic of China maintains a favorable balance of trade with the United States, Japan, and Hong Kong—its main trading partners. The Republic of China now boasts of having one of the healthiest and most stable economies in Asia.

NIXON'S CHINA VISIT.

Relations with the United States and the People's Republic of China improved greatly in 1972 after President Richard Nixon visited China. Chairman Mao and President Nixon (left) shake hands. At a conference Zhou En-lai (above) is at the left next to an interpreter. Henry Kissinger, National Security Advisor, is at Nixon's left. President and Mrs. Nixon (below) also visited the Great Wall of China. Why was Nixon's visit a turning point for China in its world relations?

lic took Taiwan's place as one of the five permanent members of the UN Security Council.

In the fall of 1972 President Nixon visited China and met with Chairman Mao. American–Chinese relations improved greatly after President Nixon's historic visit. Both countries undertook to station official representatives in the other's capital. Trade and cultural relations slowly got under way. China was opened to American tourists, and delegations of Chinese from the People's Republic began to visit the United States. But official recognition of the People's Republic by the United States would come much later. By this time new leaders had replaced the aging Mao and Zhou. Nonetheless, China's place among the world's leading nations was now assured.

Check Your Understanding

1. **a.** What was the background of the Korean War? **b.** How did China become involved in the Korean War? **c.** How did the war affect China's plans for Taiwan?
2. **a.** What effect did the Korean War have on United States policy toward China? **b.** Toward Taiwan?
3. Describe the changing relations between the United States and the People's Republic of China during the Mao years.
4. *Thinking Critically:* In what parts of Asia did Communist China pursue an aggressive foreign policy? What did Communist China hope to achieve through this type of policy? Where did this policy succeed? Where did it fail?

CHAPTER REVIEW

■ **Chapter Summary**

Section 1. Once Mao Zedong and the Chinese Communists had driven the Nationalists from mainland China, they took firm measures to tighten their hold over the country through such repressive measures as a reeducation program, spy networks, and censorship. A brief lifting of censorship called the Hundred Flowers Campaign began in 1956, but censorship was quickly restored when criticism flowed too freely. The

Communists also instituted a new system of government in which all positions of real power were entrusted only to loyal members of the Communist Party.

Section 2. With crash programs such as the First and Second Five-Year Plans, the Communists tried to increase China's industrial output in a short time. While China was rich in many natural resources, it lacked skilled workers and capital, which made progress painfully slow. Communist leaders attempted to make agriculture more efficient by organizing the peasants, first in cooperatives, and later in communes. Agricultural produce was used not only to feed the population but also to buy the necessities for industrialization. But China pushed too fast and too hard. Production quotas were not met, natural disasters led to a series of bad harvests, and social and political turmoil interrupted further progress in industrialization until the mid-1970's.

Section 3. Once in power the Communists attempted to form a new set of traditions and allegiances, but many traditional customs and beliefs endured. The Communists tried to undermine the importance of the family and to raise the status of women. They used educational reform to instill Communist views in the young. They cleaned up cities and erected hundreds of new buildings. They also began public health programs that helped reduce disease and increase life expectancy.

Section 4. The most far-reaching changes in Chinese society took place under the Great Proletarian Cultural Revolution, which lasted from 1966 to 1976. Historians believe that Mao began this period of great turmoil because he needed to bolster his power and because he felt China's people needed to become redirected toward the ideals of a classless society. But the Cultural Revolution, while it maintained Mao in power, plunged China into a decade of turmoil and disruption. The "reforms" carried out by the Red Guards in their drive to abolish the "Four Olds"—old thoughts, old culture, old customs, and old habits—undermined China's educational system and deprived China of many of the very people needed in its drive toward industrialization. The Cultural Revolution did not end until Mao's death in 1976.

Section 5. In making every effort to provide for their nation's security, the Communist leaders in China consistently involved themselves in the affairs of India, Korea, and other nations adjoining China. They also challenged the Soviet Union for world leadership of the Communist movement. For many years the United States refused to recognize China's Communist government. It was also instrumental in denying the People's Republic of China a seat at the United Nations. But in 1971 in a major foreign policy shift, President Nixon relaxed United States opposition to Communist China's admittance to the United Nations. He also visited China in 1972 where he met with the aging Mao Zedong and Zhou Enlai, both of whom died in 1976. Their deaths signalled that a new era of leadership was about to begin for China.

■ Vocabulary Review

Define: counterrevolutionary, reeducation, totalitarianism, censorship, democratic centralism, capital, nationalization, heavy industry, light industry, consumer goods, rationing, black market, cooperative, commune, demilitarized zone, truce

■ Places to Locate

Locate: North Korea, Yalu River, Taiwan, Vietnam, Lhasa

■ People to Know

Identify: Mao Zedong, Zhou Enlai, Jiang Qing, Red Guards, Lin Biao, Liu Shaoqi, Deng Xiaoping, Jawaharlal Nehru, Richard Nixon

■ Thinking Critically

1. Why is the People's Republic of China considered to be a totalitarian state?
2. How is China's totalitarian nature reflected in its government structure?
3. Evaluate China's plan to change the traditional Chinese family system, given its place in more than 2,000 years of Chinese history.
4. Why does the author call the Cultural Revolution "a bizarre episode" in China's history?
5. Discuss the motives that underlay China's relations with the Soviet Union, with the other nations that adjoined its borders, and with the United States in the period from 1949 to 1976.

■ Extending and Applying Your Knowledge

1. Using the card catalog of your local library or your school, research diaries and eyewitness accounts in books, news

magazines, or journals that describe events surrounding the Cultural Revolution and the activities of the Red Guards. Prepare a summary of one of these reports for the class. One such book is *After the Nightmare* by Liang Heng and Judith Shapiro, published in 1986 by Alfred A. Knopf.

2. Using the *Readers' Guide to Periodical Literature*, research news magazine and other reports about President Nixon's visit to China in 1972. Prepare a chronology that lists the major events of Nixon's visit and the people he met with. Include with the chronology a report describing how reporters and other analysts assessed the importance of the visit at that time.

10

China Under Deng Xiaoping

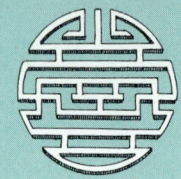

In May and June of 1989, television viewers worldwide watched in fascination as thousands of Chinese thronged into Beijing's Tiananmen Square in support of democracy in China. The 1989 demonstrations with television reporters broadcasting live from the square suggested the extent of the changes that had taken place since President Nixon's 1972 visit and the degree to which China had opened its doors to the world.

Following the death of Mao Zedong in 1976 and the rise of Deng Xiaoping in 1978, the pace of change in China quickened. Deng's policies differed sharply from the policies that had been in effect under Mao, and under Deng's leadership China embarked on far-reaching economic reforms. Agricultural and industrial production rose. International trade multiplied several times over, and the government encouraged foreign investments in China. At the same time many Chinese students went abroad to study. In addition, China opened its doors to tourists who flocked to China to see the changes for themselves. Overall China became a much freer country, as foreigners and Chinese exchanged opinions and ideas.

But in June 1989 television viewers were shocked and outraged as the Deng regime sent troops into Beijing to suppress the pro-democracy movement. Fighting followed, and hundreds of defenseless people lost their lives. Viewers were reminded that repression has been an enduring characteristic of China's history. The government's reaction to the pro-democracy movement suggested that perhaps China had changed much less than many people had been led to believe.

1. The Rise of Deng Xiaoping

For more than 25 years, Mao Zedong had guided the destiny of China. Mao's death in 1976 created a vacuum of power within the Party and the government. Complicating matters further, Communist China had no clearly defined method of choosing a successor. On Mao's death the competition for political leadership between the Maoists and the moderates that had begun in the early 1970's continued. The leader of the Maoists, Jiang Qing, who was Mao's widow, and three others, together were called the Gang of Four. Among the leaders of the moderates was Deng Xiaoping. Immediately after Mao's death the Maoists seemed to have the upper hand, but as events unfolded the moderates managed to win the struggle for control of the Communist Party and China's government, first under Hua Guofeng (HOO-WAH gwah-FUHNG) and then under Deng Xiaoping. Deng's resignation in November 1989 elevated Jiang Zemin to the position of head of the Central Military Commission. It is widely believed that as long as he is able, however, Deng will continue to be the dominant power in China.

The Succession Battle

The death of Zhou Enlai in January 1976 started a struggle for active control of the Party. Zhou Enlai had been Deng Xiaoping's patron and protector. Zhou's death weakened Deng's position in the Party hierarchy, and at a Politburo meeting Hua Guofeng, not Deng, was made acting prime minister to succeed Zhou. In April large demonstrations in Zhou's memory took place in several cities, including Tiananmen Square in Beijing. For many of the demonstrators, Zhou apparently symbolized opposition to the policies of the Maoist radicals. When the Beijing gathering in Tiananmen Square turned into a riot, the Maoist radicals blamed Deng, who was made the object of an immediate **purge** from the Party leadership. It seemed the Maoists led by Mao's widow, Jiang Qing, were now firmly in control.

Mao died on September 9, 1976. Jiang Qing felt that she should become the Party's leader. Within a month of Mao's death, Jiang Qing and the other three members of the so-called Gang of Four were arrested, possibly for plotting a **coup.** Chinese everywhere were overjoyed and toasted the gang's arrest in various celebrations. Accused of a wide variety of crimes, including framing innocent people and ordering their torture, the Gang of Four went on trial in 1980–1981. Two of the four were given long prison sentences. Jiang Qing and the fourth member received suspended death sentences.

> # TIMETABLE
>
> ### China Under Deng Xiaoping
>
> | | |
> |---|---|
> | 1976 | Naming of Hua Guofeng as prime minister and Communist Party leader |
> | | Gang of Four's arrest and imprisonment |
> | 1978 | Beginning of Four Modernizations program |
> | | United States diplomatic recognition |
> | 1978–1989 | Rule of Deng Xiaoping as senior leader |
> | 1978–1979 | Democracy Wall Movement |
> | 1979– | Beginning of responsibility system |
> | 1980 | Replacement of Hua Guofeng as prime minister with Zhao Ziyang |
> | 1980–1981 | Trial of Gang of Four |
> | 1981 | Replacement of Hua Guofeng as Party leader with Hu Yaobang |
> | 1984 | Agreement between the United Kingdom and China on the return of Hong Kong to China in 1997 |
> | 1986 | Replacement of Hu Yaobang as Party leader with Zhao Ziyang |
> | | Naming of Li Peng as prime minister |
> | 1989 | Beginning of pro-democracy movement |
> | | Visit of Mikhail Gorbachev to China |
> | | Replacement of Zhao Ziyang as Party leader with Jiang Zemin |
> | | Massacre in Tiananmen Square; crackdown on protestors and dissidents |
> | | Resignation of Deng Xiaoping |
> | | Jiang Zemin named head of Central Military Commission |

Hua Guofeng's Leadership

Mao's designated successor, Hua Guofeng, became prime minister and leader of the Communist Party. "With you in charge," Mao reportedly told him before his death, "I am at ease." Hua Guofeng was what might be termed a moderate Maoist. Although he sympathized with some aspects of Mao's **egalitarianism,** he

CHINA'S CHANGING LEADERSHIP. When Deng Xiaoping (top) came to power soon after Mao Zedong's death, he had his closest allies in top positions by 1981: Zhao Ziyang (center, left) as prime minister and Hu Yaobang (center, right) as Party leader. When Hu lost favor with Deng in 1986, Zhao was made Party leader and Li Peng (bottom, left) was made prime minister. Following the 1989 revolt, Zhao fell from favor and was replaced by Jiang Zemin (bottom, right), who later that same year replaced Deng.

was willing to compromise with the moderate side of the Party. Most Party leaders were in agreement that the Gang of Four had to be removed from power. But there was no consensus as to what policies the nation needed to pursue—continuing the program of the Cultural Revolution or ending it and beginning a new phase.

To solidify his leadership of the Party, Hua needed to keep Deng in political exile. But Hua was unable to block Deng's rehabilitation and the restoration of his former power. Deng thus became the second most powerful person in China. At the same time, Hua was officially confirmed as leader of the Party.

Below the surface a fierce struggle raged between the Hua and Deng camps. Hua's supporters tried to develop a personality cult for him but without much success. Gradually, Deng's supporters took control. By 1977 they had taken charge of China's foreign policy and had begun to introduce agricultural reforms. In 1980 Hua Guofeng was removed as prime minister and was replaced by Zhao Ziyang (JOW dzuh-YAHNG), a Deng ally. Then in 1981 Hua Guofeng was dropped as Party leader and was succeeded by Hu Yaobang (HOO YOW-BAHNG), another Deng ally.

Deng's Leadership Style

During his rise to power, Deng found it unnecessary to assume the highest positions within the Party or the government. His power came from the personal relationships he had cultivated during his several decades of service in the Party. Also his many years of seniority gave him an aura of legitimacy and authority. Deng was content to place his closest allies in key positions of power. He was a pragmatist, willing to try out new ideas even if they appeared to conflict with Communist doctrine. This attitude had gotten him into trouble more than once.

Like Deng, Zhao had been persecuted during the Cultural Revolution. In 1967 the Red Guards had paraded him through the streets of Guangzhou wearing a dunce cap, and he had been sent to the countryside for four years to do manual labor. Hu had a close working relationship with Deng, going back to the 1940's. During the Cultural Revolution, Hu had been forced to perform two years of agricultural work and then had been placed under house arrest for five years.

The Four Modernizations

Under Deng's behind-the-scenes leadership, China embarked on a program of far-reaching economic reforms called the Four Modernizations. The program included the modernization of agriculture, industry, science and technology, and national defense. The desire to modernize was not new. But the priority given to modernization and the willingness to ignore Maoist emphasis upon egalitarianism and national self-sufficiency was.

In the drive toward modernization, the system of centralized planning was cut back and the economic bureaucracy was streamlined. Agricultural and industrial workers were offered material incentives for hard work. China flung its doors open to international trade and foreign investment. On the whole, Deng's economic reforms gave China the best years it had seen in the twentieth century.

Bureaucratic Reforms

In order to facilitate economic development and to modernize society as a whole, Deng, Hu, and Zhao tried to overhaul the state and Party bureaucracies. At the same time, these three leaders were also seeking to remove political opponents from positions of power and to put their own people in place. The state bureaucracy was vastly overstaffed and the three men set about cutting it back.

When Deng took over the reins of power, the Party organization was filled with uneducated, incompetent officials, many of whom were too elderly to carry out the functions of their jobs. Within the Party and the state, corruption and other types of illegal behavior were rife. The Deng regime made an effort to weed out dishonest and inept officeholders and to bring in those who were younger and better educated. Salaries were raised so that officials would not have to resort to taking bribes in order to make ends meet.

Deng's efforts to eliminate corruption failed. In fact, Chinese society became far more corrupt as the 1980's proceeded. In part, the problem was that the country's economic expansion provided many opportunities for graft for those in key positions. As foreign trade increased and foreign investments flooded into China, the opportunities for payoffs and other illegal activities rose accordingly. Deng and his supporters rarely moved against corruption and **nepotism** in high places. Whom one knew became far more important than hard work or the law. In part, the Deng camp was probably afraid to take action against corruption and nepotism because many Party leaders took advantage of their privileged positions. Indeed even Deng himself was willing to use his personal influence to help family members.

By the mid–1980's considerable opposition to Deng's programs had developed in the Party. Many Party officials feared that the reforms were undermining the prestige and power of the Party. Some called for a return to greater centralized control, while others merely insisted that the pace of change be slowed down. Many Party leaders complained that the reforms had led to a disturbing rise in materialism, selfishness, and rebelliousness throughout Chinese society. They noted that the peoples' commitment to Communist values and objectives was waning and thought that the younger generation seemed preoccupied with acquiring Western goods and in imitating Western styles of behavior and thought. It also seemed that some young people were questioning the Party's wisdom. However, many of the Communist leaders who had made these charges were all too willing to take advantage of corruption and nepotism to make certain that they themselves lived well.

The Democracy Wall Movement

The Chinese Communists were far more cautious about political liberalization than about economic reform. The Chinese approach contrasted sharply with the Soviet experience, which has shown more willingness to undertake political reform than to overhaul their economy. When Mao died, many Chinese hoped that the new regime would permit greater individual freedom. For a brief time it seemed as if their hopes would be realized.

For several months, from November 1978 to March 1979, the government allowed the people considerable freedom to express political views. New journals appeared urging a wide range of demands, including freedom of expression and religion, reform of the Communist Party, and the creation of a multiparty system. Statements that questioned government policy were placed on a particular Beijing wall, which came to be called the Democracy Wall. Thus the entire episode became known as the Democracy Wall Movement.

Suddenly in March 1979, Deng clamped down. The people were forbidden to place posters on the Democracy Wall, and many leaders of the protest movement were arrested. Deng, like Mao in the Hundred Flowers Campaign, learned that freedom of expression resulted in harsh criticism of the regime. By his response, Deng showed a contrast between his willingness to experiment in economic matters and his unwillingness to permit even a modest challenge to Communist Party power.

The Fall of Hu Yaobang

The issue of political freedom remained quiet until 1986. In that year a number of high-ranking political leaders, including Hu

Yaobang, began urging a measure of cultural and political freedom. The call for freedom spread to a number of universities. In December Professor Fang Lizhi, a prominent astrophysicist, encouraged his students to speak out in favor of free elections on the local Party level. Soon students at a number of universities were staging protests demanding democracy and a respect for human rights. In January 1987, after college students in Beijing began to demonstrate, the government banned further protests and warned that violators would be punished. The students' campaign then disintegrated. Many in the Party were furious with Hu Yaobang, claiming that he had encouraged the movement and that when it had gotten out of hand he had been too slow in moving against it. Deng demanded Hu's resignation as a Party leader. In order to maintain the impression of Party harmony, however, Hu was allowed to keep his seat on the Politburo. Zhao Ziyang became the new Party chief, and Li Peng (LEE PUHNG) was named prime minister.

The Pro-Democracy Movement of 1989

In his analysis of the French Revolution, Alexis de Tocqueville wrote that most revolutions do not occur because conditions have gotten worse. More commonly, he explained, revolts take place when a tyrannical regime relaxes its grip. In late spring of 1989 massive protests rocked China. It was the most serious challenge to Communist Party rule in 40 years. Such turmoil had not been seen since the Cultural Revolution. The democratic outbursts that had erupted in 1978–1979 and in 1986–1987 paled next to those in 1989, which started with Hu Yaobang's death on April 15.

The day after Hu died a number of students gathered in Beijing's Tiananmen Square to mourn his passing. The students saw Hu as a leader who had been sympathetic to student demands for greater democracy and more rapid economic reform. The demonstrations grew rapidly in size as more and more students joined and as other segments of the populace began to participate. At one point a million people clogged Tiananmen Square. Soon, too, there were massive demonstrations in Shanghai, Wuhan, and other Chinese cities—an indication that the government had lost control of the situation.

In the United States, the demonstrations were quickly labeled "the pro-democracy movement." But it would be a mistake to assume that the protesters were defining democracy in the same way as Americans and many other Westerners would. The protesters' demands were vague and ill-defined. They called for the freedoms of speech, assembly, and association, and they criticized the nepotism and corruption that pervaded the Party leadership. Many of the demonstrators insisted that Deng, Zhao, and Li step down. At the same time, many of the dissidents emphasized their continuing commitment to Communism and few called for an end to one-party rule.

When the demonstrators refused to disperse, the government declared **martial law** and threatened to use the army. But for several weeks no action was taken. Many in China and abroad were surprised by the slowness with which the government moved to quell the demonstrations. China scholars in the West surmised that a power struggle was under way weeks before the protests began. At the same time that Prime Minister Li Peng threatened to use force in quelling the demonstrations, Zhao Ziyang, the Communist Party leader, was proclaiming his support of the students. With no one clearly in charge, the government could not act decisively. In addition, Mikhail Gorbachev was visiting China for the first Sino–Soviet talks in 30 years. Retaliation at this time would have been embarrassing to the Chinese. The government also seemed to have had considerable difficulty finding troops that were willing to fire on their fellow Chinese. But on the night of June 3, army units began attacking defenseless demonstrators in Tiananmen Square. The attack became a massacre as several hundred people died and many more were injured in the ensuing fighting. The government later claimed that only a handful of protesters had been killed, or none at all.

In the weeks following the Tiananmen Square massacre, the government tightened its grip over the country. The Chinese pro-democracy movement was silenced—at least for the time being. Thousands of participants were arrested and questioned. Some were tried and executed, and some fled the country. Fang Lizhi, who had encouraged the 1986–1987 democracy movement, and his wife took refuge in the American Embassy in Beijing. The Chinese government issued warrants for their arrest and mounted a huge propaganda campaign to convince the Chinese people that the protests had been part of a counter-revolutionary plot led by Zhao, Fang, and other malcontents. Zhao was stripped of his Party posts, and Jiang Zemin (JEE-AHNG dzuh-MEEN), the former Party leader in Shanghai, was chosen in June 1989 to be the new Party leader. In November, Jiang was named head of the powerful Central Military Commission upon Deng Xiaoping's resignation. As Deng's hand-picked successor, Jiang is expected to continue Deng's policies.

THE PRO–DEMOCRACY MOVEMENT. In the student pro-democracy protest of April 1989, the government and army at first held back. A lone demonstrator was able to bring a column of tanks to a standstill (top). But on June 3, helmeted soldiers began lashing out at students in Tiananmen Square (bottom). By early the next morning, the "Goddess of Democracy" statue (center), which bore a marked resemblance to the Statue of Liberty, had been crushed by a tank, and the army had mounted its bloody assault against the defenseless protestors.

China has likely entered a period of prolonged political instability. The unrest does not mean that China is necessarily moving in the direction of Western-style democracy. The leadership confronts enormous challenges. To millions of Chinese, particularly to those who are better educated, the Party has lost its legitimacy, its so-called "mandate of heaven." China's millions do what the regime tells them to do, but only out of fear. They no longer regard the Party and its leaders with any respect. The issue of freedom aside, the Chinese people crave a much higher standard of living, but this desire is likely to go unfulfilled because the economy is experiencing difficulties. (See Section 2.) Western governments have been distancing themselves from a regime that they regard as ruthless. Most foreign business people are wary of making new investments in China.

Check Your Understanding

1. Why did Mao's death create a political power vacuum?
2. How did Deng's leadership style help to make him China's uncontested leader?
3. **a.** How did Deng attempt to modernize the bureaucracy of the state and the Party? **b.** How successful were these attempts?
4. Why did opposition to Deng's programs develop?
5. Compare the Democracy Wall Movement with Mao's Hundred Flowers Campaign.
6. *Thinking Critically:* What started the Chinese pro-democracy movement of 1989? What were its effects for the students? for the Chinese people as a whole? for the Party?

2. Economic Progress Under Deng

During the 25 years that Mao was in power, China's economy made some noticeable gains. That growth, however, was characterized by periods of spurts and slumps. Once Deng Xiaoping was in power, he began to introduce far-reaching economic changes. Not only did the changes speed up the growth of the economy, they also had an impact on Chinese society. Many changes introduced elements of capitalism into China's Communist system, leading to a blossoming of international trade and an increase in foreign business investments in China. Yet China remains a terribly poor country, and the recent political struggles indicate that its economy is again headed for trouble.

Two Views on Modernization

The Cultural Revolution left China's economy in a shambles. Not until the early 1970's did any economic growth resume. Hua Guofeng knew that the economy had to be modernized quickly. The question was how. Very much an advocate of centralized planning, Hua Guofeng in 1978 announced a 10-year economic plan that was far too ambitious. When Deng and his supporters won the battle for control of the government and the Party, the plan was abandoned. By 1979 Deng was ready to launch new economic initiatives.

Deng argued that those who made the greatest contributions toward modernization should enjoy the greatest rewards. He had no use for anti-intellectualism and the egalitarianism of the radicals. In Deng's view China needed all the help it could get from professional managers, scientists, educators, and skilled administrators. Deng spoke angrily of the Cultural Revolution's practice of requiring senior scientific personnel to spend a good part of their time doing manual labor. Summing up his views, Deng said: "The Academy of Sciences is an academy of sciences . . . and not an academy of cabbage cultivation." Deng was also willing to try out ideas even if they appeared to conflict with Marxist doctrine.

Agricultural Reform

Deng's first steps to invigorate the economy were taken in agriculture. He reasoned that since the large majority of the Chinese people worked on the land, a rise in agricultural productivity would have an immediate impact on the entire economy. In 1979 Deng began to break up the commune system. In its place he established a new agricultural system that allowed peasants considerable autonomy and that rewarded them for hard work. The new policy was based largely on experiments carried out between 1975 and 1979 by Zhao Ziyang in Sichuan province. Zhao's approach emphasized material incentives and was called the **responsibility system.**

The responsibility system spread rapidly throughout China. In this system production teams, usually individual peasant families, were alloted land to use. In return for the use of government land, these peasants agreed to turn over a fixed amount of produce at a stipulated price. Peasants were also allowed to keep any surplus. They could consume it themselves, or sell it on the open market at whatever price they could get. To further encourage the peasants, the government raised the price it paid for many items.

Agricultural production soared, and farm income shot up, doubling between 1978 and 1985. The dramatic rise in peasant income stimulated rural construction and service industries. Some peasant families were even able to afford such luxuries as washing machines and television sets. To some degree urban China also benefited from agricultural reforms. Greater quantities and a wider variety of food were available in city markets. The improvement in the quality and quantity of the food supply demonstrated to urban dwellers that reforms in the economy could bring tangible results.

Deng's agricultural reforms had their critics. Some Party members bemoaned the decline in the Party's control over the agricultural sector. Other critics were troubled by the emergence of a wealthy peasant elite. Still others were concerned over the lack of attention paid to the rural **infrastructure.** The communes had been able to assign farm personnel to irrigation projects, road repair, and soil reclamation. With the breakdown of the commune system, responsibility for these projects was left to local governments. A more widespread criticism of the system came from people in the cities who now could buy more goods on the free market but had to pay higher prices for them.

Changes in Industry

Deng's industrial changes centered around three themes: a weakening of central planning, the introduction of material incentives, and the use of market-related pricing policies. In essence Deng expected each enterprise to show a profit rather than relying on government subsidies to make up for its losses. Decision making by distant bureaucrats was replaced by on-the-spot decision making by local managers. Managers and workers were to be justly rewarded for their good efforts.

Beginning in 1979, a limited number of enterprises, or work units, were selected for an experimental program. Each enterprise received a production quota. Once the quota was filled, the enterprise was free to do as it pleased. It was also able to keep a share of any profit and to purchase materials from any source. In 1982 and again in 1984 the new approach was extended to other enterprises. In addition managerial authority was expanded. However, such heavy industries as iron, steel, coal, and concrete remained under centralized control.

CHANGES IN CHINA'S ECONOMY. The 1980's saw drastic changes in China's economy: a movement away from collectivist austerity and toward individual enterprise. Farmers were allowed to sell their surplus produce on the open market (top, left). Small businesses, like this shoe repair service (top, right), were encouraged. As a result of these changes, the economy grew but so did inflation. Chinese flocked to the gold exchange to buy gold as a hedge against inflation (bottom).

The results of industrial reform have been mixed. Many factory managers and their workers have responded with creativity and hard work. Some enterprises have made large profits. But many others have progressed very little. With about one third in financial difficulty, the government has shown a surprising unwillingness to close down unprofitable enterprises, a promise made when it began reforms.

But industry has been harder to reform than agriculture because of the lack of skilled workers and inexperience in managing businesses without government directives. Furthermore the government has been reluctant to allow managers to fire irresponsible or unproductive workers. The government has also been unwilling to allow market forces to set prices. Rather, bureaucrats decide the prices for most items regardless of how much or how little demand there is for them. In this type of business environment, even enterprises with highly competent managers and workers can easily lose money.

Encouragement of Private Business

In a stunning break with the past, the Deng government decided to permit the creation of privately owned businesses. In the cities millions of people were unemployed. The urban economy was simply not growing quickly enough to absorb all those who were entering the work force each year. Furthermore the cities suffered from a shortage of consumer goods and services. To solve both these problems, the government began in the early 1980's to encourage unemployed city dwellers to set up small businesses. By 1984 more than two million licenses had been issued to hopeful **entrepreneurs.** Many established restaurants, beauty shops, and small textile and appliance manufacturing operations. Many peasants also started privately owned rural industries, such as food processing and manufacturing. Many entrepreneurs have done well, and a few have become quite wealthy.

China's Opening to the West

In the early 1970's Deng Xiaoping and Zhou Enlai tried to reverse China's Maoist course of practicing self-sufficiency, but with only limited success. Both men believed that China would be able to industrialize much more rapidly with the help of Western technology, capital, and management expertise. Following the normalization of diplomatic relations with the United States in December 1978, China began to pursue in earnest economic contact with Western nations. The new policy involved not only the expansion of foreign trade, but also the establishment of foreign business ventures in China.

To encourage foreign investment in China, the Deng regime in 1979 designated four cities on the southeastern coast as special economic zones, or SEZs. In subsequent years several other cities have been added to the list. In the SEZs, investors have been offered various incentives, such as free use of land, tariff exemptions on imports, and reduced taxes. At first many investors were attracted by the cheap labor, a vast domestic market, and the government's incentive package. But difficulties of doing business in China soon emerged. **Red tape,** lack of skilled workers, and hiring and wage practices have hampered business operations. The clampdown following the repression of the pro-democracy movement also caused many foreign investors to withdraw plans and to cut back operations.

Assessing China's Economic Growth

Between 1979 and 1989 China's foreign trade increased greatly, even though it accounted for only 2 percent of the world's trade. Imports are concentrated mainly in the area of technology, with the aim of modernizing China's petroleum industry, the transportation and communication networks, and electric power. China exports textiles, petroleum, food, and handicrafts. China's most important trading partners are Hong Kong, Japan, and the United States. But several conditions that exist in China are likely to hamper China's future economic growth.

Although China has huge resources of coal, oil, and gas, it suffers from a shortage of energy. As China's economy expanded, so did its energy needs, but China's industries use fuel very inefficiently. Oil is one of China's major exports. The income from oil exports helps to pay for China's imports. But the exporting of oil takes away from domestic needs. The problem of fuel shortages is likely to continue unless China uncovers new oil reserves on land or in coastal waters.

China's economy has grown at an impressive annual rate of about 10 percent. But inflation is running at a rate of about 25 to 30 percent a year. Most Chinese people continue to live barely above the subsistence level even though China's **gross national product,** at 286 billion dollars in 1987, was one of the largest in the world. With a population of more than one billion, however, the gross national product translates into a **per capita income** of only about $400 in U.S. currency. While income distribution was far more equal under Deng than it was under Mao, wide disparities in income levels still existed. The higher-level Party and government officials earned far more than the national average of $280. So, too, did many professionals, skilled workers, and successful entrepreneurs.

Another aspect that affects China's economic future is the new assessment that tourists and foreign investors have of China in the 1990's. China needs to reattract foreign investments and income from tourism, which fell off drastically after the Tiananmen Square massacre. For China to continue to attract foreign investments and tourism, its leaders need to make still more political changes if they are to minimize the damage to China's economy.

Social Effects of Economic Reforms

China's society today is a sometimes startling mix of the old and the new. But many of the promises made at the start of the Communist takeover of mainland China have not been fulfilled, especially those regarding the equality of women and men. Forty years after the takeover, women are still experiencing discrimination in employment practices. Women are habitually channeled into lower-paying, less skill-oriented jobs. In general, it is widely accepted that women should be paid less than men, even when they do the same level or amount of work as men. Women also experience discrimination in the Party, the government, and the bureaucracy. Almost all top-level positions are held by men.

The Communists' determined and successful efforts to improve health care throughout China have resulted in a decrease in the death rate and an increased life expectancy for China's newborn. As China moved into the decade of the 1990's, its population exceeded 1 billion. Increases in population seemed to minimize the effects of improvements in the economy for the majority of China's people. Nor have vast numbers of the population ever experienced any improvement in their standard of living.

In an effort to reduce its population growth, China has made family planning a national priority. In 1979 China began to pursue a "one-child family" plan. Preferences in housing, employment, and medical care have been given to those families having only one child. The children of such families are given the opportunity to attend the better schools. At the same time, families having more than one child are likely to be penalized. Peasant families, in particular, have been inclined to ignore the government's one-child limit. The government, however, has been reluctant to penalize farm families because of the tradition-

CHINA IN THE 1980'S. Before the Tiananmen Square massacre, China had gradually expanded its foreign contacts. Imports like this refrigerator began to flow into the country (right). Tourists came in increasing numbers; an American shops in a Beijing market (bottom, right). Some Chinese, like this women's Olympic volleyball team, had a chance to sample the outside world directly (bottom, left).

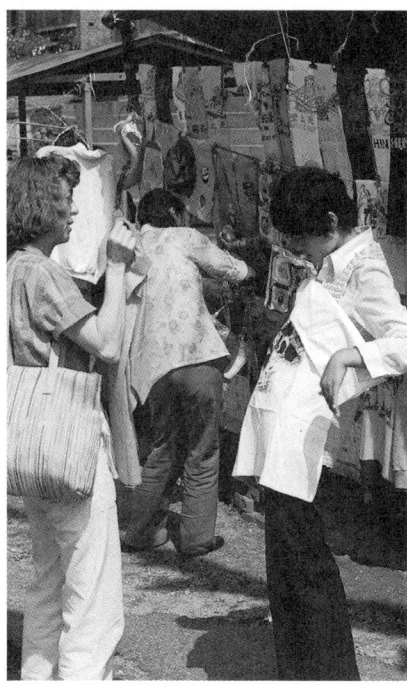

al peasant view that children are a source of labor and provide needed security for elderly parents.

China has made impressive gains in education. Today more than three fourths of the population is literate. After Mao's death in 1976, academic standards were restored to higher education. Only a small number of students, about 4 percent of the student population, has an opportunity to obtain an advanced education.

Check Your Understanding

1. Which of Deng's economic reforms introduced elements of capitalism into China's Communist system?
2. **a.** Why did Deng start his economic reforms in the agricultural sector? **b.** How did critics respond to changes in agriculture?
3. **a.** How did Deng's industrial reforms weaken central planning? **b.** How were material incentives made a part of industrial reform? **c.** In what other ways was China's economy reformed?
4. *Thinking Critically:* A country's politics and its economy are often closely interwoven. What changes in China's economic structure might have affected the people's desire for more freedom? How might China's new-found entrepreneurial spirit be affected by a return to more government control as a result of the pro-democracy movement?

3. China's Foreign Policy Under Deng

If there is a dividing point in China's foreign policy in the last several decades, it is President Nixon's visit in 1972. In the years after this historic meeting, China gradually expanded its contacts with the outside world, and particularly with the West. By breaking out of its diplomatic isolation, China hoped to establish counterweights to Soviet power. Equally important was the hope that Western technology and capital would help stimulate the Chinese economy. Under Deng, China established diplomatic relations with the United States. It shifted in its relations with the Soviet Union from outright hostility to a cautious reserve and a willingness to renew ties of friendship. With Japan, a close economic relationship developed. But China's response to the pro-democracy movement in 1989 cast a chill on its foreign relations with other nations.

Sino-Soviet Relations

During the 1970's, Sino-Soviet relations remained hostile. The Chinese were deeply concerned over Soviet support for Vietnam's invasion of Cambodia in 1978 and the Soviet Union's invasion of Afghanistan in 1979. From China's perspective both attacks were attempts to extend Soviet influence in Asia.

During the Vietnam War, China had limited its involvement in the fighting to military aid and diplomatic support. Over time, the North Vietnamese had established increasingly close relations with the Soviet Union. This trend toward friendly Soviet relations continued after North and South Vietnam were united in 1975. China was not happy about having a Soviet ally on its border. For thousands of years a major objective of China's foreign policy had been to surround itself with friendly, if not submissive, states.

Sino-Soviet relations deteriorated even further when the Soviet Union and Vietnam signed a mutual defense treaty in 1978 that was obviously directed against China. From that time on, China viewed Vietnam's actions with the same hostility it directed toward the Soviet Union. After Vietnam invaded Cambodia in 1978, China attacked Vietnam in an effort to convince it to withdraw from Cambodia. Although Vietnam's forces were badly battered in the short war that followed, Vietnam did not withdraw from Cambodia. China still looks with suspicion on Vietnamese actions in Cambodia. If it can, China will find a way to have an influence on resolving Cambodia's political turmoil.

Sino-Soviet relations reached their lowest point in December 1979 when the Soviet Union invaded Afghanistan. That country, on the Soviet Union's southern border, had an unstable pro-Communist regime. To keep that government in power and to maintain influence in the country, the Soviets sent in troops, deposed the existing ruler, and established a puppet government. Here was one more example, the Chinese said, of the Soviet Union's aggressive designs in Asia.

In 1982 the Soviet Union began to signal its desire for improved relations with China. China showed an interest because it had begun to feel less threatened by Soviet power. China's agricultural reforms had been a great success. China's leaders had high hopes for its industry and the reforms that were under way. Meanwhile, the Soviet economy seemed mired in stagnation. Internationally the Soviet Union was on the defensive.

Soviet leader Mikhail Gorbachev (left) is greeted by Chinese leader Deng Xiaoping (right) prior to talks at the Great Hall in Beijing in May 1989. Their meeting was the first Sino–Soviet summit in 30 years.

With a positive response from China, trade and cultural exchanges between the two countries grew rapidly during the rest of the 1980's. But China insisted that a real improvement in relations would have to await a fundamental shift in the Soviet Union's Asian policy. The Soviet Union would have to pull out of Afghanistan and would have to pressure Vietnam to withdraw from Cambodia. Finally the Soviet Union would have to remove some of its forces from the Sino–Soviet border.

For several years the Soviet Union took no steps to meet the conditions imposed by the Chinese. Then in 1986 Mikhail Gorbachev (gor-buh-CHAWF), the new Soviet leader, announced his determination to establish closer ties with China. By early 1989 the Soviet Union had pulled out of Afghanistan and had withdrawn some of its forces from the Sino–Soviet border. Meanwhile the Soviet Union was pressuring Vietnam to remove its forces from Cambodia.

In May 1989 Gorbachev traveled to China to meet with Deng Xiaoping. It was the first meeting between a top-ranking Chinese and Soviet leader since Khrushchev and Mao met in 1959. The Gorbachev–Deng meeting was the culmination of a gradual improvement in relations that had begun in the early 1980's.

Contact between the two countries was friendlier than it had been in a long time. The relationship may continue to improve, but China and the Soviet Union are unlikely to achieve the closeness they had before Khrushchev's denunciation of Stalin.

One stumbling block is the Chinese insistence on being treated as an equal with the Soviet Union in the worldwide Communist movement. The Soviet Union, however, has never been willing to share leadership in the movement with any nation and is unlikely to change its attitude anytime soon. An important reason for the coolness is that the Soviet Union can do little for China's economic development. China needs Western nations as trading partners and for capital investment.

Sino-American Relations

In the wake of the Nixon visit to China in 1972, Sino-American trade and cultural exchanges rose rapidly. But the diplomatic relationship, while improved, remained at a standstill. During the years 1973–1978, the United States and China maintained a non-diplomatic liaison office in each other's capital. Finally in December 1978, the two countries agreed to establish diplomatic relations as of January 1, 1979.

As part of that agreement, the United States recognized the People's Republic of China as the sole legitimate government of China and broke off diplomatic relations with the Republic of China on Taiwan. The United States also terminated its mutual defense treaty with Taiwan. China for its part made no objection to a continuing economic relationship between the United States and the Republic of China. The Chinese Communists further agreed to the sale of a limited number of defensive weapons to the Taiwan government. In the United States, Congress immediately passed the Taiwan Relations Act, which made possible an on-going, but unofficial, diplomatic relationship with Taiwan. The act created a quasi-official United States agency, the American Institute in Taiwan, and also provided for continued arms sales to Taiwan.

Sino-American relations then improved rapidly, motivated by a joint need to contain Soviet aggression. The United States supplied China with equipment for an electronic observation post near China's border with the Soviet Union. China, in turn, agreed to share the surveillance data with the United States. The United States also began to sell some advanced technology to China.

In 1981–1982, however, Sino-American relations became a bit cooler. The Chinese had apparently concluded that the Soviet threat had ebbed. Also the Chinese were irritated by the unwillingness of the United States to distance itself from Taiwan and by American restraints on Chinese exports to the United States. What the new relationship of the 1980's had lost in closeness, however, it seemed to make up in stability, and throughout the 1980's contact between China and the United States continued to broaden. Two-way trade grew and United States businesses made important investments in China. China's need for United States technology, capital, and markets also continued. The large number of cultural exchanges gave the Chinese and the American people a better understanding and appreciation of each other's culture and history. As the 1980's drew to a close, more than 250,000 Americans were visiting China annually. At the same time, 40,000 Chinese scholars and students were enrolled at United States universities.

In the wake of the Tiananmen Square massacre and the repression that followed, however, Sino–American relations entered another cooling-off period. On the Chinese side, the Deng regime blamed the United States for having encouraged a counterrevolutionary movement. At the same time, the Chinese government announced that it had no intention of altering its domestic political policies to pacify Western political opinion. Still China emphasized its desire for continued investments from the United States and other Western nations. The United States cautiously protested the actions of China, and Congress placed a ban on certain trading policies, acting warily so as not to jeopardize future relations.

China's Taiwan Overtures

Following United States recognition in 1978, the People's Republic of China began to push for reunification with Taiwan. While not renouncing the possibility of using force, Communist China focused on diplomacy to achieve its goal. China's leaders sought to assure the people in Taiwan that reunification did not mean that they would have to live under a Communist system. They put forward the concept of "one country, two systems." Taiwan would be able for many years to retain its capitalist economy and considerable political autonomy. Under the plan, however, sovereignty would be transferred to the People's Republic of China, and Taiwan would become a Special Administrative Region. As such it would have the power to tax and to elect its own legislature. The People's Republic would provide for defense and would appoint a representative to oversee the island's affairs.

Taiwan quickly responded to China's overtures by proclaiming its "three noes" policy: no contact between islanders and mainlanders, no negotiations, and no compromise. By the late 1980's, however, the Taiwan government began to soften its no-compromise stance. In the fall of 1988, Taiwan began to

SIDELIGHT TO HISTORY

Hong Kong and China

In treaties negotiated in 1842 and 1860, China ceded in perpetuity Hong Kong Island and the Kowloon Peninsula to Great Britain. These areas were formed into the British Crown Colony of Hong Kong. In 1898 Great Britain signed a 99-year lease with China for other nearby islands and the part of the mainland adjacent to the Kowloon Peninsula and joined them to the Crown Colony of Hong Kong as the New Territories. The New Territories gave Hong Kong more room for its rapidly growing population, which in the late 1980's was 5.7 million. The majority of the population is Chinese, most of whom are refugees from Communist China.

After the Chinese Communists took over China in 1949, they had the military strength to seize the Crown Colony. But for China it was economically important that Hong Kong remain stable and prosperous because it serves as an intermediary for the two-way trade between China and the West. In 1982 Great Britain and China began negotiations over the leased lands and the rest of Hong Kong. In 1984 Great Britain and China signed an agreement that called for all of the Crown Colony of Hong Kong to revert to Chinese control in 1997. At that time Hong Kong is to become a Special Administrative Region of the People's Republic. For 50 years thereafter, China promised to maintain the colony's capitalist economy and existing social structure. China has further promised that the people of Hong Kong would be accorded considerable local autonomy.

The "one country, two systems" approach of the 1984 agreement is meant to reassure the people of Hong Kong that they will not have to live under a Communist system. Nevertheless, Hong Kong residents have remained apprehensive about the future. In the years since 1984 a slow but steady stream of people, often the more affluent and better educated, have left Hong Kong. After the Chinese government's crackdown of the 1989 pro-democracy movement, requests for emigration visas accelerated. At stake is Hong Kong's status as the financial hub of Southeast Asia and its top-ranked export economy.

allow its citizens to visit relatives on the mainland, and the government looked the other way as indirect trade developed between Taiwan and the mainland.

Even before China smashed the pro-democracy movement, many people found it difficult to imagine Taiwan willing to accept reunification with the mainland. They pointed to the many differences between Taiwan and China, especially the wide gap in living standards. In 1988 China's per capita income was about $400, while Taiwan's approached the $4,000 mark. Yet during the 1980's the People's Republic managed to convince many Taiwanese of its peaceful intentions. The Taiwan government was fighting a losing battle trying to convince its citizens to distrust the Communists. By their actions in 1989, however, the Chinese Communists undid their own propaganda.

Sino-Japanese Relations

Economic relations between China and Japan was negligible for many years following World War II. In the wake of the Nixon visit to Beijing in 1972, Japan extended diplomatic recognition to the People's Republic. Trade increased rapidly, and by 1975 Japan was China's principal trading partner. In the years since Deng Xiaoping's rise to power, trade between China and Japan has continued to grow. In general the Chinese export raw materials and labor-intensive products to Japan and import advanced technology goods and capital equipment. Japan is also the largest foreign investor in China. Japanese business people see China as a source of cheap labor and as a massive market for their many manufactured products.

Although China and Japan have developed a mutually beneficial relationship, the Chinese remain wary of their island neighbors. The Chinese people remember all too well Japan's

Symbolic of Hong Kong's capitalist economy is its stock exchange, shown here. By agreement with Britain, China takes control over Hong Kong in 1997, but has promised to allow capitalism to continue there for at least fifty years.

aggression of the past. Continued suspicion of the Japanese has exerted a retarding influence on the economic contacts between the two nations.

More so than any other Western nation, Japan was reluctant to criticize the repression in China in the late 1980's. Given Japan's record of aggression in China, the Japanese government tried hard to avoid even the appearance of interference in China's internal affairs. Also Japan did not want to risk disrupting its economic ties with China.

Check Your Understanding

1. **a.** What events affected Sino–Soviet relations under Deng Xiaoping? **b.** What caused the turn-around that resulted in renewed ties of friendship?
2. **a.** To what extent did Sino–American relations change under Deng? **b.** What effect did the Tiananmen Square massacre have on Sino–American relations?
3. **a.** What overtures did the People's Republic make toward Taiwan regarding unification? **b.** How did the Taiwanese government respond to these overtures?
4. What special relationship exists between China and Hong Kong?
5. *Thinking Critically:* Discuss the effects of China's 1989 repression of the pro-democracy movement on its foreign relations. What actions do you think China needs to take to overcome what one journalist has called "China's Great Leap Backward"?

CHAPTER REVIEW

■ Chapter Summary

Section 1. After Mao's death in 1976, radicals and moderates vied for power, with the moderates eventually winning out. Changes in leadership took place whenever a crisis arose. After 1978, however, Deng Xiaoping was firmly in power, although he preferred to have his friends in outward positions of leadership. Under Deng, China began its period of Four Modernizations, instituting many reforms in the bureaucracy.

Several periods occurred in which the people were allowed some leeway in expressing opinions, but each period of free expression was short-lived as repression followed. The most severe repression occurred when the government sent the army to put down the pro-democracy movement in Tiananmen Square. Jiang Zemin was named head of the Party in June and head of the Central Military Commission in November 1989, following Deng Xiaoping's resignation.

Section 2. Economic changes that smacked of capitalism helped China to make rapid progress toward industrialization and increase agricultural productivity. Private businesses were encouraged, and foreign investments helped to spur China's economy. Many economic reforms had an impact on society in China, although some promises made by the Communists never materialized. One notable lack of progress was in equality of the sexes. While improvements in women's lot were made, discrimination in employment, in the government, and in the bureaucracy existed. Efforts to curb China's rapid population growth resulted in a one-child family campaign.

Section 3. A turning point in China's relations with foreign nations occurred after President Richard Nixon of the United States visited China in 1972. From that point on, China was recognized by many foreign governments, including the United States in 1978. Sino–Soviet relations, however, remained cool during most of the 1980's because of China's view that the Soviet Union was overly aggressive in Asia. Efforts to induce Taiwan to join with the mainland continued to fail. But repercussions from the Tiananmen Square massacre have continued to affect China's relations with the outside world.

■ **Vocabulary Review**

Define: purge, coup, egalitarianism, nepotism, martial law, responsibility system, infrastructure, entrepreneur, red tape, gross national product, per capita income

■ **Places to Locate**

Locate: Hong Kong, Taiwan, Beijing, Shanghai, Vietnam, Soviet Union, Cambodia

■ **People to Know**

Identify: Hua Guofeng, Jiang Qing, Zhao Ziyang, Hu Yaobang, Li Peng, Jiang Zemin, Mikhail Gorbachev

■ **Thinking Critically**

1. Why have corruption and nepotism continued to plague China regardless of the ruling group in power?
2. Which reforms begun under Deng do you think are likely to be long-lasting? Explain your reasoning.
3. Why is China's size both an advantage and a disadvantage in its drive toward modernization and industrialization?

■ **Extending and Applying Your Knowledge**

1. Using reports from newspapers, news magazines, and other journals, draw up a chronology of events concerning the pro-democracy movement in China, beginning with the death of Hu Yaobang. Use the chronology to develop a timeline of events showing democracy's progress, or lack of it, in China.
2. Using various statistical sources, such as almanacs and yearbooks and data from the Population Reference Bureau, prepare a chart showing China's population growth in the twentieth century. Indicate projections of China's growth up to the year 2100.

APPENDIX

BIBLIOGRAPHY

General Works

A Source Book in Chinese Philosophy, compiled and translated by Chan Wing-tsit. Princeton University Press, 1963. A challenging collection of philosophical works.

Chang Kwang-chih, ed. *Food in Chinese Culture: Anthropological and Historical Perspectives*. Yale University Press, 1977. This is a fascinating study of food as a reflection of Chinese culture, not a book of recipes.

Ebry, Patricia Buckley. *Chinese Civilization and Society: A Sourcebook*. The Free Press, 1981. A book of primary source materials focusing on sociological and anthropological issues.

Fairbank, John K. *The United States and China*, 4th ed., enlarged. Harvard University Press, 1983. A comprehensive history that includes an extensive bibliography.

Fairbank, John K., Edwin O. Reischauer, and Albert M. Craig. *East Asia: Tradition and Transformation*. Houghton Mifflin, 1989. A masterful survey of East Asian history.

Gernet, Jacques. *A History of Chinese Civilization*, trans. by J. R. Foster. Cambridge University Press, 1982. A comprehensive survey of Chinese history focusing on the pre-republic period.

Hsü, Immanuel C. Y. *The Rise of Modern China*, 37th ed. Oxford University Press, 1984. A solid history of China from the Qing dynasty to the early 1980's that emphasizes political and diplomatic developments.

Rodzinski, Witold. *The People's Republic of China: A Concise Political History*. The Free Press, 1988. A solid political analysis.

Sivin, Nathan, ed. *The Contemporary Atlas of China*. Houghton Mifflin, 1988. A modern atlas that surveys the land and people of China with authority, depth and precision.

Sources of Chinese Tradition, compiled by William Theodore de Bary, Chan Wing-tsit, and Burton Watson, 2 vols. Columbia University Press, 1960. A compilation of traditional Chinese thought, admirably translated.

Tregear, T. R. *A Geography of China*. Aldine Publishing Company, 1965. A detailed examination of China's geography.

Van Slyke, Lyman P. *Yangtze: Nature, History, and the River*. Addison Wesley Company, Inc., 1988. An examination of the famous river against the backdrop of Chinese history.

Ancient and Imperial China: Chapters 1–6

Carter, Thomas F. and L. Carrington Goodrich. *The Invention of Printing in China and Its Spread Westward*, 2nd ed. Ronald Press, 1955. A fascinating volume useful for the study of the cultural history of both Asia and Europe.

Creel, Herrlee G. *Confucius and the Chinese Way.* Harper, 1960. An outstanding study of the life and thought of China's great philosopher.

Grousset, Rene. *Conqueror of the World,* trans. by Marian McKeller and Denis Sinor. Orion Press, 1966. An exceptional biography of Ghenghis Khan in a fine English translation.

Hart, Henry H. *Marco Polo: Venetian Adventurer.* University of Oklahoma Press, 1967. A lively account of the celebrated traveler in imperial China.

Hucker, Charles O. *China to 1850: A Short History.* Stanford University Press, 1978. A solid introduction to Chinese history until the mid-nineteenth century.

Keightley, David N., ed. *The Origins of Chinese Civilization.* University of California Press, 1983. A collection of 17 articles that looks at the emergence of Chinese civilization during the period 5000 to 500 B.C.

Loewe, Michael. *Everyday Life in Early Imperial China During the Han Period, 202 B.C.–A.D. 220.* A look at government and ordinary life in Han China.

O'Connor, Richard. *The Spirit Soldiers: A Historical Narrative of the Boxer Rebellion.* Putnam, 1973. A lively account of the anti-foreign explosion in China at the opening of the twentieth century.

Reischauer, Edwin Oldfather. *Ennin's Travels in T'ang China.* Ronald Press, 1955. The adventures and observations of a Japanese Buddhist monk who visited China in the ninth century.

Spence, Jonathan. *The Death of Woman Wang.* Viking Press, 1978. A portrait of daily life in seventeenth century China.

Wright, Arthur Frederick. *Buddhism in Chinese History.* Stanford University Press, 1959. An illuminating interpretation of the role and influence of Buddhism in Chinese history.

The Republic: *Chapters 7 and 8*

Barnett, A. Doak. *China on the Eve of the Communist Takeover.* Praeger, 1964. A collection of absorbing first-hand reports written in 1948–1949.

Bianco, Lucien. *Origins of the Chinese Revolution, 1915–1949,* trans. by Muriel Bell. Stanford University Press, 1971. A challenging interpretation of the Chinese Revolution.

Clubb, O. Edmund. *Twentieth Century China,* rev. ed. Columbia University Press, 1972. A detailed and informative review of China in recent times.

Payne, Robert. *Chinese Diaries (1941–1946).* Weybright and Talley, 1969. A gifted writer's reminiscences of life in China during World War II.

Pruitt, Ida. *Old Madam Yin: A Memoir of Peking Life.* Stanford University Press, 1979. Life in Peking (Beijing) during the turbulent 1920's.

Schiffren, Harold Z. *Sun Yat-sen: Reluctant Revolutionary.* Little Brown, 1981. A solid biography of the Chinese revolutionary.

Tuchman, Barbara. *Stilwell and the American Experience in China, 1911–1945.* Bantam Books, 1972. A beautifully written biography of a famous American army officer who spent much of his military career in China.

China Under the Communists: *Chapters 9 and 10*

Butterfield, Fox. *China, Alive in the Bitter Sea.* Bantam Books, 1983. A fascinating portrait of Chinese society in the early 1980's.

Heng, Liang and Judith Shapiro. *Son of the Revolution.* Alfred A. Knopf, 1981. An eyewitness account of the Cultural Revolution.

Meisner, Maurice. *Mao's China and After, A History of the People's Republic.* rev. ed. The Free Press, 1986. A solid analysis of China under Communist rule.

Salisbury, Harrison. *The Long March: The Untold Story.* Harper and Row, 1985. No new revelations, but well done.

Satzmann, Mark. *Iron and Silk.* Random House, 1986. The autobiographical account of an American college student who taught English and studied martial arts in China.

Schell, Orville. *In the People's Republic.* Random House, 1977. A perceptive eyewitness account of China in the mid–1970's.

Wilson, Dick. *Zhou Enlai: A Biography.* Viking, 1984. A balanced and readable biography of the famous Chinese leader.

Wolf, Margery. *Revolution Postponed: Women in Contemporary China.* Stanford University Press, 1985. An examination of women's status in post-revolutionary China.

Worden, Robert L., et. al. eds. *China: A Country Study.* United States Government, 1988. A solid survey of contemporary China.

GLOSSARY

This Glossary contains definitions for the social studies terms used in this volume about Chinese history. These terms are printed in bold type the first time they appear in the text. The page number following each definition tells you the page on which the word is first used. Often words have more than one meaning. The definitions given below are the ones that will be most helpful to you in reading this book.

acculturation process by which a culture absorbs the characteristics of another culture (28)
alliance association of nations or groups based upon mutual purpose, interest, or advantage (180)
ambassador diplomatic representative (112)
annexation the process of adding territory to an existing country (137)
aristocracy privileged upper class (38)
autonomous region territory governed as an administrative or political unit of China, either originally or largely inhabited by ethnic minorities (3)

balance of trade conditions that exists between imports and exports of a country; the balance is favorable when exports exceed imports, unfavorable when imports exceed exports (114)
banner Manchu military division (100)
black marketeer person who buys or sells goods illegally (193)
blockade action that closes, or seals off, an area (178)
block printing type of printing in which sheets of paper are pressed against inked blocks of carved wood containing raised characters (84)
boycott organized refusal, often to purchase goods (155)
brotherhood organization, such as the White Lotus Society that promoted rebellion against oppressive Qing rulers (108)
buffer region or territory located between unfriendly powers that acts as a deterrent to war (173)
bullion uncoined precious metal, such as gold or silver, usually in the form of ingots, or bars (114)

calligraphy expert use of the brush in Chinese writing (63)

capital resources used to produce goods and services (208)

catapult ancient military device used to fling rocks, bombs, and other types of missiles (84)

censor traveling investigator of the Qing censor system (103)

censorship policy of stopping publication and distribution of literature, art, or any creative material found objectionable by the government or other authority (203)

censor system practice of the Qing dynasty that used traveling investigators to search out abuses of power and corruption in government (103)

central government kind of government in which authority is concentrated in a single organization or unit (54)

China Proper the east central section, or heartland of Greater China (2)

civilization level of society determined by technical and intellectual achievement (1)

clan group of families or a small tribal community (26)

classical age period during which a flowering of art, thought, and other forms of culture arose (43)

commune agricultural unit larger than a cooperative formed by the Chinese Communists that was operated for the benefit of the government (211)

communism system of government in which the state owns all land and controls production of goods and services; one political party maintains power with the goal of distributing all goods equally to the people (164)

compromise settlement of differences through concessions (149)

Confucianism philosophy based on the teachings of Confucius (44)

constitution document that sets forth the guiding principles and basic laws of a constitutional government (140)

consumer someone who buys and uses goods and services (156)

consumer goods materials such as food and clothing purchased by people for their own use (208)

cooperative agricultural unit formed by the Chinese Communists that was operated for the benefit of the government (211)

counterrevolutionary person who opposes a revolution and attempts to restore the government previously in power (202)

coup sudden overthrow of a government (241)

cultural diffusion spread of cultural characteristics from one group to another (28)

demilitarized zone area established along the 38th parallel between North and South Korea that was to be free of military installations and forces (227)

democracy system of government in which citizens govern directly or through elected representatives (162)

democratic centralism underlying principle of Communist Party policy that all major issues must be discussed at all levels of the Party before final decisions are reached; in practice decisions are made by the Politburo (205)

dialect language variation (25)

dictator ruler exercising absolute authority over the government (150)

diplomatic mission building that housed an ambassador (112)

divination art of trying to foretell the future (38)

double-cropping practice of growing a second crop within a single growing season (6)

dynasty line of families that transfers its right to rule by inheritance (2)

egalitarianism policy espoused by Mao Zedong under which all people in China were to be treated equally, peasants and officials alike (242)

empire state and the conquered lands that it rules (2)

entrepreneur person who starts up and operates his or her own business (254)

ethical system basis for judging the behavior of individuals and groups (44)

extraterritoriality provision by which Western nations were granted special privileges in China (125)

factory place in China where an artisan worked (68)

feudalism economic, social, and political system in which upper-class landowners gave lower classes protection and land in exchange for labor or military service (42)

filial piety Confucian ideal of good behavior (45)

gross national product total value of goods and services produced annually in a country (255)

guerrila warfare type of fighting characterized by surprise attacks and hit-and-run tactics (177)

heavy industry manufacture of steel, machines, transportation equipment, and machinery to make these goods (208)

nationalism feeling of devotion to and pride in one's country (162)
nationalization policy of bringing privately owned resources or industries under government control and ownership (208)
Neo-Confucianism philosophy of Zhuxi that combined the teachings of Confucianism, Buddhism, and Taoism into a unified system (91)
nepotism corrupt policy under which relatives of government officials and Party leaders receive favorable treatment (245)
nirvana Buddhist term for a state of enlightenment (71)

oral tradition stories, folk tales, poetry, and songs passed from one generation to the next by word of mouth (35)

paddy wetland in which rice is grown (15)
parliament legislative body that creates the laws of a state (140)
per capita income average income of the people in a nation (255)
philosopher someone who studies philosophy (44)
phonetic alphabet set of symbols based on spoken sounds that form a written language (30)
pictograph picture used in writing, especially by ancient Chinese (28)
Pinyin phonetic system of writing Chinese using the Western alphabet (30)
prehistoric characteristic of the time before people kept written records (2)
prejudice adverse view or hostility held by one individual or group toward another without just grounds (68)
protectorate nation, state, or territory that depends on a stronger country for defense and foreign affairs (6)
province territory governed as an administrative or political unit of China (3)
puppet emperor ruler who fronts for the person or persons who really exercise the ruling power (71)
puppet government political organization controlled by a foreign power (174)
purge persecution, exile, and possible execution of Communist Party members to eliminate opposition or to punish mistakes (167, 241)

queue hair style called a pigtail imposed on Chinese males by the Qing rulers as a sign of subjugation (105)

ideograph combination of symbols in Chinese writing, us[ed to] convey an idea (28)
illiteracy inability to read and write (157)
imperialism policy by which a nation extends its control [over] other lands to gain an economic or political advantage (1[ ])
indemnity compensation for war damages (116)
industrialization movement of an economy away from ag[ricul]ture and trade and toward industry and technological adv[ance]ment (30)
infrastructure equipment, roads, railroads, airports, comm[uni]cation networks, buildings, and other basic works that en[able a] nation's economy to function (252)

khan prince of Mongolia (79)
kowtow elaborate system of behavior consisting of nine bow[s or] prostrations, that signaled utmost respect of an inferior to [a] superior, usually the emperor (111)

Legalism Chinese philosophy of third century B.C. that assumed people were evil and selfish and lived well only unde[r] strict rules (47)
Legalist follower of Legalism (49)
legation official residence of a diplomatic representative, suc[h] as a minister or ambassador (137)
light industry manufacture of foods, textiles, and other good[s] that do not require large machines (208)
literacy ability to read and write (29)
loess fertile soil composed of fine particles deposited by the wind (5)
Long March journey of Mao Zedong and thousands of support[]ers across China to escape Nationalist forces (178)

Mandate of Heaven traditional Chinese belief that rulers needed the gods' approval to stay in power (46)
martial law control of an area by military rule (248)
mercenary paid professional soldier (122)
modernization process of replacing traditional ideas and systems with more recent ones (7)
monopoly control of a service or product and its price by a single source (63)
monsoon seasonal winds that bring torrential rains when they blow over oceans before reaching land or that bring periods of drought when they blow over land toward the oceans (6)

rationing system of distributing goods equally during times of scarcity (208)

red tape bureaucratic rules and regulations that often result in delay (255)

reeducation process used by Chinese Communists to bring the thinking of non-Communists into line with Communist thought (202)

regent acting ruler; often used when a sovereign ruler is under age (128)

republic government in which citizens elect representatives to govern them (141)

responsibility system economic approach established by Deng Xiaoping that established work units and free enterprise zones and that emphasized material incentives (251)

revolutionary someone who advocates revolution (146)

scholar-official member of China's government bureaucracy (64)

Silk Road route that silk merchants traveled westward from ancient China to India, Persia, and the Mediterranean (10)

social class division of society (63)

socialism political and economic system under which the government owns and controls the means of production and operates them for the welfare of all citizens in society (163)

social order ranking of class divisions within a society (65)

sovereign relating to supremacy or authority to rule (125)

sovereignty supremacy of authority or rule (40)

sphere of influence region in which another nation claims the right to exercise economic and political control (135)

strategic location area with strong military defense possibilities (11)

Taoism Chinese philosophy based on discovering the Tao, or "way," of the universe and living in harmony with nature (47)

tariff tax on imports (126)

terrace leveled strips of land on the sides of hills and mountains (6)

totalitarianism form of government in which one person or party exercises complete control over all aspects of life and excludes all opposition to its policies (202)

trade union group of workers in the same trade organized to promote their interests (156)

tradition set of enduring customs and patterns from the past that influence the present (62)

treaty port coastal trade center in China in the 1800's where Westerners were allowed to conduct business (116, 156)

tributary system process, beginning with the Han and continuing through all subsequent dynasties, by which the Chinese allowed rulers of border states to stay in power through an exchange of tribute and the development of familial ties (54)

tribute money and goods paid to Han dynasty rulers by local rulers of border states (57)

truce period of cease-fire (230)

unequal treaty one of a series between Qing China and Western nations in the 1800's that forced China to accept trade conditions dictated by foreigners (125)

veto power authority to nullify an action (126)

warlord ruler of a limited area, usually exercising power through force (150)

ACKNOWLEDGMENTS

Text Credits

Chau Ju-kua: His Work on the Chinese and Arab Trade in the Twelfth and Thirteenth Centuries, translated by Friedrich Hirth and W. W. Rockhill, (St. Petersburg, Imperial Academy of Sciences, 1911) pp. 33–34. Hummel, Arthur W., ed. *Eminent Chinese of the Ch'ing [Qing] Period, (1644–1912)*, 2 vols. (Washington D. C., United States Government Printing Office, 1943) Vol. I, p. 300. Marshall, George C. "Personal Statement by the Special Representative of the President, January 7, 1947," in *United States Relations with China* (Department of State Publication 3573, August 1949) p. 687. *Memories of Father Ripa*. selected and trans. from the Italian by Fortunato Prandi (New York, John Wiley, 1849) pp. 59–60. Polo, Marco, *The Travels of Marco Polo the Venetian* (New York, E. P. Dutton, 1908), p. 118. Rodzinski, Witold, *The People's Republic of China: A Concise Political History*. (New York, The Free Press, 1988) p. 119. Reprinted with the permission of The Free Press, a division of Macmillan, Inc., and William Collins, PLC, London. Sun Yat-sen, *San-min chu-i: The Three Principles of the People*, trans. by Frank W. Price (Chungking, Ministry of Information of the Republic of China, 1943.) pp. 113–114, 168–169, 171. *The Jade Mountain: A Chinese Anthology, Being Three Hundred Poems of the Tang Dynasty, 618–906*, trans. by Witter Bynner, p. 53. Copyright 1929 by Alfred A. Knopf, Inc., copyright renewed 1957 by Alfred A. Knopf, Inc. Reprinted by permission.

Art Credits

Book designed by George McLean.
Cover concept and design by Hannus Design Associates.
Cover photograph: P. & G. Bowater/The Image Bank.
Maps: Precision Graphics.
Title Page and Chapter Opener art: Leslie Evans.
Calligraphy, p. 29, by Zunvair Yue

Photographs   **3** Peter Carmichael/Aspect Picture Library Ltd.; **5** Heather Angel; **12** Paolo Koch, Rapho Guillumette/Photo Researchers; **16** *(top)* Emil Schulthess/Black Star, *(bottom)* Marc Riboud/Magnum; **19** *(top and center)* Sovfoto, *(bottom)* Cary Wolinsky/Stock Boston; **22** *(top)* Pan Asia Photo News/Black Star, *(bottom)* Cary Wolinsky/Stock Boston; **29** Sovfoto; **34** American Museum of Natural History; **37** Courtesy of Dr. Shigeki Kaizuka; **39** *(top and bottom right)* Smithsonian Institution, Freer Gallery of Art, Washington, D.C., *(center)* The Cleveland Museum of Art, Anonymous Gift, *(bottom left)* Museum of Fine Arts, Boston, Jacob Hirsch Hecht Fund; **55** Der Stern/Black Star; **63** The Nelson–Atkins Museum of Art, Kansas City, Missouri; **66** *(top)* Museum of Fine Arts, Boston, Ross Collection, *(center)* The Cleveland Museum of Art, Edward L. Whittemore Fund, *(bottom)* Sovfoto; **70** *(top left)* The Cleveland Museum of Art, Mr. and Mrs. Severance A. Millikin Collection, *(top right)* Field Museum of Natural History, *(bottom)* Paolo Koch/Black Star; **79** *(top)* Sovfoto, *(bottom)* Historical Pictures Service, Chicago; **82** From *San ts'ai t'u hui*, Harvard–Yenching Library, Harvard University; **84** Illustration from *History of Rocketry and Space Travel*, © 1966 by Wernher von Braun, Frederick I. Ordway III, and Harry H–K Lange, Thomas Y. Crowell Company, New York; **86–87** Museum of Fine Arts, Boston; **87** *(top left)* The Cleveland Museum of Art, Mr. and Mrs. Severance A. Millikin Collection, *(top right)* The Metropolitan Museum of Art, Rogers Fund; **90** *(top)* The Cleveland Museum of Art, Gift of Hanna Fund, *(bottom)* Fogg Art Museum, Harvard University, Gift of Charles L. Coolidge; **94** Nieuhof: *An Embassy from the East Indian Company of the United Provinces to the Grand Tartar*, Rare Book Room, New York Public Library; **105** From *Ch'ing-tai ti-hou hsiang*, Harvard–Yenching Library, Harvard University; **110** Musée Guimet; **113** Huntington Hartford Collection; **115** Peabody Museum of Salem; **129** Oriental Collection of the late Ernst von Harringa; **131, 132** Essex Institute, Salem, Massachusetts; **136** Charles A. Killie Collection, Hoover Institution; **139** Methodist Prints; **147** Sovfoto; **151, 161** *(top)* Wide World Photos; **155, 161** *(bottom)* European Picture Service/FPG International; **167** Nym Wales; **175** *(top)* Paul Dorsey/*LIFE Magazine* © Time, Inc., *(bottom)* European Picture Service/FPG International; **186, 189, 191** *(bottom)* Wide World Photos; **191** *(top)*, **196, 205** *(top left)* Sovfoto; **205** *(top right)* Bruno Barbey/Magnum, *(bottom)* Bettmann Newsphotos; **206** *(top)* Sovfoto, *(bottom)* Marc Riboud/Magnum; **210, 214, 216** *(bottom)* Sovfoto; **216** *(top left)* Emil Schulthess/Black Star, *(top right and center)* Marc Riboud/Magnum; **217, 222** *(top and center)* Sovfoto; **222** *(bottom)* Frank Fischbeck/*LIFE Magazine* © Time, Inc.; **232** *(top and bottom)* Bettmann Newsphotos, *(center)* Patrick Zachmann/Magnum; **235** *(top and center)* Magnum, *(bottom)* Bettmann Newsphotos; **243** *(top)* FPG International, *(center and bottom)* Wide World Photos; **249** *(top and center)* Stuart Franklin/Magnum, *(bottom)* J. Langevin/Sygma; **253** *(top left and right)* Susan Van Etten, *(bottom)* Alon Reininger/Contact Press Images; **257** *(top)* Jean–Pierre Laffont/Sygma, *(bottom left)* David Burnett/Contact Press Images, *(bottom right)* Susan Van Etten; **260** Wide World Photos; **264** COMSTOCK, INC./Hartman–Dewitt.

INDEX

This index includes references not only to the text of the book but also to charts, graphs, maps, and pictures. These may be identified as follows: *c* refers to a chart; *g* refers to a graph; *m* refers to a map; *p* refers to a picture.

A

acupuncture, 88, *p*217, 218
Afghanistan, 258, 259, 260
Afro-Asian Conference, 228–229
agriculture, *m*4; of North China, *p*3, 5–6, 15, 16, 17; of South China, *p*5, 6, 15–16, 17; of Northeast China, 7; and peasants, 67; during Qing dynasty, 107–108; reforms in, 181–182; cooperatives, 182, 211; under Communist government, 209, 211, 213; under Deng Xiaoping, 245, *p*253, 251–252; communes, 251, 252; responsibility system, 251–252
Allied Expeditionary Force, 137, 138
Allies, of World War I, 154; of World War II, 184, 188
All Men Are Brothers, 92
American Institute (Taiwan), 261
Amur River, 109, 127
ancestors, veneration of, 23
Anyang, 37–38
architecture, housing 13; use of walls in, 36
Army of the Green Standard, 103
art and artisans, of Shang dynasty, 38, *p*39; of Zhou dynasty, *p*39; of Tang dynasty, *p*66; and Confucian class system, 67–68; Buddhist, *p*70; of Song dynasty, *p*90, 91; of Ming dynasty, *p*90, 91

B

backyard furnaces, *p*210
Baihua **(common language),** 158
Bandit Extermination Campaign, 178, *p*183
Bandung Conference, 228–229
banks, peasant, 182
Banners (Manchu military), 100–101
bauxite, resources of, 207
Beijing, *m*8–9; as governmental municipality, 3; Russian diplomatic mission in, 112; English and French capture of, 126; and Boxer Uprising, 137, 138; during warlord period, 151; as capital, 167, 197; changes in, under Communists, 215; Democracy Wall Movement, 246; demonstrations in, 240, 241, 247–250, *p*249. See also Beiping
Beijing University, 154
Beiping, 167, 197; in Second Sino-Japanese War, 185. See also Beijing
Benlong people, *p*19
black market, 193, 209
Bo Gu, *p*167
Borodin, Michael, 160, 165, 167
Boxer Fellowships, 140
Boxer Uprising, 136–138, *p*136
Britain. See Great Britain
bronze work, of Shang dynasty, 38–39, *p*40; of Zhou dynasty, 42
Buddha, 44, 60, *p*70, 71
Buddhism, origin of, 69, 71; art of, *p*70; beliefs of, 71–72; spread of, in China, 72; opposition to, 72–73, 89
Burma, 2, 128; as tributary state, 110, *m*125
Burma Road, *m*183, 187
business, under Communists, 254. See also economics

C

calligraphy, *p*29, 63, 64
Cambodia, 128, 230–231, 259
Canton. See Guangzhou
catapults, 84
Cathay, 77
Catholic missionaries, *p*94, 96
celestial clock, 88
censor system, 103
Central Asia, and spread of Islam, 73
Chagatai, Khanate of, *m*78
Changan, as Han capital, 57
Chang Jiang River, 3, 13–14, *m*18, *m*41, 77
Cheng Ho, *m*78
Chennault, Claire, 187
Chiang, Madame, *p*189
Chiang Ching-Kuo, 234
Chiang Kai-shek, commands Whampoa, 161, *p*161; as leader of Kuomintang, 164–169; and Northern Expedition, 165, 168–169; battles against Communists, 165, *m*166, 167, 168, 172, 177–179, 190–192, *p*191, 193–198, *m*194, *p*196; and

283

Japanese attacks, 176; Bandit Extermination Campaign, 178; kidnapping of, 179–180; in Second Sino–Japanese War, 186, *p*186, 188, *p*189; on Taiwan, 197, 231, 232, *p*232, 234

children, *p*232; and traditional family, 21; and Confucianism, 45; and one-child families, 213, 214–215, 256

China Incident, 184

China Proper, *m*8–9; and Great Wall, 2; population of, 3; geography of, 2–6, *m*4; rivers of, 12–14, *p*12; and Manchu invasion, 100

"China's First Hundred," 131

"China's Sorrow," 13

Chinese people, minority groups, *p*19; physical characteristics of, 20; way of life, 20–24, *p*22

Chongqing, *m*8–9, 13, *m*125; as capital of Free China, *m*183, 185, *m*194

Christianity, and Jesuit missions, *p*94, 96; in Tang dynasty, 73

Churchill, Winston, 188, *p*189

cities, importance of walls around, 36; Communist changes in, 215, 254

civil service examinations, 63, 64

Cixi. See Empress Dowager

Classical Age, 43–46

Classic of Filial Piety, 64

Classic of the Way and Its Power. See Tao Te Ching

class system, and Confucianism, 65–68; and Great Proletarian Cultural Revolution, 220–221

climate, 5–6

clocks, 88

coal, 209; resources of, 207, *m*212, 252

Comintern, 160

commerce. See Foreign trade; Trade

commune system, 211, 215, 251, 252

Communist International, 160

Communist Party (Chinese), and Sun–Joffe Agreement, 160, 164; origin of, 164; battles with Chiang Kai-shek, 165, *m*166, 167, 168, 172, 177–180, 190–192, *p*191, 193–198, *m*194, *p*196; Long March, 178–179, *m*183, *m*189; foreign policy of, 201, 226–236; and Great Proletarian Cultural Revolution, 201, 209, 220–225, *p*222; education policy of, 202, 214, 215, *p*216, 221, *p*222, 223; and censorship, 202–203; and totalitarianism, 202–206; organization of, 204–206; economic policies of, 207–213; social changes under, 214–219, *p*214, *p*216, *p*217; Hua Guofeng as leader of, 241, 242, *p*243, 244, 250–251; Deng Xiaoping as leader of, 244–264, *p*243; bureaucratic reforms in, 245–246; and pro-democracy movement, 240, 247–250, *p*249, 255, 258, 262. See also government; Mao Zedong; People's Republic of China

Communist Party (Russian), 160, 180

compass, 83

Complete Library of the Four Treasuries, 104

Confucian Classics, 46, 62, 64

Confucianism, and Zhou dynasty, 44–46; under Qin dynasty, 62; under Han dynasty, 62–63; and education, 64–66; and class system, 65–68; and opposition to Buddhism, 72–73, 89; and Neo–Confucianism, 89, 91; and tributary system, 109–110

Confucius, 33, *p*70; and value of the past, 23–24; teachings of, 44–46, 49

Constitutional parliamentary government, 140. See also Government Consumer goods, 208, *p*257

cooperatives, 182, 211

copper, resources of, 207, *m*212

corn, *m*4, 107

cotton, 17

coup, 241

Cutural Revolution. See Great Proletarian Cultural Revolution

D

Da Gama, Vasco, 94

Dalai Lama, 11

dance, *p*214, *p*232

defense. See military

demilitarized zone, 227

democracy, Sun Yat-sen theory of, 162–163; and pro-democracy movement, 240, 247–250, *p*249, 255, 258, 262

Democracy Wall Movement, 246

democratic centralism, 205

Deng Xiaoping, as vice-premier, 224; and pro-democracy movement, 240, 247–250, *p*249, 255, 258, 262; and the Four Modernizations, 244–245; as leader of Communist Party,*p*243, 244–264; economic policies of, 244–245, 250–256, *p*253, *p*257; foreign trade under, 254–256; education policies of, 257; foreign policy of, 258–264, *p*260; and Taiwan policy, 262, 264; relations with Japan, 264

dietary habits, 17

divination, 38
double-cropping, 6
"double ten", 147
dragon bones, 37, *p*37, 38
drama, 92
Du Fu, 61
Dutch, trade with, 95, 113–114, *m*126
dynasties. *See* Names of individual dynasties

E

Early Imperial Age, 54–73, *m*58
East Asia, use of term, 95
East India Company, 113–114, 115
East India trade, 95
economics, banks, 182; black market, 193, 209; following World War II, 193; of Communist government, 207–213; under Deng Xiaoping, 244–245, 250–256, *p*253, *p*257; special economic zones, 255
education, and language, 27; and Confucianism, 64–65; under Kangxi, 104; Chinese students abroad, 131, 140, 240, 262; reforms in, 139–140; following World War I, 157–159; reforms under Kuomintang, 183–184; Communist system of, 202, 208, 214, 215, *p*216, 221, *p*222, 223; student demonstrations, 246–247; under Deng Xiaoping, 257
egalitarianism, 242, 244
Eightfold Path, 71
Eighth Route Army. *See* Red Army
elderly, and traditional family, 21
Empress Dowager, 128–130, *p*129, 132; death of, 133, 141; and Boxer Uprising, 137; and government reforms, 140
energy shortage, 255
England. *See* Great Britain
entrepreneurs, 254
Ephedrine, 88
Europe, and Qing dynasty, 112–116
"Ever Victorious Army," 123
extraterritoriality, 125–126

F

family, traditional, 21; and Confucianism, 45; one-child, 213, 214–215, 256
famines, 6, 16
Fang Lizhi, 247, 248
Far East, use of term, 95
Far West, use of term, 95
Feng Yuxiang, *p*151
feudalism, in Zhou dynasty, 42–43
filial piety, 45

firearms, 130, 131; invention of, 84, *p*84
First Emperor, 55
First Treaty Settlement, 124–126
Five Principles of Coexistence, 229
Five-Year Plans, 208–209. *See also* economics
Flying Tigers, 187
foreign mud, 114
foriegn policy, during Qing dynasty, 112–116, 124–128; during warlord period, 152; of Mao Zedong, 201, 226–236, *p*235; of Deng Xiaoping, 258–264
foreign trade, and tributary system, 57; during Qing dynasty, 113–116, *m*125; and balance of trade, 114; boycott of Japanese goods, 155, *p*155, 176; under Deng Xiaoping, 254–256. *See also* trade
Formosa. *See* Taiwan
Four Modernizations, 244–245
Four Noble Truths, 71
Four Olds, 221
France, 113–114, 124, *m*125; and invasion of Beijing, 126; in Indochina, 128; spheres of influence, 135
Free China, 185, 187, 188

G

Gang of Four, 242, 244
Guatama, 69, 71
Generalissimo. *See* Chiang Kai-shek
Genghis Khan, 79–80, *p*79
geography, of China Proper, 2–6, *m*4; of North China, 5–6; of South China, 6; of Northeast China, 7
Germany, 184; spheres of influence, 135
Gobi Desert, 10, *m*18
"Goddess of Democracy" (statue), *p*249
gold, *p*253; resources of, 207
Golden Horde, *m*78
"Golden Rule," 45
Gorbachev, Mikhail, 248, 260, *p*260
Gordon, Charles George, 123
government, current divisions of, 3; and autonomous regions, 6–7; attitude toward Taoists, 49; attitude toward Legalists, 49–50; of Qin dynasty, 50; of Early Imperial Age, 54; and civil service examinations, 63; of Qing dynasty, 102–104, *m*102, 106, 108, 140–141; and tributary system, 109–111, *p*110; reforms in, 140–141, 181–184; republic formed, 145–151; attempts to restore imperial dynasty, 150; in Nanjing, 167–169; Manchukuo puppet government, 174–175, *p*175. *See also* Kuomintang; People's Republic of China

285

Grand Canal, *m*8–9, 14, *m*78
Great Britain, trade with, 95, 113–114, *m*125, 152, 153; and Opium War, 115–116, 124; and Hong Kong, 116, 263; and invasion of Beijing, 126; territorial gains of, in China, 127–128; spheres of influence, 135; and Open Door Policy, 137
Great Hall of the People, 215
Great Khan, Khanate of the, *m*78
Great Leap Forward, 209, 211
Great Proletarian Cultural Revolution, 201, 209, 220–225, *p*222
Great Wall, *m*8–9, *p*235; and extent of China Proper, 2; building of, *p*55, 56, *m*58, 59–60
Green Standard. *See* Army of the Green Standard
gross national product, 255
Guangxu, 128, 133, 149
Guangzhou, *m*8–9, 14, *m*78, *m*102, *p*115, *m*125, 156, *p*186, *p*196
Guanyin, *p*70
guerilla warfare, 177, 192; and Nien rebellion, 123, *m*125
gunpowder, 84
Guo Xi, 91
Guomindang. *See* Koumintang

H

Han dynasty, 57–60, *m*58; Confucianism under, 62–63; and civil service examinations, 63; porcelain of, 86
Hankou, 13, 147; in Second Sino–Japanese War, 185
Hanyang, 147
Han Yu, 60
Hawaii, 184, 188
Hay, John, 136, 137
health care, *p*217, 218–219, 256
Heilongjiang, 7, *m*8–9
Henry the Navigator, 82, 94
Hermit Kingdom. *See* Korea
Hideyoshi, 93
histories, written, 23; oral, 35–37
Hitler, Adolf, 184
Ho Chi Minh, 229–230
Hong Kong, *m*8–9, 14, *m*125; and Great Britain, 116, 255; industry in, 156; demonstrations in, 157; trade with, 255; and People's Republic of China, 263; stock exchange, *p*264
Hong Xiuquan, 120–121, 122
housing, 13
Hsi River. *See* Xi River
Hua Guofeng, 241, 242, *p*243, 244, 250–251
Huai River, 5
Huang He River, 2, 3, 12–13, *p*12, *m*18, *m*41; and Grand Canal, 14

Hundred Days' Reform, 133
Hundred Flowers Campaign, 203
Hu Shi, 158
Hu Yaobang, *p*243, 244–247
hydroelectric power, 14, *p*210, *m*212

I

ideographs, 28. *See also* Writing systems
illiteracy, attempts to end, 157–158. *See also* education
India, Buddhism in, 69, 71; trade with, 81; China's foreign policy with, 228–229
Indochina, 128; as tributary state, 110, *m*125 Indoctrination, policy of, *p*206, 214
Indus River, *m*41
industry, beginnings of, 132–133, *p*132; following World War I, 156–157; under Communist Party, 207–209, *p*210, *p*212; under Deng Xiaoping, 245, 252, 254
inflation, 255. *See also* economics
International Settlement, 156–157, 176, *p*186
invasions, during Age of Disunity, 58–59; from Mongolia, 77, 79–80; from Manchuria, 77, 100; by Japanese pirates, 93; by England and France, 126
inventions, 83, 84–85, 88
iron, 209, *p*210; resources of, *m*212, 252
Iron Age, 42
Islam, 10; spread of, in China, 73

J

Japan, and Mongols, 82; and Neo–Confucianism, 91; pirates of, 93; refused to join tributary system, 111; territorial gains of, in China, 127; and Korea, 134–135, 153; and First Sino–Japanese War, 134–135; and Qing dynasty, 134–138; Taiwan ceded to, 135; Russo–Japanese War, 153; in World War I, 153; attempts to gain power in China, 153–154; boycott of, 155, *p*155; wars with, 172–176, *p*175; and Manchurian takeover, 173–176, *p*175; and Second Sino–Japanese War, *m*183, 184–188, *p*186, 190–192; trade with, 255; relations with Deng Xiaoping, 264–265
Java, *m*78, 82
Jesuits, *p*94, 96, 104
Jews, 73
Jiang Qing, *p*205, 221, 224; as member of Gang of Four, 241, 242
Jiang Zemin, *p*243, 248
Jiaozhou Bay, *m*125, 135, 153

Jilin, 7, *m*8–9
Joffe, Adolf, 160
Journey to the West, 92

K

Kangxi, Emperor, 104, 106, *p*105
Karluks, *m*58
Kazakh people, *p*19
Khanbalik. *See* Beijing
Khitan people, 77
Khmer Rouge, 231
Khrushchev, Nikita, 227
Kipchak, Khanate of, *m*78
Kissinger, Henry, 230, *p*235
kites, 88
Korea, and Neo–Confucianism, 91; invaded by Hideyoshi, 93; as tributary state, 110; and Japan, 134–135, 153; and Korean War, 226–227, 231. *See also* North Korea; South Korea
Korean War, 226–227, 231
Kowloon Peninsula, *m*125, 128, 263
kowtow, custom of, 111–112
Kublai Khan, *p*79, 80
Kuomintang, formation of, 146; and Sun Yat-sen, 159–163, *p*161; under Chiang Kai-shek, 164–169, *m*166, *m*183; reforms of, 181–184; loses support, 188, 190; battles with Communists, 190–192, *p*191, 193–198, *m*194, *p*196, 202; downfall of, 198; and policies of Communist Party, 202. *See also* government

L

land policy, under Kuomintang, 182
language, description of, 24–26; *putonghua*, 25, 26, *p*29; Mandarin, 25, 27; dialects of, 25–26; homonyms, 26–27; and education, 27; written, 28–30; and literacy, 29, 30; *baihua*, 158; reforms in, 158–159
Laos, 2, *m*8–9, 128, 230
Laozi, 47
Late Imperial Age, 76–96; Qing dynasty, 99–117
Later Han dynasty, 57
League of Nations, 174, 176
Ledo Road, *p*189
Legalism, 62
Legalists, 49–50
Lhasa, 228
Liang Lingzan, 88
Liaodong Peninsula, *m*125, 135
Liaoning, 7, *m*8–9
Li Bo, 60–61
Li Hongzhang, 130–131, *p*131, 132
Lin Bao, 223–224
Li Peng, *p*243, 247–248
Li people, *p*19

literature, of Tang dynasty, 60–61; of Song dynasty, 91; of Ming dynasty, 91–92; of Southern Song dynasty, 92
Liu Shaoqi, 204
loess, *p*3, 5, 12
Long March, 178–179, *m*183, *m*189
Lon Nol, 230–231
Luxun, 132
Lytton Commission, 174

M

Macau, *m*8–9, 94
Malay States, *m*125, 128
Manchukuo, 174–175, *p*175, *m*183. *See also* Manchuria
Manchuria, 7, 109, *m*125; invasions from, 77; Japan's takeover of, 173–176, *p*175, *m*183; civil war in, *m*194, 195, 197; protected by Mao, 227. *See also* Manchukuo
Manchus, conquests of, 100; military of, 100–101; and scholarofficials, 101, 102; traditions of, 105–106; and tributary system, 109–110; ouster of, 145. *See also* Qing dynasty
Mandarin, 25, 27
Mandate of Heaven, 46
manganese, resources of, 207, *m*212
Mao Zedong, 26; organizes Communist Party, 164, *p*167, 168; as president of People's Republic of China, 172, 204, *p*205; Long March, 178–179, *m*189; battles with Kuomintang, 190–192, 193–198, *m*194, *p*196; and Great Proletarian Cultural Revolution, 201, 209, 220–225, *p*222; foreign policy of, 201, 226–236, *p*235; and Hundred Flowers Campaign, 203; and Great Leap Forward, 209, 211; and communes, 211; and Richard M. Nixon, *p*235, 236; death of, 240, 241
Marco Polo, *p*79
Marco Polo Bridge, 184
Maritime Province, *m*125, 128
marriage, 22–23, *p*22; under Communist system, 214–215
Marshall, George C. 193, 194
martial law, 248
May Fourth Movement, 154–155
medicine, and dragon bones, 37; acupuncture, 88, *p*217, 218; ephedrine, 88; under Communist system, *p*217, 218–219. *See also* Health care
"Memorial on the Bone of Buddha" (Han Yu), 60
Mencius, 46, 49
merchants, and Confucian class system, 68
Middle Kingdom, 2, 145

military, under Han dynasty, 57; and Confusian class system, 68–69; of Manchus, 100–101; and Taiping Rebellion, 121–123; reforms of, 131–132, 139; and Revolution of 1911, 147–149; under Chiang Kai-shek, 165, m166, 167. See also Red Army
Ming dynasty, sea power of, m78, 81–82, p82, 93–94; porcelain of, 86–87; art of, p90, 91; literature of, 91–92; and attack by Hideyoshi, 93; and Catholic missionaries, p94, 96; and Manchu invasion, 100
minority groups, p19
missionaries, Jesuit, p94, 96, 104
Mohammed, 73
money, paper, 84–85
Mongol Empire, m78, 80
Mongolia, m8–9, 10; invasions from, 77, 79–80; under Genghis Khan, 79–80, p79; sea power of, 81–82; under Qing dynasty, m102, 109
Monkey, 92
monsoons, 6
most-favored nation status, 126
Muslims, rebellions by, 123

N
Nanjing, p12, 13; as Taiping capital, 121; as center of Kuomintang, 167; in Second Sino–Japanese War, m183, 185
Nanjing, Treaty of, 116, 124
nationalism, p155; Sun Yat-sen's goals, 160–161; principles of, 161–163
Nationalist China. See Taiwan
Nationalist Party. See Kuomintang
Nationalization, process of, 208
National People's Congress, 204
Nation–People–Party. See Kuomintang
natural resources, 207, m212
nature, attitudes toward, 21; in art of Song dynasty, p90, 91
navigation, 83
Nehru, Jawaharlal, 229
Neo–Confucianism, 89, 91. See also Confucianism
Neolithic Age, 35
nepotism, 245
Nerchinsk, Treaty of, 112
newspapers, censorship of, 202–203
New Stone Age, 35; ceramics of, 86
New Territories, 263
Nien rebellion, 123, m125
Nirvana, 71
Nixon, Richard M., 230, 232; visit to China, p235, 236, 258, 261
North China, geography of, 5–6; agriculture of, p3, 5–6, 15, 16, 17
North China Plain, 3, m41

Northeast China, 7
Northern Expedition, 165, 168–169
North Korea, m8–9, 226–227, 231. See also Korea; South Korea
North Vietnam, 229–230, 259. See also South Vietnam; Vietnam
Nurhachi, 100, 101

O
oil, m212, 255
Okhotsk, Sea of, 109
Okinawa, 128; as tributary state, 110, m125
"Old Buddha," 128–130, p129
Old Stone Age, 34
"One country, two systems," 262, 263
Open Door Policy, 136, 137; and United States, 126
opium, 114–115
Opium War, 115–116, 124
Oracles bones, 37, 38
oranges, 107
outsiders, and Confucian class system, 68–69

P
painting. See art and artisans
Paleolithic Age, 34
paper, invention of, 84–85
Pathet Lao, 230
peanuts, 107
Pearl Harbor, 184, 188
peasants, and Confucian class system, 67; uprisings of, 99, 108, 120–121; under Qing dynasty, 103, 107; and rebuilding of Communist Party, 178; and Red Army, p191, 192; and communes, 211; and responsibility system, 251–252
Peking Man, 34–35, p34, m41
People's Liberation Army, 11, 226
People's Republic of China, m8–9; Mainland China becomes, 172; proclaims new government, 197; United States acknowledges, 232, 236, 261; and Hong Kong, 263. See also Communist Party (Chinese)
per capita income, 255
Persia, m78
Pescadores Islands, m125, 135
petroleum, resources of, 207
philosophy. See Confucianism; Legalism; Neo–Confucianism; Taoism
pictographs, 28. See also writing systems
Pinyin alphabet, 30. See also writing systems
piracy, 93
PLA. See also People's Liberation Army
playing cards, 88
Politburo, 204–205

Polo, Marco, 85, 93
population, *g*20; of China Proper, 3; of autonomous regions, 7; of Northeast China, 7; of river valleys, *m*18; between 1600–1700, 106; growth of, under Communist government, 213; in 1990s, 256
porcelain, 86–87, *p*87, 114
Port Arthur, *m*125, 132, 135, *m*183
Portugal, 82, 94, 95
potatoes, 107
power plants, 208, *p*210
Po Zhuyi, 61
Prehistoric China, 34–35, *p*34, *m*41
printing, 84, 88
pro-democracy movement, 240, 247–250, *p*249, 255, 258, 262
propaganda, *p*206, *p*222
protectorates, 6–7
provinces, 3
Putonghua (dialect), 25, 26, *p*29
Pu-yi, 149, 176, *p*175

Q

Qian Long, Emperor, 104, 106, 108, *p*110, 112
Qin dynasty, 33, *m*41, 54, *m*58; name of China derived from, 2; government of, 50; overthrow of Zhou dynasty, 50; Legalism in, 50; and Shihuangdi, 55–57; fall of, 56–57; Confucianism under, 62
Qingdao, 153
Qing dynasty, use of kites, 88; peasant uprisings, 99, 108, 120–121; establishment of, 100–101; and scholar-officials, 101, 102; government of, 102–104, *m*102, 106, 108, 140–141; emperors of, 104; and Manchu traditions, 105–106; agriculture of, 107–108; and tributary system, 109–111, *p*110, 127–128; and Europe, 112–116; foreign trade during, 113–116, *m*125; and Opium War, 115–116, 124; decline of, 119–141; foreign policy of, 124–128; and Empress Dowager, 128–130, *p*129, 132, 133, 137, 140, 141; military reforms, 131–132; Hundred Days' Reform, 133; and Japan, 134–138; reforms during, 138–141; overthrow of, 145, 146–148. *See also* Manchus
Qinghai, 3, *m*8–9
Qinling Shan Mountains, 5
Quangzhou, 113, 116, *p*115, *m*125
queues, 105
"Quiet Thoughts at Night" (Li Bo), 60–61

R

railroads, 14, 132, *p*132, 182, 208, 209, *m*212

rationing, 208–209
Red Army, 178, 179, 190–192, *p*191, 193–198, *m*194, *p*196; and policies of Communist Party, 202
Red Guards, 221, *p*222, 223
reeducation. *See* education, Communist system of
reforms, during Qing dynasty, 138–141; literacy movement, 157–158; language, 158–159; agricultural, 181–182; of Kuomintang, 181–184; under Deng Xiaoping, 245–246
religion. *See* Buddhism; Christianity; Confucianism; Islam; Jews; Muslims; Taoism
Republic, founding of, 141, 145–151
Republic of China. *See* Taiwan
responsibility system, 251–252
Revolution of 1911, 145–148
Ricci, Matteo, 96
rice, *m*4, 15, *p*16, 107
Ripa, Father, 111
rivers, 12–14, *p*12, *m*18, *m*212
road systems, 182, 187, *p*189, *m*212
Romance of the Three Kingdoms, 58, 92
Roosevelt, Franklin D.. 188, *p*189
Russia, trade with, 95–96, 112, *m*125; and Chinese borders, 109, 127; territorial gains of, in China, 127; spheres of influence, 135; and Boxer Uprising, 138; Russo–Japanese War, 153; assistance to Sun Yat-sen, 160–161; Communist Party in, 180. *See also* Soviet Union
Russo–Japanese War, 153

S

Schall, Father Adam, *p*94
scholar-officials, and Confucian class system, 64, 65, 67; under Neo–Confucianism, 91; and Manchus, 101, 102; and Qing dynasty, 101, 102
science, under Deng Xiaoping, 245
Second Treaty Settlement, 126–127
SEZ. *See* special economic zones
Shandong Question, *m*8–9, 154
Shang dynasty, 37–39, *p*37, *p*39
Shanghai, *m*8–9, 13, *m*125, 176; as governmental municipality, 3; in Taiping Rebellion, 123; industry in, 156; and International Settlement, 156–157, 176, *p*186; captured by Chiang Kai-shek, 165
Shenyang, *m*8–9, 173, 195
Shihuangdi, 55–57
Shimonoseki, Treaty of, 134–135
shipbuilding, 83, 131, 132
Shu Han monarchy, 58
Siam, as tributary state, 110, *m*125

289

silk, 16, 85, p86, p87, 114
Silk Road, 10, 85, 93; trade along, 57, m58, 59
silver bullion, in foreign trade, 114
Sinitic language family, 24
Sino–Japanese War, First, 134–135
Sino–Japanese War, Second, 184–188, p186, 190–192
Sino–Portuguese Agreement, 94
Suno–Tibetan language family, 24
socialism, 163
social reforms, under Communist Party, 214–219, p214, p216, p217; under Deng Xiaoping, 256, p257
Society of Harmonious Fists, 136
Song dynasty, m41, m78; reign of, 77; and maritime trade, 81; and invention of firearms, 84, p84; invention of paper money, 84–85; art of, p90, 91; literature of, 91
sorghum, m4, 107–108
South China, geography of, 6; agriculture of, p5, 6, 15–16, 17
Southeast Asia, 81, 229
Southern Song dynasty, 77, m78, 80; literature of, 92
South Korea, m8–9, 226–227, 231. *See also* Korea; North Korea
South Vietnam, 229–230, 259. *See also* North Vietnam; Vietnam
Soviet Union, and Chinese border, 109, 127; and downfall of Kuomintang, 198; split in relations with China, 227–228; and Cambodia, 231; relations with, under Deng Xiaoping, 259–261, p260. *See also* Communist Party (Russian); Russia
soybeans, m4, 17, 107
Spain, 95
special economic zones (SEZ), 255
spheres of influence, 135
Stalin, Joseph, 180, 227
standard of living, 208–209
steel, 209, p210, 252
Stilwell, "Vinegar Joe," 187
Stimson, Henry, 176
Sui dynasty, 59–60
Sun–Joffe Agreement, 160, 164
Sun Yat-sen, background of, 146, p147; and Kuomintang, 146, 159–163; conflicts with Yuan Shi-kai, 149–150; goals of, 160–163; and principles of nationalism, 161–163; and communism, 165
Su Song, 88

T

Taipei, m8–9, m194, p232, 234
Taiping Rebellion, 120–121, 122
Taiwan, m8–9, m125, 172, m194; migration to, 107; under Qing dynasty, 109; ceded to Japan, 135; Chiang Kai-shek retreated to, 197; Nationalist government on, 231, 232, p233, 234; United States severs relations with, 261; attempts at reunification, 262, 264
Taiwan Relations Act, 261
Takla Makan, 10, m18
Tang dynasty, reign of, m58, 60–61; literature of, 60–61; women of, p63; art of, p66; and Empress Wu, 71; persecution of Buddhists, 72–73; fall of, 77
Taoism, 33, 47–49, 73, 89
Tao Te Ching, 47, 48
tariffs and taxes, 126, 181–182
tea, m4, 16, 107, p113, 114
technology, under Deng Xiaoping, 245
Temujin. *See* Genghis Khan
terraces, 6
textile mills, 156
Thailand, as tributary state, 110
Thousand–Character Classic, 64
Three Principles of the People (Sun Yat-sen), 161
Tiananmen Square, demonstrations in, 240, 241, 247–250, p249
Tianjin, m8–9; as governmental municipality, 3; industry in, 156; in Second Sino–Japanese War, 185
Tibet, m8–9, 11, m18, 228; people of, p19, m58; under Qing dynasty, m102, 109
tin, resources of, 201, m212
tobacco, 107
Tocqueville, Alexis de, 247
Tongking, 109
totalitarianism, 202–206
trade, along Silk Road, 57, m58, 59; and merchant class, 68; maritime, 81–82; with Portugal, 82, 94, 95; East India, 95; with Spain, 95; with Great Britain, 95, 113–114, m125, 152, 153; with Dutch, 95, 113–114, m125; with Russia, 95–96, 112, m125; with France, 113–114, 124, m125; with United States, 124, m125, 255; following World War I, 156–157. *See also* foreign trade
trade, balance of, 114
trade unions, 156
transportation, via riverways, 12–14, p12; reforms in, 182; under Communist system, 207, 208, m212. *See also* railroads; road systems
treaty ports, 116, m125, 156
tributary system, m102, m125; and foreign trade, 57; under Qing dynasty, 109–111, p110; destruction of, 127–128
Trimetrical Classic, 64
Truman, Harry S, 193, 194

tungsten, 207
Twenty-one Demands, 153–154

U

Uighurs, 10–11, m58
umbrellas, invention of, 88
Unequal treaty system, 125–126, 152, 154; renegotiation of, 169
United Nations, and Nationalist China, 188, 193, 231–232; and Korean War, 226–227, 231; admits People's Republic of China, 232, 236
United States, trade with, 124, m125, 255; and Open Door Policy, 126, 136, 137; Chinese students in, 131, 140; reactions to Twenty-one Demands, 153–154; refuses to acknowledge Manchukuo, 176; support for Free China, 187, 188; aid to Nationalist China, 193–194, 231–232; and Korean War, 226–227, 231; in Vietnam, 230; and Taiwan, 231, 232, 234; acknowledges People's Republic of China, 232, p235, 236, 261; and pro-democracy movement, 247; Taiwan Relations Act, 261; foreign relations with, under Deng Xiaoping, 261–262

V

Versailles, Treaty of, 154
Vietnam, 2, m8–9, 128, 229–230, 259; and Neo–Confucianism, 91. See also North Vietnam; South Vietnam
Vladivostok, m125, 127
Voltaire, 106

W

Wang Zhen, 88
Ward, Frederick Townsend, 122–123
Warlord period, 150, 151, m166, 168
Warring States period, m41, 43
Water Margin, 92
Wei monarchy, 58
Wen, Emperor, 60
Whampoa, 161, p161
wheat, 15
White Lotus Society,
Wilson, Woodrow, 154
women, p19; and traditional family, 21; and marriage, 22–23, p22; and Confucianism, 45; of Tang dynasty, p63; Empress Wu, 71; and silk industry, p86, p87; in Chinese drama, 92; during Taiping Rebellion, 122; Cixi as Empress Dowager, 128–130, p129, 132, 133, 137, 140, 141; in Communist society, 214–215, p214; Jiang Qing as Communist Party leader, 241; role of, under Deng Xiaoping, 256
work units (enterprises), 252
World War I, China remains neutral, 153; China joins Allies, 154; Shandong Question, 154
World War II, 184–192, p186, p189, p191
writing systems, 28–30, p29, c29, 64; Pinyin, 30; of Shang dynasty, 38
Wu, Empress, 71
Wuchang, 146, 147
Wuhan, m8–9, m18, 147
Wu monarchy, m41, 57

X

Xavier, Francis, 96
Xia dynasty, 33, 36–37
Xian, 179
Xinjiang, 3, m8–9, 10–11, m125; during Han dynasty, 57; and Islam, 73; under Qing dynasty, 109; Muslim rebellions in, 123
Xi River, 3, p5, 14, m212
Xuan Tong, 149, p175, 176

Y

Yalu River, m212, 226
Yan'an, m183, p191
Yang, Emperor, 60
Yangtze River. *See* Chang Jiang River
Yellow River. *See* Huang He
Yen, James Y.C., 157
Yi Xing, 88
Yuan dynasty, 80; porcelain of, 86
Yuan Shikai, 139, p147, 149–151; and Twenty-one Demands, 153–154
Yunnan, m8–9; Muslim rebellions in, 123

Z

Zhang Heng, 88
Zhang Xueliang, 173, 179–180
Zhao Ziyang, p243, 244–245, 247–248, 251
Zheng He, 82
Zhongguo (Middle Kingdom), 2
Zhou dynasty, m41; reign of, 40, 42; art of, p39; feudalism in, 42–43; and the Classical Age, 43–46; and Confucianism, 44–46; philosophies of, 47–50; overthrow of, 50
Zhou Enlai, p167, 168, p235; as premier of Communist Party, 204, p205, 213; as president, 224; at Bandung Conference, 228–229; death of, 241
Zhu De, p167, 168
Zhuxi, 89, 91
Zi poetry, 91